W9-CKJ-529

Infection Control in the Child Care Center and Preschool

Seventh Edition

Infection Control in the Child Care Center and Preschool

Seventh Edition

Edited by

Leigh B. Grossman, M.D.

Professor of Pediatrics
Chief, Division of Pediatric Infectious Diseases
University of Virginia Health System
Charlottesville, Virginia

silverchair

SCIENCE + COMMUNICATIONS, INC

Charlottesville, Virginia

Project Manager: Heidi L. Pennington
Production Supervisor: Lisa K. Cunningham
Publisher/Compositor: Silverchair Science + Communications, Inc.
Printer: RR Donnelley, Crawfordsville, IN

© 2006 by Leigh B. Grossman

All rights reserved. This book is protected by copyright. No part of this book may be reproduced in any form or by any means, including photocopying, or utilized by any information storage and retrieval system without written permission from the copyright owner. Materials appearing in this book prepared by individuals as part of their official duties as U.S. government employees are not covered by the above-mentioned copyright.

Printed in the USA

Library of Congress Cataloging-in-Publication Data

Infection control in the child care center and preschool / edited by
    Leigh B. Grossman. -- 7th ed.
        p. ; cm.
    Includes index.
    ISBN-13: 978-0-9787436-0-4
    ISBN-10: 0-9787436-0-1
    1. Communicable diseases in children--Prevention. 2. Day care
centers--Health aspects.   I. Grossman, Leigh B.
    [DNLM: 1. Communicable Disease Control. 2. Child Day Care
Centers. 3. Child, Preschool. 4. Infant. 5. School Health Centers.
6. Schools, Nursery.   WA 110 I425 2006]
RJ401.I528 2006
618.92'9--dc22
                                                        2006020101

Accurate indications, adverse reactions, and dosage schedules for drugs are provided in this book, but it is possible that they may change. The reader is urged to review the package information data of the manufacturers of the medications mentioned.

This text is provided for educational purposes and contains general information and recommendations concerning infection control for health care workers. Please consult and comply with your own institution's infection control policies.

06 07 08

1 2 3 4 5 6 7 8 9 10

To my children,
Nick and Jeff,
who were role models
of what healthy child care years
can and should be
for all children.

Preface

In 2001, the U.S. Department of Education reported that 61% of children not yet in kindergarten (more than 15 million children ages 0–6) received some form of child care from persons other than their parents.

The prevention of the spread of infectious diseases in the child care and preschool setting has been addressed by attempting to exclude sick children from attending child care during their illness. However, experience has shown that these exclusionary rules do not prevent isolated cases and outbreaks of infection that then extend beyond the child care and preschool attendees to their families and the surrounding community. One of the reasons for the very high rate of infectious disease among child care and preschool attendees is that this is our most infection-susceptible age group. Infants and children under the age of 5 lack prior exposure to most infectious pathogens, and thus there is rapid spread of infection in this susceptible population. Their close contact, care, and play, coupled with their lack of hygienic practice, further facilitate transmission of infectious agents. Isolation of infected cases is further hampered in that many children are infectious before they become symptomatic, are chronic carriers of pathogens, or have mild to asymptomatic infections that go undiagnosed but can spread to other children or adults.

The goal of this book is to provide child care and preschool providers, pediatricians, family practitioners, and public health officials with a current and easy-to-read reference on infections and infection control for children in day care. This book provides:

- An overview of how infections are spread.

- An overview of the appropriate use of antibiotics.

- Suggested policies for enrollment requirements, staff education, and employee health.

- Guidelines for children at greater risk of infection (e.g., infants, immunocompromised children, and children with chronic diseases).

- Guidelines for investigation and management of outbreaks.

- Information on specific pathogens with information on the reservoir, transmission, incubation, infectious periods, and suggested management of each infection in this unique setting.

In conclusion, I wish to thank my assistant, Arlene Estrada, who single-handedly organizes, edits, and provides the secretarial assistance that makes each edition of this book better than the last. I also would like to acknowledge the authors of this text who not only provide their expertise, time, and scholarship in writing this book, but who, as respected colleagues and pediatricians, have spent their lives treating and preventing the spread of infection in children.

Leigh B. Grossman, M.D.

Contributing Authors

Stuart P. Adler, M.D.
Professor and Division Chairman
Pediatric Infectious Diseases
Virginia Commonwealth University School of Medicine
Medical College of Virginia Campus
Richmond, Virginia

Susan M. Anderson, M.D.
Associate Professor of Clinical Pediatrics
Division of Developmental Pediatrics
Kluge Children's Rehabilitation Center
University of Virginia Health System
Charlottesville, Virginia

E. Lee Ford-Jones, M.D.
Associate Professor of Pediatrics
Division of Infectious Diseases
University of Toronto Faculty of Medicine
The Hospital for Sick Children
Toronto, Ontario
Canada

Anne A. Gershon, M.D.
Professor of Pediatrics
Director, Division of Pediatric Infectious Diseases
Columbia University College of Physicians and Surgeons
New York, New York

Charles M. Ginsburg, M.D.
Marilyn R. Corrigan Distinguished Chair in Pediatrics
Professor and Chairman
Department of Pediatrics
University of Texas Southwestern Medical Center
Dallas, Texas

Kenneth E. Greer, M.D.
Professor and Chair
Department of Dermatology
University of Virginia Health System
Charlottesville, Virginia

Leigh B. Grossman, M.D.
Professor of Pediatrics
Chief, Division of Pediatric Infectious Diseases
University of Virginia Health System
Charlottesville, Virginia

Moses Grossman, M.D.
Professor of Pediatrics, Emeritus
University of California, San Francisco, School of Medicine
San Francisco, California

Caroline Breese Hall, M.D.
Professor of Pediatrics and Medicine, Infectious Diseases
University of Rochester School of Medicine and Dentistry
Rochester, New York

Scott A. Halperin, M.D.
Professor of Pediatrics
Dalhousie University
Izaak Walton Killam Health Centre
Halifax, Nova Scotia
Canada

Margaret R. Hammerschlag, M.D.

Professor of Pediatrics and Medicine
Director, Division of Pediatric Infectious Diseases
State University of New York
Downstate Medical Center
Brooklyn, New York

Gregory F. Hayden, M.D.

Professor of Pediatrics
Division of General Pediatrics
University of Virginia Health System
Charlottesville, Virginia

J. Owen Hendley, M.D.

Professor of Pediatrics
Division of Pediatric Infectious Disease
University of Virginia Health System
Charlottesville, Virginia

Mary Anne Jackson, M.D.

Professor of Pediatrics
Chief, Section of Pediatric Infectious Diseases
Children's Mercy Hospital
University of Missouri at Kansas City, School of Medicine
Kansas City, Missouri

Richard F. Jacobs, M.D.

Horace C. Cabe Professor of Pediatrics
University of Arkansas for Medical Sciences
President, Arkansas Children's Hospital Research Institute
Division of Pediatric Infectious Diseases
Arkansas Children's Hospital
Little Rock, Arkansas

Barbara A. Jantausch, M.D.

Associate Professor of Pediatrics
Division of Infectious Diseases
Children's National Medical Center
Washington, D.C.

Deborah L. Kernested, R.N.
Winnipeg, Manitoba
Canada

William C. Koch, M.D., F.A.A.P.
Associate Professor of Pediatrics
Virginia Commonwealth University School of Medicine
Medical College of Virginia Campus
Richmond, Virginia

Andrew D. Lynk, M.D., M.S.C., C.T.M., F.R.C.P. (C)
Consultant Pediatrician
Cape Breton Regional Hospital
Sydney, Nova Scotia
Canada

S. Michael Marcy, M.D.
Clinical Professor of Pediatrics
UCLA Center for Vaccine Research
Harbor-UCLA Medical Center
Torrance, California

Marian G. Michaels, M.D., M.P.H.
Associate Professor of Pediatrics and Surgery
Division of Infectious Diseases
Children's Hospital of Pittsburgh
Pittsburgh, Pennsylvania

Jonathan P. Moorman, M.D., Ph.D.
Associate Professor, Infectious Diseases
James H. Quillen College of Medicine
East Tennessee State University
Johnson City, Tennessee

Trudy V. Murphy, M.D.
Medical Epidemiologist
National Immunization Program
Centers for Disease Control and Prevention
Atlanta, Georgia

Ross A. Pennie, M.D.

Medical Director, Laboratory Services
Brantford General Hospital
Brantford, Ontario
Canada

Philip A. Pizzo, M.D.

Dean, Stanford University School of Medicine
Stanford, California

Keith R. Powell, M.D.

Vice President and Dr. Noah Miller Chair of Medicine
Department of Pediatrics
Children's Hospital Medical Center of Akron
Akron, Ohio

Michael F. Rein, M.D.

Professor of Medicine
Division of Infectious Disease and International Health
University of Virginia Health System
Charlottesville, Virginia

Karen S. Rheuban, M.D.

Professor of Pediatrics
Division of Pediatric Cardiology
University of Virginia Health System
Charlottesville, Virginia

William J. Rodriguez, M.D., Ph.D.

Pediatric Science Advisor
Office of New Drugs, CDER
Food and Drug Administration
Silver Spring, Maryland

Theresa A. Schlager, M.D.

Associate Professor of Pediatrics and Emergency Medicine
University of Virginia Health System
Charlottesville, Virginia

Gwendolyn B. Scott, M.D.
Professor of Pediatrics
Director, Division of Pediatric Infectious Disease and Immunology
Leonard M. Miller School of Medicine
University of Miami
Miami, Florida

Eugene D. Shapiro, M.D.
Professor of Pediatrics and Epidemiology
Department of Pediatrics
Yale University School of Medicine
New Haven, Connecticut

Ziad M. Shehab, M.D.
Professor of Clinical Pediatrics and Pathology
Department of Pediatrics
University of Arizona College of Medicine
The University of Arizona Health Sciences Center
Tucson, Arizona

Jane D. Siegel, M.D.
Professor of Pediatrics
Division of Infectious Disease
The University of Texas Southwestern Medical Center
Dallas, Texas

Stephanie H. Stovall, M.D.
Assistant Professor
Department of Pediatrics
College of Medicine
University of Arkansas for Medical Sciences
Little Rock, Arkansas

Ciro V. Sumaya, M.D., M.P.H.T.M.
Dean, School of Rural Public Health
Cox Endowed Chair in Medicine
Texas A & M University System Health Science Center
College Station, Texas

Timothy R. Townsend, M.D.
Associate Professor of Pediatrics
Johns Hopkins University School of Medicine
Baltimore, Maryland

Ronald B. Turner, M.D.
Professor of Pediatrics
Division of Pediatric Infectious Disease
University of Virginia Health System
Charlottesville, Virginia

Judy M. Vincent, M.D.
Colonel (Retired), Medical Corps, United States Army
Pediatrician and Consultant in Pediatric Infectious Disease
Pearl Harbor Pediatric Clinic
Pearl Harbor, Hawaii

Linda A. Waggoner-Fountain, M.D.
Associate Professor of Pediatrics
Division of Pediatric Infectious Disease
University of Virginia Health System
Charlottesville, Virginia

David A. Whiting, M.D., F.A.C.P., F.R.C.P. (Ed)
Clinical Professor of Dermatology and Pediatrics
University of Texas Southwestern Medical Center
Medical Director, Baylor Hair Research and Treatment Center
Dallas, Texas

Richard J. Whitley, M.D.
Loeb Eminent Scholar Chair in Pediatrics
Professor of Pediatrics, Microbiology, and Medicine
University of Alabama at Birmingham
Children's Hospital of Alabama
Birmingham, Alabama

Terry Yamauchi, M.D.
Professor and Vice-Chair
University of Arkansas for Medical Sciences
College of Medicine
Department of Pediatrics
Infectious Disease Section
Chair, Infection Control
Arkansas Children's Hospital
Little Rock, Arkansas

Contents

Section IV. Specific Infections

How Germs
Are Spread

J. Owen Hendley

Child day care centers provide a unique setting conducive to transmission of infectious agents. Preschool aged children who are susceptible to virtually every infection congregate daily with their peers. Each child brings viruses, bacteria, and parasites from his or her own family to share. The gathered children have habits of personal hygiene that are either questionable (at best) or deplorable (on the average). A child who acquires an infection may generously share these germs with adult workers in the child care center, with his or her own parents and siblings, and with peers at the center.

This book would not be needed if we had an easy and practical method to prevent transmission of pathogens in the child care or preschool environment. Since we do not have such a method, I will highlight what we know about transmission of infectious agents as a basis for at least limiting spread.

Three steps are required for transmission of an infectious agent from an infected individual to an uninfected person (Table 1.1). First, the pathogen must be excreted by the infected person from a site such as the nose or the mouth or in the feces. Excretion does not occur through the skin (except from boils, impetigo, or varicella) or through clothes. Second, the excreted pathogen must be transferred to the well person. Transfer could be through the air (aerosol spread), or by direct contact (hand-holding), or by way of an intermediary surface (door knobs). Finally, the infecting agent must reach a susceptible site (usually the mouth, the nose, or the eye) to infect the well person. A

Table 1.1.   Pathogens Transmitted in the Child Care Center

	Bacteria	Viruses	Parasites
Direct	Group A streptococci *Staphylococcus aureus*	Herpes simplex Herpes zoster	Pediculosis Scabies
Respiratory	*Bordetella pertussis* Group A streptococci *Haemophilus influenzae* *Mycobacterium tuberculosis* *Neisseria meningitidis*	Adenovirus Influenza Measles Parainfluenza Respiratory syn-cytial virus Rhinovirus Varicella	
Fecal-oral	*Campylobacter* *Escherichia coli* *Salmonella* *Shigella*	Enteroviruses Hepatitis A Hepatitis E Rotavirus Calicivirus Astrovirus	*Cryptosporidium* *Giardia lamblia* Pinworms
Contact with infected blood and secretions (urine, saliva)		Cytomegalovirus Hepatitis B Hepatitis C Herpes simplex Human immuno-deficiency virus	

pathogen on the skin of a well person does not infect that person unless it is inoculated onto a susceptible mucosa.

The sites from which organisms are excreted by an infected child are known. Agents (viruses, bacteria, and parasites) that infect the gastrointestinal tract are excreted in the feces. Viruses and bacteria that infect the respiratory tract are excreted in respiratory tract secretions (nasal mucus, droplets in cough or sneezes) and not in feces. Cytomegalovirus is excreted in both saliva and urine (Table 1.1).

Table 1.2.   Three Steps Required for Transmission of an Infectious Agent[a] from an Infected to an Uninfected Person

Excretion	Pathogen must be excreted from site(s) by infected person
Transfer	Pathogen must be transferred to well person
Inoculation	Pathogen must reach susceptible site in well person

[a]Infectious agent could be bacteria, viruses, or parasites.

The three transmission steps (Table 1.2) may be illustrated with two examples. In the first, transmission of a virus causing gastroenteritis (such as rotavirus) would begin with excretion of the virus in the diarrheal stool of the sick child. Transfer to a well person would result from contamination of the hands of the person with stool while changing the diaper of the infant. The final step, inoculation of a susceptible site, requires that the well individual put his or her hands or contaminated articles into his or her mouth. The virus, after being swallowed, then would infect the lower gastrointestinal tract. Transmission by this fecal-oral route could be interrupted by removing the contaminating virus from the hands of the individual by the use of soap and water.

A second example is provided by transmission of respiratory viruses (rhinovirus, respiratory syncytial virus), which are excreted in nasal secretions and may be in droplets expelled during coughing. These viruses in droplets may be transferred to the well person by way of the air. Susceptible mucosal sites would be inoculated as the well person breathes the droplet-contaminated air. The frequency of transmission of agents through the air is probably small, although this is not known for certain. On the other hand, viruses in nasal secretions may contaminate the hands of the sick person and articles in the environment by way of the hands. Transfer to the hands of the well person occurs during contact with contaminated articles or the hands and nasal secretions of the sick child. Inoculation, the final step in transmission, requires that the hands of the well person contact the lining of his or her nose or eye so as to deposit the virus on the mucosa. This self-inoculation step could be interrupted by rinsing the virus off the hands before mucosal contact, such as occurs from nose or eye rubbing.

What can be done to prevent transfer of infectious pathogens in the child care setting? Constant cleaning of the diaper changing area is an obvious means of reducing environmental contamination with fecal material. Frequent handwashing by adults working in the child care center is one control measure that all could agree is needed to prevent both self-inoculation and transfer of pathogens contaminating hands to other children. The availability of handwashing facilities and the importance of the repetitive use of these facilities by children and personnel cannot be overemphasized.

Section II

Policies

Guidelines for Attendees and Personnel

Terry Yamauchi

With the steady increase in the numbers of children attending child care centers and preschools, the need for infection control guidelines for this special population also has increased.

GENERAL POLICIES OF THE CENTER

Liaison with Parents and Physicians.   Child care and preschool staff are potentially a very valuable resource in health promotion and maintenance. They should maintain a close working relationship with parents and physicians to ensure that vaccinations are up to date and health problems are promptly identified and adequately managed. Transition times with parents at the beginning and end of the day should be used thoughtfully. Parents should be asked to identify symptoms of any infection in the child or household members at drop-off time.

Liaison with Public Health.   Child care and preschool staff should maintain a close working relationship with their local public health departments. Personnel should appreciate the public health care provider's responsibility for all children as opposed to the parents' primary concern for their own child and the private physician's primary concern for his or her patient.

Physical Organization.   There should be separate rooms and caregivers for diapered and nondiapered children. Food preparation areas must be separate from diaper change areas; each should have handwashing facilities. Bathrooms must include handwashing facilities. Cribs should be separated by at least 3 feet to decrease the transmission of airborne pathogens, and bedding and mattresses should not be shared unless thoroughly cleaned between users.

Staffing Issues.   A staff:child ratio of 1:3 or 1:4 and a small group size (8 to 12 infants maximum) are required. Staff require training and ongoing supervision of their work. Assignment of a primary caregiver will reduce exposures and thus the risk of infection. Responsibilities for diaper changing and food and formula preparation should be assigned to different staff as much as possible. Infants should also be protected from other children and caregivers who are ill with colds or other infections. Handwashing and personal hygiene of all staff should be stressed.

ATTENDEE POLICIES

Children attending day care or preschool should be free of known infectious disease unless the center has specific facilities for care of the sick child. Behavioral characteristics of the preschool child attendee make for easy transmission of infectious agents. Because of the difficulty in identifying contagious illnesses during the incubation period and the well-known fact that contagium may be present well before symptoms develop, it is imperative that when an infection is recognized, alternative child care be arranged. Parents or guardians should be carefully questioned as to symptoms of infection in the attendee as well as other family members (siblings and parents). Symptoms such as fever, lethargy, poor feeding, decreased activity, or unusual behavior should be a warning that prodrome to illness may be occurring. Although these symptoms do not necessarily warrant exclusion from the child care facility, close observation for further developing illness is indicated.

Alternate Care for the Sick Child.   Symptoms such as fever, diarrhea, vomiting, rash, skin lesions, wound infections, cough, or runny nose should alert personnel to the strong likelihood of an infectious disease (Table 2.1). The symptoms listed above may also be the result of other conditions not related to infectious agents; however, most often they are associated with transmissible microbial organisms,

Table 2.1. Common Signs and Symptoms of Childhood Infection

Coughing	• Respiratory infections, bronchiolitis, sinusitis, pneumonia caused by respiratory syncytial virus, parainfluenza, influenza, adenovirus, pertussis, *Haemophilus influenzae*, pneumo-coccus, and others
Diarrhea	• Multiple infectious agents including *Salmonella, Shigella, Campylobacter, Yersinia, Giardia*, cryp-tosporidium, rotavirus, enterovirus, and parasites
Fever	• May be a general symptom of viral or bacterial diseases
Headache and/or stiff neck	• May be a symptom of many illnesses but with fever may represent bacterial or viral meningitis
Infected skin or sores	• May represent impetigo, herpetic infection, chickenpox, or wound infection, and child should not be allowed in day care without physician consent
Irritability that is unusual or unexplained crying	• May be a symptom of many illnesses but with fever may represent bacterial or viral meningitis
Itching of body or scalp	• Close observation for lesions or agents such as scabies or lice
Lethargy	• May be a general symptom of viral or bacterial diseases
Pink eye	• Tearing, itching of eye, swelling, and tenderness, along with redness and/or discharge from the eye represents conjunctivitis, either viral or bac-terial in nature
Rapid or altered breathing	• Respiratory infections as above
Rash	• Generally must be evaluated on a case-by-case basis; whenever there is a question of etiology, physician should be consulted
Sore throat	• Respiratory infections, pharyngitis, tonsillitis, viruses, and group A streptococcus (strep throat)
Stomatitis	• May be a symptom of viral gingivostomatitis (coxsackie, herpes)
Vomiting	• May be a general symptom of viral or bacterial diseases
Yellow skin and/or eyes	• May be a symptom of hepatitis, and child should not be allowed in day care without physician consent

and whenever possible another care source for these children should be sought. On enrollment, the parent needs to provide the alternate arrangements to be made when a child is identified as ill during the day. Parents must understand the center's policies on ill children and the exclusion guidelines set out by public health authorities.

Attendee Immunizations.   Child care and preschool attendees should be up-to-date on their immunizations. The following vaccines are highly recommended for children attendees to day care and preschool facilities: diphtheria, *Haemophilus influenzae* type b, hepatitis A, hepatitis B, influenza, mumps, pertussis, pneumococcus, polio, rubella (German measles), rubeola (measles), tetanus, and varicella (chickenpox) (Table 2.2). Stronger recommendations may be made during outbreaks and/or epidemic situations.

Attendee Medical History.   Every effort should be made to acquire an adequate medical history on all attendees. Essential medical information should include immunization records, known allergies, past illnesses, infections, trauma, and medications. Any child from a high-risk setting should be screened for tuberculosis prior to enrollment.

PERSONNEL POLICIES

Child care and preschool personnel should be free of known infections and maintain high standards of personal hygiene. A medical history should be obtained from the day care employee. The history should recognize employee susceptibility by documenting previous infections, immunizations, and medications. Especially important is the history of childhood illnesses such as measles, mumps, rubella, and chickenpox to determine the child care workers' current immune status to the vaccine-preventable diseases. This information takes on added importance in that the immunity induced by some vaccines appears to lessen over a period of time (pertussis and measles vaccines); other vaccines do confer lifelong protection, and the protected and unprotected employee should be identified. Specific immunization recommendations for child care and preschool personnel are outlined below.

Personnel taking medications that may suppress the immune response are at increased risk for infections. Although corticoster-

Table 2.2. Recommended Vaccines for Child Care Center and Preschool Attendees

Vaccine	Comment
Diphtheria (killed)	• Immunization at 2, 4, 6, and 18 months of age, repeated at school entry and every 10 years throughout life
Haemophilus influenzae type b conjugate (killed)	• Immunization at 2, 4, 6, and 15 months of age
Hepatitis A (killed)	• Two doses 6 to 12 months apart, starting at 12 months of age
Hepatitis B (killed)	• Immunization at birth, 1, and 6 months of age
Influenza (killed)	• Yearly
Mumps (live, attenuated)	• Immunization at 15 months, repeated at 4 to 6 years of age
Pertussis, acellular (killed)	• Immunization at 2, 4, 6, and 18 months of age, repeated at school entry and every 10 years throughout life
Pneumococcus (killed)	• Immunization at 2, 4, 6, and 12 to 15 months of age
Polio (killed)	• Immunization at 2, 4, and 18 months, repeated at 4 to 6 years of age
Rubella (live, attenuated)	• Immunization at 15 months, repeated at 4 to 6 years of age
Rubeola (live, attenuated)	• Immunization at 15 months, repeated at 4 to 6 years of age
Rotavirus (live, attenuated)	• Immunization at 2, 4, and 6 months of age
Tetanus (killed)	• Immunization at 2, 4, 6, and 18 months of age, repeated at school entry and every 10 years throughout life
Varicella (live, attenuated)	• Immunization at 12 to 18 months of age

oids are the medications more frequently associated with decreasing the immune response, the usual dosage for acute treatment (i.e., allergic reactions) is not enough to compromise the normal host response. Even long-term corticosteroid therapy for such diseases as asthma or systemic lupus erythematosus does not suppress the normal host response enough to cause concern. Higher doses of corticosteroid or chemotherapeutic agents used in cancer and/or transplant patients are the only conditions that place the child care worker at increased risk of infection. If there is any question regarding the employee's immune status, a statement clarifying the current status from his or her prescribing physician is suggested. As stated above, the employee should be free of known infections and maintain high standards of personal hygiene.

Preemployment Physical Examination. A physical examination should be obtained to ensure that personnel are physically able to carry out the tasks assigned for the area of employment. Obvious physical disorders that may be conducive to transmission of infectious diseases, such as dermatitis, must be cleared by a physician before the employee is allowed to work in areas of child contact. Child care workers should be screened with an intradermal tuberculin skin test prior to employment.

Preemployment Culturing of Personnel. Culturing for enteric pathogens is still required in some states, and individual state health regulations should be reviewed. In general, culturing of child care personnel before employment is of little value and should not be necessary. However, personnel should be informed that culturing may be required if surveillance data so indicate during an outbreak investigation.

Personnel Immunizations. The following vaccines are highly recommended for day care and preschool employees: diphtheria, hepatitis A, hepatitis B, influenza, mumps, polio, rubella (German measles), rubeola (measles), tetanus, and varicella (chickenpox) (Table 2.3).

Diphtheria-tetanus toxoid vaccines have been widely used in the United States and have markedly decreased the incidence of these diseases. Because of the seriousness of these two diseases and the fact that child care workers may be at higher risk, diphtheria-tetanus toxoid vaccination should be carried out every 10 years. It may be necessary to reimmunize personnel who have encountered wounds thought to be contaminated and if more than 5 years have lapsed since the vaccines were last administered.

Rubeola (measles), mumps, rubella (German measles), and varicella (chickenpox) vaccines are live, attenuated viruses. Although live

Table 2.3. Immunization Recommended Vaccines for Child Care Center and Preschool Personnel

Vaccine	Comment
Diphtheria (killed)	• Booster if none in past 10 years
Hepatitis A (killed)	• Proof of immunization or disease in the past
Hepatitis B (killed)	• Proof of immunization or disease in the past
Influenza (killed)	• Yearly
Meningococcal (killed)	• Prevention of disease outbreak caused by serogroup C
Mumps (live, attenuated)	• Proof of immunization or disease in the past
Pertussis, acellular (killed)	• Booster effect when given with diphtheria tetanus vaccine (DTap)
Pneumococcal (killed)	• For child care workers over age 65
Polio (inactivated)	• If no immunization in past or booster is found to be needed
Rubella (live, attenuated)	• Proof of immunization or disease in the past
Rubeola (live, attenuated)	• Proof of immunization or disease in the past
Tetanus (killed)	• Booster if none in past 10 years
Varicella (live, attenuated)	• Proof of immunization or disease in the past

vaccines, there is little evidence to prove that they pose any risk of infection to an immunized adult or child. They are available as combination or single vaccines. Each vaccine should be considered separately in regard to its efficacy and use by child care personnel. Child care personnel lacking a history of disease or immunity (antibody) by laboratory testing (if available) should receive the vaccines.

Poliomyelitis is a disease that has almost disappeared in the United States, and this accurately reflects the efficacy of the poliovirus vaccines. The inactivated poliomyelitis vaccine (IPV) is currently the recommended vaccine for childhood immunization in the United States. It is advised that child care and preschool personnel be fully immunized against poliovirus. The inactivated poliovirus vaccine is the vaccine of choice for the unvaccinated child care worker.

The current drop-off in use of the pertussis vaccine for infants has resulted in an increase in whooping cough in infants and children.

Speculation has also been raised as to the increased susceptibility of previously immunized adults. In 1994, adolescents and older individuals were found to be the second-largest group (after infants) to contract pertussis. Pertussis in these older persons is atypical, with protracted cough, mild illness, but continued infections. Transmission of whooping cough from infants and children to adult caretakers has been demonstrated. Of perhaps greater concern is the transmission of this bacteria from the adult caretaker to the unprotected infant or child. Reimmunization with the acellular pertussis vaccine has been shown to boost protection to pertussis in adults without risk for adverse events.

Influenza virus infections are well known in the child care facility. The influenza vaccine is a killed virus vaccine and is recommended for all child care personnel. Unfortunately, the influenza virus undergoes periodic changes, and if those changes occur after the vaccine strains have been selected, the vaccine may not be protective. Since the influenza virus vaccine induces protective antibodies with a relatively short life, annual immunization is necessary for maximum protection. Because the immune response to the vaccine requires about 2 weeks for antibody levels to become protective, in times of epidemics it may be necessary to prophylactically administer an antiviral agent if the employee has been exposed and has not been immunized.

The hepatitis A vaccine is effective and safe and should be used for all child care workers. Although this illness is generally mild or even asymptomatic in children, it can easily spread in this setting, and the adult disease can be severe, debilitating, and prolonged.

Hepatitis B virus vaccine is recommended for all child care workers, but, most importantly, for staff of institutions for the mentally retarded and staff who care for children from high-risk families.

The varicella vaccine should be administered to all nonimmune child care workers. This is a live, attenuated vaccine that may produce a few atypical pox lesions but is effective and safe in immunocompetent adults who we know will be exposed to this pathogen in the child care setting.

Other vaccines that may benefit child care workers include:

1. **Meningococcal:** useful in the control of serogroup C disease
2. **Pertussis:** the acellular pertussis vaccine has been found to be effective in boosting protection to pertussis without increased risk for adverse events when administered with diphtheria tetanus vaccine (TDaP)
3. **Pneumococcal:** the pneumococcal vaccine is recommended for the child care worker aged 65 years or over

PET AND ANIMAL POLICIES

Pets and animals may be advocated for use in some day care settings. The benefit of these programs remains to be demonstrated. In many states, it is illegal to bring animals other than Seeing Eye dogs into facilities involved in child care. It is advisable that the child care facility remain in compliance with federal and state licensure regulations.

Remember that pets may be vehicles for diseases. They may initiate allergic reactions in some children, they may cause accidents, unpleasant odors may result, and they may infringe on other children's rights. Animals brought into a strange new environment may not act as they normally do in more familiar surroundings.

The list of diseases associated with pets and animals is extensive. There are many microorganisms, including bacteria, viruses, fungi, and para-sites, associated with animals commonly used as pets. With this background information, child care centers and preschools considering the use of pets or other animals within the facility must carefully weigh the potential benefits against the potential risks of exposure of each and every individual (child and staff) within the facility. Until further information is available, it seems prudent to limit the area in which and the extent to which pets and animals can be used in a center.

RECOMMENDED CLEANING AND DISINFECTION

The child in day care is frequently one who crawls and explores the environment with his or her mouth. Likewise, many day care children are incontinent of urine and feces. For these reasons it is important that the environment be kept as clean as possible. Because of the increased numbers of children and the usual higher ratio of children to adults in the child care setting than in the home, it may be more difficult to maintain cleanliness.

Regularly scheduled environmental cleaning, such as vacuuming, sweeping, dusting, and washing, is an essential element of preventing the spread of infectious agents. Standard household cleaning materials are adequate for most environmental surfaces. Care should be taken to ensure proper dilutions and removal after use because of the potential toxicity of many standard products.

Special care may be needed in certain locations such as food preparation and consumption, diaper changing, toilet, and sleep areas, as these are higher in risk for transmission of infectious agents.

Contaminated Surfaces.   Special cleaning of contaminated surfaces requires removal of organic material, followed by application of a commercial cleansing agent. With the concern over acquired immune deficiency syndrome caused by the human immune deficiency virus, additional precautions are indicated. Blood and body fluids contaminated with blood (blood is visible) should be flooded with a bleach solution diluted 1 part bleach to 10 parts water. Many commercial cleansing agents are also acceptable for this purpose, but the label should be carefully reviewed for this use. After thorough soaking, the mixture (contaminated material plus cleansing agent or bleach solution) should be carefully removed, and the area cleaned with the routine product.

Bedding.   Individual bedding should not be shared and must be washed at least weekly.

Carpets.   Carpets are a special surface that are extremely difficult to maintain. In general, the same principles apply, but because carpet may remain wet for long periods of time and thus retain infectious material, the drying of the carpet following cleanup, as for other surfaces described above, is imperative. I would consider previously contaminated carpets to be of high risk for transmitting infectious agents, even if cleaned, until they have dried.

Toys and Play Equipment.   In the child care setting, toys and play equipment may be shared by many children, and the potential for transmitting infections is obvious. Toys are especially challenging because of the varying materials and textures involved. In general, soft, cuddly toys should be discouraged, as they require washing and drying, which may be much more difficult than toys of impervious materials. Infants may play with washable toys that are disinfected before and after use by another infant. To clean, wash toys with dishwashing detergent and water, then rinse in a dilute (1:10 to 1:100) bleach solution. Infants should not be given shared, nonwashable soft toys that may be contaminated with infectious secretions.

HANDWASHING PROCEDURES

The importance of handwashing cannot be taken lightly. Hand transmission of infectious agents has been recognized for more than 100 years. Handwashing is the single most important procedure for preventing the transmission of infections in the child care and preschool setting. For example, 50% reduction rates in diarrhea were observed in centers adopting a careful handwashing regimen.

Handwashing is the mechanical removal of infectious agents. In the child care center, soap and water are all that is needed to carry out this procedure. What must be taught and reinforced is the importance of performing handwashing correctly and frequently.

Day care employees should be taught that handwashing prevents the employees from infecting themselves or their family members, as well as protects the children in their care.

For routine handwashing, the hands should be wet, and soap applied with vigorous rubbing together to lather on all surfaces for at least 10 seconds, followed by thorough rinsing under running water and drying. Liquid soap is preferable. If bar soap is used, it should be stored in a manner to allow complete drainage of water.

Handwashing should be carried out when visible contamination or soiling occurs, after use of the toilet, following diaper changes, after handling any body fluids, before eating or feeding, and after tending children with known infections.

To facilitate correct, frequent handwashing, a sink, running water, soap, and clean, preferably disposable, dry towels are necessary.

DIAPERING PROCEDURES

Since so many children in the child care setting are not toilet-trained, diaper changes are necessary. Correct changing of diapers is required to prevent the spread of infectious agents in the fecal material. Even asymptomatic children may harbor infectious microorganisms in their stools. Spread of diseases via the fecal-oral route is well documented but can be prevented if proper procedure is followed.

It is essential that the diapering area is separated from areas of food preparation and feeding. Disposable diapers are the preferred materials. Cloth diapers may be stored with the paper diapers, but both should be kept far from the area of the soiled diapers to prevent contamination. The changing surface should be away from other child activities and covered with a smooth, moisture-resistant, cleanable cover.

A tightly covered container with a foot-operated lid is preferred for the soiled diapers. A plastic trash bag or disposable container should be placed into the plastic container. This must be emptied and cleaned daily, or more frequently as needed.

When changing the soiled diaper, disposable gloves may be used if so desired or available. The removed soiled diaper should be folded inward to cover fecal material. The child's skin is then cleansed to remove stool. Soap and water may be needed to remove visible soiling. After the clean diaper has been applied and the child has been removed from the changing area, the soiled diaper is placed in the covered container. The changing surface is cleansed with a detergent spray or soap and water and allowed to dry. Hands of the child and caregiver must be carefully washed whether gloves are used or not.

FOOD PREPARATION

Food preparation areas require sinks and towel supplies separate from diaper change facilities. Hands must be washed before food and formula preparation and before feeding an infant. Food should be refrigerated, and any unused food or formula discarded within 24 hours.

Guidelines for the Appropriate Use of Antibiotics

S. Michael Marcy

Excessive and inappropriate use of antibiotics has been a source of concern almost since their introduction into the practice of medicine in the late 1940s. As these medications achieved easy availability and widespread use, the problem became ever more acute, to the extent that by the early 1990s, children in this country were receiving an average of almost one oral antibiotic prescription per year, in many cases for the treatment of self-limited viral upper respiratory infections. For example, in a recent study of pediatric office visits, it was found that an antibiotic was prescribed for almost half of children with a common cold and 75% of those with "bronchitis," conditions for which antibiotics offer no significant benefit. Overall, it has been estimated that of the 85,000,000 courses of antibiotics prescribed in 1992 for these and other upper respiratory infections (e.g., common cold, pharyngitis, acute otitis media, acute bacterial sinusitis, cough illness/bronchitis), up to 50,000,000 were probably unnecessary.

Although this problem has improved to some extent in the last decade, over-prescribing of antibiotics continues to be prevalent and a major public health concern.

The reasons for over-prescribing are multiple and can be laid at the feet of parents, health care providers, managed care organizations, and even child care centers and schools. Parents, misunderstanding the role of antibiotics and intent on returning their child to some form of day care as soon as possible, demand antibiotic treatment "just to be on the safe side," even if told it will be ineffective. In many cases, both parents have employment outside the home, making the need to send their child to a child care center or preschool both imperative and urgent. These facilities, in turn, provide additional impetus for demanding antibiotics by policies that call for any "sick" child to be on antibiotic treatment before being allowed to return. Finally, health care providers, cognizant of these perceived needs, intent on retaining parental approval and managed care endorsement, respond to the pressure and acquiesce to these demands.

The public health consequences of these behaviors are profound. It has been stated that antibiotics are unique in the sense that, unlike other medications, treatment of an individual can affect an entire community. Thus, the use of antibiotics will, after a relatively short period of time—sometimes after only a *single* dose—select out antibiotic-resistant bacteria for survival in the upper respiratory tract. These antibiotic-resistant organisms can then readily be spread via unwashed hands or respiratory secretions to any close contacts: siblings, parents, playmates, and child care center and preschool personnel. They, in turn, can pass these resistant bacteria on to their contacts. Because resistant organisms tend to die out after several months and are replaced by antibiotic-susceptible bacteria, this problem is not permanent. However, every time a child receives an antibiotic, the potential for reinstituting the cycle begins once again. When the exposed community is a child care center or preschool, each child on unnecessary antibiotic treatment represents a potential threat to all children attending that facility. When the facilities require antibiotic treatment as a criterion for the return of a sick child, they are, in a sense, perpetuating a situation that, under more conservative policies, would resolve on its own.

How does injudicious use of antibiotics affect the community, particularly the childhood community? The adverse effects of anti-biotics can have direct consequences for the individual receiving them. It has been estimated that up to 10% of persons taking antibiotic therapy will experience at least one side effect. These are usually relatively minor and can include allergic rash; abdominal pain, diarrhea, nausea and vomiting; vaginal or skin yeast infection; and far less frequent but more serious reactions such as anaphylactic shock, hemolytic anemia, life-threatening vasculitis, and hepatitis. Notably, any of the more common reactions can require home care, often for several days, negating the presumed advantages of treating "just to be on the safe side."

Of no less importance are the indirect effects engendered by acquisition and transmission of antibiotic-resistant bacteria. When children who carry these organisms in their nose and throat acquire an ear infection, sinusitis, or pneumonia, treatment with standard primary therapy will often fail, resulting in a delay in appropriate treatment, prolongation of illness, possibly more severe infection, and the need for additional therapy with an antibiotic possessing a broader spectrum of action, with higher cost and generally more side effects. At the present time, between 15% and 40% of pneumococci in the United States are resistant to amoxicillin, the antibiotic generally recommended for first-line therapy of otitis media and sinusitis, two of the most common pediatric bacterial upper respiratory infections caused by this organism. In contrast, in Holland, where antibiotic use is voluntarily restricted by practitioners, the incidence of pneumococcal amoxicillin resistance is around 2 to 5%. Among many of the organisms considered in other chapters in this book, antibiotic resistance has been a considerable problem. Thus, in addition to pneumococcal infection, those caused by staphylococci, streptococci, meningococci, *Haemophilus influenzae*, salmonella, shigella, gonococci, and tuberculosis are all very likely to be due to an antibiotic-resistant organism.

SPECIFIC PEDIATRIC UPPER RESPIRATORY TRACT INFECTIONS

Acute Otitis Media.   The clinical manifestations of acute otitis media include irritability, sleep disturbance, poor appetite, and pulling at the ear in preverbal infants. Older children may complain of ear pain, difficulty hearing, and vertigo. Sometimes, pus or bloody discharge from the ear is present. Fever occurs in one-third to two-thirds of children with ear infections. Acute otitis media is often preceded by a viral cold with runny nose and cough.

Most infections are caused by the pneumococcus. The other major etiologic agents are *H. influenzae* (nontypeable strains), *Moraxella catarrhalis*, and group A streptococcus (particularly during the winter).

The diagnosis of acute otitis media is made with a history of rapidly (usually less than 48 hours) progressing signs and symptoms together with otoscopic examination of the tympanic membrane. Pain alone is never a sufficient criterion to make this diagnosis. Discomfort felt in the ear can be caused by numerous conditions other than acute otitis media, including tonsillitis, a blocked eustachian tube, fluid in the ear (otitis media with effusion), infection or foreign body in the ear canal, or infection of the soft tissues and structures around the ear (mumps parotitis, lymphadenitis, dental abscess).

Antibiotics are generally recommended for persistent signs and symptoms of acute otitis media. Recent recommendations encourage an "observation option" with pain medication but no antibiotics for 48 hours for children over 2 years of age who are not toxic or experiencing severe pain. Clinical worsening or failure of resolution by the end of that time warrants antibiotic therapy. It is estimated that 80% to more than 90% of ear infections will resolve without antibiotic therapy. Pain (acetaminophen, ibuprofen, codeine) and fever (acetaminophen, ibuprofen) control is an essential part of treatment.

Influenza vaccine can be effective in preventing acute otitis media during the influenza season. Pneumococcal vaccine can prevent about 6% of all ear infections and 20% of recurrent (≥ 5/year) ear infections. Acute otitis media is not contagious, and exclusion from child care or preschool is only required until the child is free of fever and is able to participate in general activities. No special precautions are required for other children at the center, personnel, or family.

The Common Cold.   The clinical manifestations of the common cold are stuffy nose, cough, sore throat, fatigue, and poor appetite. Less frequently, children complain of headaches, muscle aches, fever, and chills. Signs and symptoms of a cold may persist or even worsen for the first few days, but gradually improve thereafter.

Typically, nasal discharge with an uncomplicated viral cold will proceed over the first week from a thin, watery discharge to a cloudy discharge, a yellow-green discharge, and then slowly resolve. Appearance of a yellow-green discharge does not indicate the presence of a secondary bacterial infection. Of those children who cough and have a runny nose with a cold, 50% may still be coughing and 25% may still be complaining of nasal stuffiness at 14 days of illness. Thus, the common cold is often a 2- to 3-week illness.

Acute otitis media may occur during the first week of a cold with additional clinical findings, particularly in infants and young children. Persistent and unimproving nasal discharge and daytime cough for 14 days or longer suggests the presence of acute bacterial sinusitis. Children with asthma may experience exacerbation of their reactive airways disease associated with upper respiratory infections.

The common causes of the common cold are the rhinovirus, coronavirus, parainfluenza virus, and respiratory syncytial virus. Less often, influenza virus, adenovirus, and enterovirus cause the common cold.

The diagnosis is usually based on clinical signs and symptoms and a history of contact with another infected person.

Antibiotic therapy is not indicated, and no specific therapy is available. Saline nasal irrigation and aspiration of nasal mucus with an ear-bulk syringe for infants, limited use of sympathomimetic nasal sprays (neosynephrine, oxymetazoline) in older children, and antipyretics and analgesics (acetaminophen, ibuprofen) can provide symptomatic relief. Placing young infants in an infant seat can help with drainage of nasal secretions.

The infectious period varies with etiologic agent, but generally is during the time that nasal secretions are present. Prevention of infection varies with the etiologic agent. Other than influenza vaccine, no vaccine is available. Exclusion from child care or preschool should only be until the child is free of fever and able to participate in general activities. Transmission to other children, personnel, and families is largely via fingers contaminated with viruses from toys, counter tops, and other environmental surfaces and can be reduced by frequent handwashing, careful secretion/excretion control, and making certain that tissues are discarded in a closed container.

Cough Illness/Bronchitis. The early clinical manifestations are those of the common cold, but within a few days cough becomes more prominent, dry at first and then productive or "wet." Fever is common the first 5 to 7 days. Mild substernal chest pain is not uncommon in older children during the early phases of the illness. Children with asthma may experience exacerbation of their reactive airway disease. The etiologic agents of cough illness/bronchitis are generally the same as those of the common cold. The diagnosis is based on signs and symptoms and a history of contact with infected people. Unimproving daytime cough lasting more than 14 days may represent acute bacterial sinusitis.

Antibiotic therapy is not indicated, and no specific therapy is available. Children over 6 months of age with a dry, nonproductive cough experiencing gagging or sleep difficulty may be given an antitussive medication such as dextromethorphan (DM). Use of codeine-containing preparations should be reserved for children over 3 years of age. Any antitussive should be used with caution in children with a productive "wet" cough and/or asthma. Antipyretics and analgesics (acetaminophen, ibuprofen) can provide symptomatic relief.

The infectious period varies with the etiologic agent, but is generally during the first week or two of cough. Prevention of infection varies with the etiologic agent. Other than influenza vaccine, no vaccine is available for prevention. Children should be excluded from child care or preschool until they are free of fever and able to participate in general activities without disruption of classes due to cough. Transmission to other children, personnel, and families can be reduced by frequent handwashing and disposal of tissues in a closed container.

Acute Bacterial Sinusitis.   The common cold is considered a viral rhinosinusitis; bacterial sinusitis is a complication identified by the severity of the illness or the persistence of symptoms. Thus, clinical manifestations include either a "severe" or "persistent" form: "Severe" acute sinusitis presents with high fever, an ill appearance, facial pain, and mucopurulent nasal discharge. The "persistent" form is far more common and presents as 14 or more days of unimproving nasal discharge of any quality together with a daytime cough (which may be worse at night). Appearance of a yellow-green nasal discharge during the first week of a common cold does not indicate the presence of acute bacterial sinusitis.

The etiologic agents that cause bacterial sinusitis are the same as those causing acute otitis media. The diagnosis of sinusitis is based on clinical findings, which are adequate in almost all cases to establish a diagnosis. Radiographs to confirm or rule out the presence of bacterial sinusitis in children 6 years of age or younger are not recommended. Although they may be useful in older children, they are rarely indicated.

Antibiotics are always indicated for the "severe" form of acute sinusitis and at 14 or more days of "persistent" sinusitis symptoms. Ancillary treatment such as that recommended for symptoms of the common cold and cough illness/bronchitis is appropriate when indicated.

Acute bacterial sinusitis is not contagious. Influenza vaccine may be effective in preventing acute bacterial sinusitis during the influenza season. Exclusion from child care or preschool is recommended until the child is free of fever and able to participate in general activities. There are no recommendations or special precautions for other children, personnel, or families.

Pharyngitis. The clinical manifestations of pharyngitis in infants and young children often include a refusal to eat, irritability, and sleep disturbances. Older children complain of sore throat and, when there is an associated cervical lymphadenitis, neck pain. *Viral pharyngitis* is often part of a common cold and accompanied by one or more of the following: rhinitis, cough, hoarseness, ulcerovesicular enanthem, conjunctivitis, or diarrhea. Presence of any of these signs is strong evidence against a "strep throat." The throat and tonsils may look normal, slightly red, or intensely red with an exudate. Fever is usually low grade and brief in duration. The pain of pharyngitis can be referred to the ear, leading to confusion with acute otitis media. The presence of an exudate does not indicate group A streptococcal (GAS) infection.

GAS pharyngitis is usually rapid in onset and can be accompanied by headache, abdominal pain, enlarged and tender cervical lymph nodes, and significant fever ($\geq 102°F$). A red, papular "sandpaper" rash may accompany the pharyngitis (scarlet fever). The pharynx and uvula are usually red and swollen. Tonsillar exudates and palatal petechiae may or may not be present but, when present, are not diagnostic of GAS infection.

The causes of pharyngitis include viruses, which represent about 80% of all sore throats and are caused by the same organisms as those responsible for the common cold. GAS is the most common bacterial etiology of pharyngitis.

The diagnosis of *GAS pharyngitis* is made with throat culture or a rapid antigen detection test. Diagnosis based on clinical appearance of the throat is highly unreliable.

No specific treatment is available for viral pharyngitis. Antibiotic therapy is indicated for treatment of laboratory-confirmed *GAS pharyngitis*.

THE ROLE OF CHILD CARE CENTERS
AND PRESCHOOLS IN PROMOTING
JUDICIOUS ANTIBIOTIC USE:

- Recognize that most childhood upper respiratory infections are caused by viruses. Do not insist that children with "a cold," "sore throat," "hoarseness," "cough," or "snotty nose" be on antibiotics or excluded from attendance. Provide assurance that this is understood by parents, health care providers, and staff.

- Recognize that the average normal infant and young child may have as many as 5 to 10 viral upper respiratory infections a year, most during the winter, each lasting from 1 to 3 weeks. Thus, having a viral cold for much of the winter would not be abnormal or unusual. The larger the child care center or pre-school, the greater the number of contacts with infected children and the greater the number of such infections.

- Utilize the guidelines provided in Table 4.3 to determine appropriate policies for treatment, exclusion, and return.

- Utilize the guidelines provided in Sections I and II on Transmission and Policies to aid in infection control.

- Most childhood upper respiratory tract bacterial infections can be treated at home with once- or twice-daily therapy. Permit children on antibiotics to attend if they are free of fever and able to participate in general activities.

- If antibiotic therapy during child care hours is required, clear instructions regarding storage, administration, and duration of therapy should be provided in writing. Ideally, a form should be provided for this purpose. Storage temperature (refrigerator, room) should be specified. A graduated syringe or dosage cup should be provided; teaspoons or tablespoons should not be used, as their volume varies widely. A masking substance (e.g., chocolate syrup, marmalade, preserves, jelly) should be available to facilitate acceptance of bad-tasting medication.

Control of Isolated and Epidemic Infection

Leigh B. Grossman

An estimated 20 million children under 5 years of age in the United States are enrolled in child care programs, either part- or full-time. These infants and young children are particularly susceptible to many infectious agents due to their limited immunity, the degree of close contact between children and staff, and the lack of hygienic practices. Infectious diseases readily spread among the children, staff, family members, and community. The child care setting carries a great potential for infectious disease outbreaks.

An outbreak or epidemic is defined as a recent or sudden excess of cases (three or more) of a specific disease or clinical symptom. Individual cases of certain diseases, such as measles, constitute an outbreak. A foodborne outbreak occurs when two or more persons experience gastrointestinal tract disease after ingesting a common food or water.

The investigation of an outbreak or suspected outbreak of a disease may not be required for every infectious problem you identify. In some situations, the factors associated with the problem may be apparent, and you can implement control measures without conducting an investigation. But if you do not know the factors (causative agent, source, and/or mode of transmission) associated with the problem, a systematic investigation of the outbreak should be conducted (Table 4.1).

Table 4.1.   Systematic Approach to Outbreak Investigation

- Verify the diagnosis of the reported or suspected case (illness).
- Implement interim infection control measures.
- Develop a case definition.
- Search for existing and new cases.
- Characterize the cause by person, place, time, and risk factors.
- Formulate a tentative hypothesis.
- Update infection control measures.
- Test the hypothesis. (In most child care centers or preschools, this step may be eliminated unless resources are available to conduct the necessary studies.)
- Write a report summarizing the results of the investigation.

EPIDEMIC INVESTIGATION

To verify a reported or suspected infectious disease in a child, contact the child's physician. The local health department may be contacted to assist in the investigation as well as follow-up of exposed persons. After the diagnosis is confirmed, a decision to proceed with the investigation depends on multiple factors such as causative agent, immune status of the children exposed, mode of transmission and incubation period of the infectious disease, and the time interval between onset of the illness in the index case and notification of the center.

If high morbidity or mortality is occurring, the problem is unique or unusual, or there is a possibility of litigation or political pressure, the problem should be investigated. If the problem has occurred previously or you know the contributing factors, implement infection control measures without an investigation.

After the diagnosis is confirmed, interim infection control measures to contain or interrupt the transmission of the infectious disease should be implemented. All members of the child care setting should be informed of the implementation of the control measures (Table 4.2). More specific control measures may be necessary as more information becomes available during the investigation.

The nature of the case or infectious problem that is occurring should be defined in order to recognize existing or new cases. The definition should be based on the causative agent, site of infection, and/or clinical

Table 4.2. Examples of Interim Epidemic Control Measures

- Wash hands with soap and water immediately after handling infants, blowing noses, changing diapers, or using toilet facilities, and before handling food. Alcohol-based hand gels are an effective alternative if hands are not visibly covered with secretions/excretions. The use of disposable gloves is helpful but not a substitute for good hand disinfection/handwashing practices.
- Discourage sharing of personal articles and toys.
- Clean soiled surfaces with a disinfectant rated by the U.S. Environmental Protection Agency or household bleach diluted 1 part bleach to 100 parts water.
- Change clothing as soon as it is soiled; place in a plastic bag to be sent home.
- Use disposable diapers; discard into a covered container.
- Cohort infected or exposed children with personnel who are not caring for noninfected or unexposed children.
- Assess staff's risk and need for intervention to ensure that all employees are protected.
- Exclude new admissions to the child care center or preschool during the outbreak.
- Notify families of the involved children; instruct them to keep the sick child or children at home (see Appendix 4.1).

---

signs and symptoms. As the investigation proceeds, further information may be obtained that will require the case definition to be revised.

The search for existing and new cases is necessary in order to estimate the magnitude of the problem. The staff should be educated regarding signs and symptoms of the illness so they can monitor exposed children and staff for the onset of the illness. Families should be asked to notify the center if their child becomes ill. To complete case findings, absences from the center should be contacted.

Characterize the data collected by person, place, time, and risk factors. The interrelationship of these factors will help formulate a valid hypothesis of the cause of the outbreak, the population at risk, and the incubation period of the infectious disease.

EPIDEMIC HYPOTHESIS

Based on the data collected, formulate a tentative hypothesis regarding the causative agent, source of infection, and mode of transmission of the infectious disease. The hypothesis should explain the majority of cases and permit intervention and control measures. Case control study, cohort study, and prospective intervention study are epidemiologic approaches to test the hypothesis.

Unless an outbreak is associated with a commercial product, considerable morbidity, or mortality, hypothesis testing is usually aborted, particularly if the outbreak clears with coincident infection control measures.

The final step in the investigation of an outbreak is a written summary of the findings and recommendations to prevent a similar occurrence in the future. The report should include facts only—no explanations. The completed report should be disseminated to management and the individuals involved in the investigation.

EPIDEMIC PREVENTION

To prevent the spread of communicable illness among children and staff, health policies must be designed to reduce the risks associated with infections in the child care setting. Employee health guidelines should define health maintenance for personnel, including immune status and requirements for updating immunizations, disease history, tuberculosis screening, and work restrictions if an employee has or is exposed to a communicable disease. The staff should be required to participate in educational programs regarding hygienic practices, modes of transmission, and signs and symptoms of infectious diseases.

Requirements for program participants should include specific preadmission requirements for physical examination and current immunization status; children must receive additional immunizations as necessary. Recommendations for exclusion of sick children from the child care or preschool setting should include specific communicable diseases as well as criteria for return to the center following an illness (Table 4.3).

The child care or preschool administrator should be observant of illnesses occurring in staff and participants to determine whether patterns of infections occur. If a pattern is detected, prompt intervention is necessary. A resource consultant (e.g., public health provider, pediatrician) should be available to assist the child care center or preschool in determining appropriate measures to prevent the spread of infectious diseases.

Table 4.3. Communicable Diseases in Child Care Centers and Preschools

Infection	Infective Material	Incubation Period	Comments
Amebiasis (*Entamoeba histolytica*)	Feces	2–4 weeks	*Case:* Exclude during acute illness, until treated and until stools are free of oocysts. *Contacts:* Symptomatic contacts should be excluded until stools are screened for oocysts.
Campylobacter enteritis	Feces Contaminated food or water	1–7 days	*Case:* Exclude until 48 hours of effective therapy or until asymptomatic, whichever is shorter. *Contacts:* Exclusion not required.
Chickenpox (varicella)	Infected exudate Respiratory secretions	10–21 days	*Case:* Exclude until lesions are dry and crusted. *Contacts:* Exclude immunosuppressed children during outbreak.
Conjunctivitis Bacterial	Purulent exudate	24–72 hours	*Case:* Exclude until 24 hours of effective therapy. *Contacts:* Exclusion not required.
Viral (adenovirus, etc.)	Purulent exudate	12–72 hours	*Case:* Exclude until exudate resolves. *Contacts:* Exclusion not required.
Cytomegalovirus	Infected urine and saliva	1 month	*Case:* Exclusion not required. *Contacts:* Exclusion not required.
Diarrhea	Feces	1–3 days	*Case:* Exclude until symptoms resolve. *Contacts:* Exclusion not required.

(*continued*)

Table 4.3. (continued)

Infection	Infective Material	Incubation Period	Comments
Escherichia coli O157:H7	Feces Contaminated food	2–6 days (usually 3–4 days)	*Case:* Exclude until two serial stool cultures negative or until 10 days after cessation of symptoms. *Contacts:* Stool cultures not indicated in absence of symptoms.
Fifth disease (erythema infectiosum)	Respiratory secretions	4–14 days (usually 12–14 days)	*Case:* Exclusion not required. *Contacts:* Exclusion not required.
German measles (rubella)	Respiratory secretions	14–21 days (usually 16–18 days)	*Case:* Exclude for 7 days after onset of rash. *Contacts:* Those who are pregnant and not immunized should seek medical advice.
Giardia lamblia	Feces Contaminated food or water	1–4 weeks	*Case:* Exclude until asymptomatic. *Contacts:* No exclusion required.
Gingivostomatitis (herpes simplex virus)	Infected secretions	3–5 days	*Case:* Exclude until cutaneous lesions are dry and crusted. *Contacts:* Exclusion not required.
Haemophilus influenzae	Respiratory secretions	2–14 days	*Case:* Exclude during acute illness until treated. *Contacts:* Seek physician's advice concerning prophylaxis.
Hand, foot, and mouth syndrome (Coxsackie A16)	Feces Respiratory secretions	4–6 days	*Case:* Exclusion not required. *Contacts:* Exclusion not required.

Disease	Source	Incubation period	Exclusion guidance
Hepatitis A	Feces	15–50 days (usually 20–30 days)	*Case:* Exclude until 10 days after onset of symptoms and symptomatically able to participate in general activity. *Contacts:* Prophylaxis should be considered for staff and children.
Hepatitis B	Infected saliva or blood	6 weeks–6 months	*Case:* Exclude during acute illness and children with chronic hepatitis B surface antigens who bite or cannot contain secretions. *Contacts:* No exclusion required.
Impetigo contagiosa (*Staphylococcus*)	Lesion secretions	7–10 days	*Case:* Exclude for 48 hours of effective therapy. *Contacts:* Exclusion not required.
Infectious mononucleosis	Saliva	5–7 days	*Case:* Exclude until symptomatically able to tolerate general activity. *Contacts:* No exclusion required.
Influenza	Respiratory secretions	1–3 days	*Case:* Exclude until symptomatically able to tolerate general activity. *Contacts:* No exclusion required. Seek physician's advice concerning prophylaxis and immunization.
Lice (pediculosis)	Infested area	Approximately 7–10 days after eggs hatch	*Case:* Exclude until treated. *Contacts:* Examine for infestation and recommend treatment if needed.
Measles (rubeola)	Respiratory secretions	6–21 days (usually 10–12 days)	*Case:* Exclude until 5 days after appearance of rash. *Contacts:* Check immunization status. Exclude immediately on signs of prodrome.

(*continued*)

Table 4.3. (continued)

Infection	Infective Material	Incubation Period	Comments
Meningitis			
Meningococcal	Respiratory secretions	2–10 days	*Case:* Exclude during acute illness and until treated. *Contacts:* Seek physician's advice concerning prophylaxis and immunization.
Mumps (infectious parotitis)	Respiratory secretions	12–25 days	*Case:* Exclude for 9 days from onset of swelling; less if swelling subsides. *Contacts:* Susceptible contacts should seek physician's advice.
Pharyngitis			
Nonspecific	Respiratory secretions	12–72 hours	*Case:* Exclude only if child has fever or is unable to participate in general activities. *Contacts:* Exclusion is not required.
Streptococcal	Respiratory secretions	1–4 days	*Case:* Exclude for 24 hours of effective therapy. *Contacts:* Exclusion not required.
Pinworms (*Enterobius vermicularis*)	Feces, contaminated fomites, clothing, house dust, etc.	2 weeks–2 months	*Case:* Exclude until treated. *Contacts:* Exclusion not required.
Pneumococcal infections (otitis media, respiratory infections, meningitis, bacteremia)	Respiratory secretions	Varies with type of infection (1–30 days)	*Case:* Exclude only if child has fever or is unable to participate in general activities. *Contacts:* Exclusion is not required. Susceptible contacts should seek physician's advice concerning immunization.

Disease	Mode of transmission	Incubation period	Exclusion guidelines
Respiratory infections (upper respiratory infections, colds, bronchitis)	Respiratory secretions	12–72 hours	*Case:* Exclude only if child has fever or is unable to participate in general activities. *Contacts:* Exclusion not required.
Roseola	Probably respiratory secretions	5–15 days	*Case:* Exclude until rash has disappeared. *Contacts:* No exclusion required.
Rotavirus	Feces	1–3 days	*Case:* Exclude until asymptomatic. *Contacts:* No exclusion required.
Salmonellosis	Feces, Contaminated food	6–72 hours	*Case:* Exclude during acute illness, usually 5–7 days. *Contacts:* Stool cultures not indicated in absence of symptoms.
Scabies	Infested areas	2–6 weeks; 1–4 days after reinfestation	*Case:* Exclude until treated. *Contacts:* Direct inspection of body.
Scarlet fever (*Streptococcus*)	Respiratory secretions	1–4 days	*Case:* Exclude for 24 hours of effective therapy. *Contacts:* Exclusion not required.
Shigellosis	Feces	1–7 days (usually 1–2 days)	*Case:* Exclude for 5 days of antibiotics or until stool cultures are negative. *Contacts:* Stool cultures indicated only in suspected outbreak.
Tuberculosis	Respiratory secretions	2–10 weeks	*Case:* Exclude until physician advises return. *Contacts:* Seek physician's advice concerning prophylactic treatment.

(continued)

37

Table 4.3. (continued)

Infection	Infective Material	Incubation Period	Comments
Whooping cough (pertussis)	Respiratory secretions	7–21 days (usually 7–10 days)	Case: Exclude until 5–7 days of effective therapy and physician advises return. Contacts: Seek physician's advice concerning prophylactic treatment.
Yersiniosis	Feces Contaminated food or water	2–11 days (usually 3–7 days)	Case: Exclude during acute illness. Contacts: Exclusion not required.

Appendix 4.1

Sample Information That May Be Sent Home to Parents or Guardians*

The disease(s) checked below are now occurring in your child's day care center or preschool, and your child may have been exposed. You may want to call your physician if any of the symptoms listed here appear. Better protection for all results when ill children are kept home until they have recovered.

—**Amebiasis (*Entamoeba histolytica*):**
Usually asymptomatic but occasionally varies from acute diarrhea with fever, chills, and bloody or mucoid diarrhea to mild abdominal discomfort with diarrhea containing blood or mucus, alternating with periods of constipation or remission. The incubation period is 2 to 4 weeks. The child will not be allowed to attend if the diarrhea contains blood or pus or is accompanied by fever. The child may return following treatment for the acute illness, and when stools are free of oocysts.

—**Chickenpox (varicella):**
Small water blisters on the scalp, neck, and covered parts of the body are usually the first signs noted. The blisters break easily. The child may become cross, tire easily, and have a fever during the first few days of disease. The incubation period is 10 to 21 days; commonly, 13 to 17 days. Sick children must be kept at home until all lesions are dry and crusted. Consult your physician for prophylactic protection if your child is immunocompromised.

---

*Adapted from the Child Care Center, University of Virginia Health System, Charlottesville, Virginia.

—Conjunctivitis:
Inflammation of the eye, causing redness, tearing, and occasionally formation of pus. The incubation period is 12 to 72 hours for viral infection and 24 to 72 hours for bacterial infection. Children with conjunctivitis must be kept at home until 24 hours after initiation of effective bacterial therapy or, in viral disease, until purulent discharge disappears.

—Cytomegalovirus:
Rarely produces symptomatic disease; when it does, it is characterized by fever, sore throat, and swollen lymph nodes (glands). The incubation period is 1 month. Children will be allowed to attend as long as they are able to function within the normal activities of their class.

—Diarrhea:
Increase of frequency and change of consistency in bowel movements from the child's normal pattern; fever may or may not be present. The incubation period depends on the causative agent (salmonellosis—6 to 72 hours; shigellosis—1 to 7 days; yersiniosis—2 to 11 days; *Campylobacter*—1 to 7 days; *E. coli* O157:H7—3 to 8 days; viral—24 to 48 hours). The child will not be allowed to attend if diarrhea is accompanied by fever or other symptoms, such as vomiting, irritability, dehydration, lethargy, blood, or pus. The child may return once the diarrhea is manageable and/or symptomatic infection has been treated.

—Fifth Disease (erythema infectiosum):
A rose-red rash (slapped-face appearance) on the face, which fades and recurs and may spread to the limbs and trunk. By the time the rash appears, the child is no longer contagious and may return to child care or preschool.

—German measles (rubella):
A light rash, mild symptoms, with glands behind the ears and neck enlarged. The incubation period usually is 14 to 21 days. Sick children must be kept at home for a minimum of 7 days after the onset of rash and until all symptoms have disappeared.

—*Giardia lamblia*:
May be associated with a variety of intestinal symptoms, such as chronic diarrhea, abdominal cramps, bloating, frequent loose

and pale greasy stools, fatigue, and weight loss. The incubation period is 1 to 4 weeks. Sick children must be kept at home until diarrhea has resolved.

—Gingivostomatitis (herpes simplex virus):
Infection may be mild to severe and is marked by fever and malaise lasting a week, accompanied by vesicular lesions in and around the mouth and nose. The incubation period is 3 to 5 days. Children must remain at home until the lesions are dry and crusted.

—Hand, foot, and mouth syndrome (Coxsackie A16):
Characterized by sudden onset, fever, sore throat, and lesions that may occur on the inside of the mouth (cheeks, gums, and sides of tongue) as well as on the palms, fingers, and soles. Occasionally, lesions appear on the buttocks. The incubation period is 4 to 6 days. Children will be allowed to attend, as long as they are able to function within the normal activities of their class, including outdoor activities.

—Hepatitis A:
Sudden onset of fever, malaise, loss of appetite, nausea, and abdominal discomfort followed by jaundice. The incubation period is 15 to 50 days. Sick children must be kept at home until physician advises return. Consult your physician for prophylactic protection of your child. Your physician may recommend hepatitis A immunization as part of a community-wide outbreak control program.

—Hepatitis B:
Characterized by loss of appetite, abdominal discomfort, nausea, and vomiting. Joint pain and rash may occur as well as jaundice and a mild fever. The incubation period is 6 weeks to 6 months. Sick children must be kept at home during acute illness, and children with chronic disease who bite or cannot contain secretions will be excluded.

—Impetigo:
Starts with multiple skin lesions, usually around the face and mouth and other exposed areas, such as the elbows, legs, and knees. The lesions vary in size and shape and begin as blisters but rapidly change to yellow crusted areas on a reddened base.

The incubation period is 1 to 10 days. Children must remain home until they have received at least 48 hours of effective antibiotic therapy.

—Infectious mononucleosis:

An acute syndrome characterized by fever, sore throat, weakness, and enlarged lymph nodes (glands), especially in the neck. The incubation period is 5 to 7 weeks. Child must be kept at home until symptoms disappear and he or she is able to tolerate general activity.

—Influenza:

An acute illness characterized by fever, chills, headache, muscle aches, mild sore throat, and cough. The incubation period is 1 to 3 days. Sick children must be kept at home until general activity is tolerated. Aspirin or aspirin-containing products should be avoided during influenza infection because of the association with Reye's syndrome. Consult your physician for advice concerning prophylaxis and immunization.

—Lice (pediculosis):

Severe itching and scratching of the scalp. Eggs of head lice (nits attached to hairs) are small round gray lumps. Children with head lice should remain at home until they have been treated. Advise examination of household and other close personal contacts, with concurrent treatment as indicated. Clothing, bedding, and other vehicles of transmission should be treated by laundering in hot water, by dry cleaning, or by application of an effective chemical insecticide.

—Measles (rubeola):

Runny nose, sneezing, coughing, watery eyes, and fever, with a red blotchy rash appearing on the third to seventh day. The incubation period is 6 to 21 days; commonly, 10 to 12 days. Sick children are to be kept home for a minimum of 5 days from the appearance of the rash. Consult your physician for prophylactic protection of household contacts who have not had measles or who have not been immunized against measles.

—Meningitis:

Meningococcal infection is characterized by sudden onset of fever, intense headache, nausea and often vomiting, stiff neck, and frequently a rash. The incubation period varies from 2 to 10 days; commonly, 3 to 4 days. Consult your physician regarding immunization and/or prophylactic treatment of your child.

Haemophilus influenzae infection has a sudden onset of fever, vomiting, lethargy, and stiff neck and back. Progressive stupor and coma are common. The incubation period is 2 to 14 days. Consult your physician regarding prophylactic treatment of your child.

—Mumps (parotitis):
Fever with swelling and tenderness in front of and below the ear or under the jaw. The incubation period is 12 to 25 days. Sick children must be kept home until the swelling of all glands involved and all symptoms have disappeared.

—Nonspecific respiratory infection:
Runny nose, sneezing, lacrimation, irritated nasopharynx, and malaise lasting 2 to 7 days. The incubation period is usually 12 to 72 hours. Child will be allowed to attend, as long as he or she has no fever and is able to function within the normal activities of the class, including outdoor activities.

—Roseola:
Characterized by sudden fever, sometimes as high as 106°F (41°C), which lasts 3 to 5 days. A rash appears on the chest and abdomen with moderate involvement of the face and extremities as the temperature returns to normal. Rash lasts 1 to 2 days. Child may return to school when rash disappears.

—Rotavirus:
Sporadic severe diarrhea and vomiting, often with dehydration. The child will not be allowed to attend until he or she is asymptomatic.

—Scabies:
Begins as itchy raised areas or burrows around finger webs, wrists, elbows, armpits, and the belt line. Extensive scratching often occurs, especially at night, with secondary sores. The incubation period is 2 to 6 weeks; 1 to 4 days after repeat exposure. Children with scabies should be kept at home until they have been treated.

—Streptococcal infections (sore throat or scarlet fever):
Sudden illness with vomiting, fever, sore throat, and headache. Usually within 24 hours, a bright red rash appears. Some cases may not have a rash, although disease is just as serious. The incubation period is 1 to 3 days. If your child has any of these symptoms, you should contact your physician. Sick children are to be kept at home until 24 hours after initiation of effective antibiotic therapy with clinical improvement.

—Tuberculosis:
Fatigue, fever, and weight loss may occur early, while cough, chest pain, hoarseness, and coughing up blood may occur in more advanced disease. The incubation period is 2 to 10 weeks. Consult your physician regarding prophylactic treatment of your child.

—Whooping cough (pertussis):
A persistent cough that later comes in spells and may have an associated whoop. Coughing may cause vomiting. Many cases have persistent cough but never whoop. The incubation period is 7 to 21 days. Sick children should be kept at home until 5 to 7 days after initiation of effective antibiotic therapy with clinical improvement. Consult your physician regarding prophylactic treatment of your child.

—Worms:
Worms passed in the stool or, occasionally, from the mouth or nose may be accompanied by wheezing, coughing, fever, diarrhea, abdominal pain, or itching around the rectum. The incubation period is about 2 months after ingestion of the worm eggs. Sick children must be kept at home until all symptoms have disappeared.

Section III

Care of High-Risk Children

Young Infants

Andrew D. Lynk
Deborah L. Kernested
E. Lee Ford-Jones

When compared with infants cared for at home, young infants in child care centers are more likely to develop both minor (nuisance) and serious (life-threatening) infections. In addition, signs of serious infection may be subtle. Child care centers are not appropriate for infants unless staff are active in health promotion and infection control activities. A young infant should be cared for by a trained, primary (regularly assigned) caregiver within a safe and stimulating environment. The total group size should be small, and the staff:child ratio should be less than or equal to 1:4. We have known for a number of years that these same measures, which reduce the risk of infection, are also important to a child's healthy emotional development.

INFECTIOUS RISKS

Young infants in child care centers are uniquely prone to potentially more frequent and severe infections for several reasons.

Increased Susceptibility. An infant's immune system (natural bodily defense against infection) is less developed and capable than that of an older child. This results in more difficulty fighting an initial infection as well as repeated illnesses with the same infectious agent.

Infants Lack Complete Immunization. Infants who have not received the diphtheria-pertussis-tetanus-polio, *Haemophilus influenzae*, hepatitis B, varicella, pneumococcal, influenza, and measles, mumps, rubella vaccinations are susceptible to these preventable infections.

Increased Exposure.   It is normal for any child entering a group situation where exposure is increased (e.g., public school) to have more infections. Infants in group care face such increased exposure from staff, other children, and even other parents. This results in ample opportunity for transmission of infectious agents, primarily via unwashed hands (very common) but also through contaminated objects and surfaces.

Infants, in general, require more handling by caregivers for changing diapers, cuddling, feeding, and cleaning of facial secretions. Without proper preventive measures (e.g., handwashing), caregivers and other children may easily transmit high doses and wide varieties of infectious agents from one infant to another.

Infants also have frequent hand-to-mouth contact. This increases their exposure to any infectious agents in their surrounding environment, which may have been contaminated by sick staff or children or by apparently healthy children or staff who are at the beginning or end of an infectious disease. Respiratory viruses, for example, will persist for hours on surfaces. Other common infectious agents causing diarrheal illness (rotavirus, *Giardia*), hepatitis A, and cytomegalovirus (CMV) diseases may live for days to weeks on toys and play mats.

Tendency to Complications.   While some infectious agents, such as respiratory viruses, are a nuisance when they occur in the older child, in the young infant they may lead to prolonged, more severe disease and complications such as ear or lung infections.

COMMON INFECTIONS

Infections in infants attending child care centers can be broken down into (a) those causing illness in infants and adults (staff, parents), such as ear, other respiratory, and diarrheal infections; (b) those causing illness only in the infants (e.g., *Streptococcus pneumoniae* bacteremia); (c) those causing clinical illness primarily in adults (e.g., hepatitis A); and (d) those causing illness only in special situations (e.g., cytomegalovirus affecting the fetus of a pregnant staff member or parent). The carriage of common bacteria, now with increasing resistance to the commonly used antibiotics, is being more frequently recognized, although resulting severe infection still remains uncommon (e.g., penicillin-resistant pneumococcus, methicillin-resistant *Staphylococcus aureus*).

Infants and children who attend child care centers are more likely to carry antibiotic-resistant bacteria and, specifically, antibiotic-resistant *S. pneumoniae* or methicillin-resistant *S. aureus*, which then places them at greater risk of serious infection with these bacteria. This emerging problem of increased incidence of antibiotic-resistant bacteria is due to both personal antibiotic use and exposure to other colonized children who receive many antibiotics.

Infants are commonly and repeatedly infected with seasonal viruses, which may cause colds, diarrhea, rashes, and fevers. Colds in infants are commonly complicated by ear or eye infections and sometimes by pneumonia. Although hepatitis A may be a common and mild infection in infants in child care, it may cause more serious disease in susceptible adults (caregivers, parents) who are secondarily exposed at work or at home.

INFECTION CONTROL

Special Infection Control Needs. Infants do require special infection control procedures. Pediatric infection control experts now recommend the same things psychologists have known for years to be important to an infant's well-being: a primary caregiver who is trained and motivated, a small group size, and a staff:infant ratio of less than or equal to 1:4.

Physical Organization. There should be separate rooms and caregivers for diapered and nondiapered children. Food preparation areas must be separate from diaper change areas; each should have handwashing facilities. Bathrooms must include handwashing facilities. Cribs should be separated by at least 3 feet to decrease the transmission of airborne pathogens, and bedding and mattresses should not be shared unless thoroughly cleaned first.

Staffing. A staff:child ratio of 1:3 or 1:4 and a small group size (8 to 12 infants maximum) are required. Staff require training and ongoing supervision of their work. Assignment of a primary caregiver will reduce exposures and thus the risk of infection. Responsibilities for diaper changing and food and formula preparation should be assigned to different staff as much as possible. Infants should also be protected from other children and caregivers who are ill with colds or other infections.

Handwashing.   Handwashing is a crucial infection control measure. Careful handwashing reduces transmission of infections dramatically. For example, 50% reduction rates in diarrhea were observed in centers adopting a careful handwashing regimen.

Diapering.   Hygienic precautions, especially handwashing and surface cleansing, must be ensured during the changing and disposing of diapers. Disposable diapers are recommended. Handwashing facilities including disposable towels are recommended.

Food Preparation.   Food preparation areas require sinks and towel supplies separate from diaper change facilities. Hands must be washed before food and formula preparation and before feeding an infant. Food should be refrigerated, and any unused food or formula discarded within 24 hours.

Toys.   Infants may play with washable toys that are disinfected before and after use by another infant. (To clean, wash toys with dishwashing detergent and water, then rinse in a dilute 1:10 to 1:100 bleach solution.) Infants should not be given shared, nonwashable soft toys that may be contaminated with infectious secretions.

Environmental Cleaning.   Individual bedding must be washed at least weekly. Other surfaces should be cleaned between use or daily, depending on the item.

Surveillance of Infants for Symptoms of Infection.   Primary caregivers must be watchful for subtle signs of infection in young infants, such as changes in feeding or behavioral patterns. These may be the only manifestations of serious infections in young infants.

Risks to Healthy Children.   Healthy children exposed to infants at child care centers do have an increased risk of infection. Staff working with diapered infants may directly (via hands) or indirectly (via food, mats, or toys) infect other healthy children if hygienic precautions (separate staff, separate areas, handwashing) are not maintained. Note that infected infants may appear well if they are just starting or ending an illness or have mild or clinically undetectable infections such as is the case with hepatitis A. It is therefore crucial to maintain hygienic precautions at *all times*. Allowing infants and older mobile children to play together increases everyone's exposure to infectious agents.

Infants who have acquired infections such as diarrhea or head and chest colds at the child care center are likely to infect 20 to 100% of their own healthy family members. In most cases, the healthy child, if older, will have milder disease, and the reason for separation of infants from healthy children is primarily to protect the infant. In the case of hepatitis A, infection is usually more severe in the older child or adult.

Exclusion from Child Care Center Attendance.   As with older children, infants should be screened daily and excluded when they have signs and symptoms of illness that require a degree of care or manpower beyond the staff's abilities and available time. The following is a list of signs and symptoms of infection in infants that should serve as attendance exclusion criteria:

- Fever (rectal temperature is greater than 101°F or 38.3°C)
- Rash with fever
- Diarrhea (loose stools that cannot be contained with a diaper)
- Vomiting
- Unusual tiredness
- Poor feeding
- Persistent crying or irritability
- Breathing difficulties or persistent coughing
- Yellow skin or eyes (jaundice)

When child care staff notice any of the symptoms above, the parents should be contacted, and medical attention sought.

Recommendations for Personnel. All personnel caring for young infants should receive specific training and ongoing supervision regarding:

- Disease transmission and prevention

- Principles and practice of
  (a) Handwashing
  (b) Diapering procedures
  (c) Food handling, preparation, and feeding
  (d) Environmental cleanliness

- First aid and cardiopulmonary resuscitation

- Recognition of behavioral variations in both healthy and ill infants

- Maintenance of daily records on each infant, based on information from staff and parents

Signs of illness in young infants may be subtle. Caregivers should consistently look after the same infants and communicate closely with their parents on a daily basis so that they may recognize which behaviors (e.g., feeding, temperament, stooling) are normal and which are not.

Caregivers should have written policies and procedures to deal with infant illnesses and emergencies. Ideally, child care centers should have access to a nurse and/or physician consultant and to copies of relevant aspects of each child's current health records.

Caregivers should not look after more than three or four infants, nor should they work concurrently with toddlers and older children.

Staff who are sick with the following illnesses should not take care of infants:

- Diarrhea and/or vomiting

- Measles, mumps, or rubella

- Chickenpox or shingles

- Skin infections

- Pulmonary tuberculosis

- Hepatitis

- Head colds and coughs

- Cold sores on lips

Parental Advice.   Young infants at child care centers are prone to more frequent minor and serious infections than are infants cared for at home and older children.

Exposure to infectious agents at any child care center is dependent on several factors:

- The total number of children at the center

- The amount of antibiotic use among attendees (i.e., increased use of antibiotics) results in a greater likelihood of antibiotic-resistant bacteria at the center

- The completeness of age-appropriate immunizations for each child

- Infant group size (ideally, not more than 8 to 12)

- The ratio of staff to infants (ideally, less than 1:4)

- Whether or not each small group of infants has an exclusive, skilled, primary caregiver

- The training and supervision of the staff in standard environmental hygiene practices (e.g., proper handwashing after diaper changing and before food preparation and feeding)

- The floor design and availability of proper equipment to ensure safe hygienic practices (e.g., number of sinks, separate diaper and kitchen facilities, 3-foot space between cribs, physical separation of infants and their caregivers from older children)

- The enforcement of specific, written exclusion policies for children and staff

- Liaison with the local department of public health

Parents must have prearranged alternative care plans for their infants in the event of illness. They should appreciate the importance and benefits of well-supervised health procedures and exclusion policies. They should always advise the child care center of the cause of any illness necessitating their child's absence.

Parents should get to know and maintain daily communications with their child's primary caregiver.

Parents should be aware that young infants, even in excellent centers, will probably have more frequent colds and febrile illnesses, most of which will be minor. However, it may be difficult for caregivers to distinguish minor from serious febrile illnesses in infants less than 3 to 6 months of age.

Parents should insure that their children are immunized at the appropriate age with all recommended vaccines. Parents should realize that their child will be exposed to and may acquire more resistant bacteria. Parents can reduce this risk by avoiding the unnecessary use of antibiotics in their children.

Children with Immunodeficiencies

Philip A. Pizzo

INFECTIOUS RISKS

Protection of a child's body against infection includes the cooperative activity and interaction of physical barriers that keep germs out of the body (e.g., lining of the mouth, intestinal and respiratory tracts) and the germ-fighting molecules produced by blood cells and the immune system to help fight invading microorganisms, in concert with the protective effects that come from the organisms that normally reside safely in various body surface areas. When any one of these components becomes impaired by either a disease or its treatment, an immune deficiency and increased susceptibility to infection can occur. Unfortunately, in a number of immunodeficiencies, more than one component is adversely affected, rendering the body at risk for a wide array of potential infectious complications.

Immunodeficiencies have traditionally been divided into either those that are congenital (i.e., child is born with) or those that are acquired (after birth). Congenital immunodeficiencies are uncommon and can affect one or more components of the immune system. These deficiencies often become manifest shortly after birth but may sometimes become apparent only during the early years of life. An acquired immunodeficiency refers to a deficit of the immune system that is the consequence of a disease or treatment occurring after birth. Of the acquired immunodeficiencies, the abnormalities consequent to cancer and its treatment, transplantation and its treatment, treatment with immunosuppressive drugs, and the severe sequelae of infection with the human immunodeficiency virus (HIV) represent the major causes of acquired immunodeficiency in childhood.

Regardless of whether the immune impairment is a defect with which the child was born or whether it occurs after birth as a consequence of disease or its treatment or a new infection such as HIV, the end result is the inability to fight off germs that either are newly acquired or have already been part of the normal microbial flora.

COMMON INFECTIONS

Immunocompromised children are subject to infection with virtually all classes of microorganisms. These include the bacteria, fungi, viruses, and protozoans. However, the risk for infection from one or more of these microorganisms can be related to the specific immune defect or constellation of immune impairments that have occurred. Accordingly, there are both similarities and differences in the types of infections that occur in children who are immunocompromised as a consequence of cancer, transplantation, immunosuppressive therapy, or HIV infection.

The child with cancer is at highest risk for infection when receiving more intensive courses of cancer cell–destroying (i.e., cytotoxic) chemotherapy. This is the period when neutropenia (low blood counts) is most common and when infection with various members of the indigenous microflora (the germs that normally live within the body) are most likely to occur. Gram-positive and gram-negative aerobic bacteria are the major causes of infection during the early stages of neutropenia. In most centers around the country, staphylococci and streptococci now predominate. In some cases, infections are related to the presence of indwelling Hickman-Broviac catheters or abnormalities of the lining of the gastrointestinal tract. In other cases, the streptococci (such as the alpha viridans streptococci) can cause serious infection as a consequence of certain types of chemotherapy or ulcerations in the oral cavity sometimes associated with the herpes simplex virus. In addition, the gram-negative bacteria *Escherichia coli*, *Klebsiella*, and *Pseudomonas aeruginosa* can also lead to serious infection during periods of neutropenia. Although fungi have become increasingly important as a cause of infection in the neutropenic cancer patient, these infections occur predominantly in patients who have more prolonged periods of neutropenia. The child with cancer is also at risk for infection with certain parasites, the most notable of which is *Pneumocystis carinii*. Reactivation infections can occur with viruses, particularly in the herpes group. The most notable pathogens are herpes simplex and cytomegalovirus. Varicella-zoster virus also represents a very notable threat. Indeed, without treatment, the occurrence of varicella-zoster virus in a seronegative child who is undergoing immunosuppressive therapy can be associated with significant morbidity and even mortality. Also, the respiratory viruses (especially respiratory syncytial virus, parainfluenza, and adenovirus) can cause serious respiratory and systemic infections in immunocompromised cancer patients. Because of its increasing frequency and the occurrence of outbreaks in recent years, measles virus must now once again be added to the list of potential pathogens for the cancer patient.

For the child who has undergone a bone marrow or organ transplant and who is receiving immunosuppressive therapy to maintain the graft, the predominant infections that occur are a consequence of depressed cellular immunity. These include, therefore, reactivation infections with *P. carinii* or with the herpesviruses or adenovirus. Of the herpesviruses, herpes simplex virus and cytomegalovirus are again most notable, and if the child has not previously been infected or immunized, exposure to varicella or measles can also result in significant morbidity. For those children who have had chickenpox and who have undergone bone marrow transplantation or who have received intensive chemotherapy, there is an increased risk for developing reactivation infection with varicella-zoster virus, which is manifested as dermatomal lesions. Depending upon the intensity of the chemotherapy, children who are significantly immunosuppressed and who develop dermatomal zoster are at heightened risk for developing cutaneous or visceral dissemination with this virus.

Children with HIV infection, like those with cancer, can develop infection with virtually all the classes of microorganisms. Although the immune abnormalities in children with cancer can be severe, they are generally intermittent and may abate when chemotherapy is not being given. In contrast, the immune deterioration associated with HIV infection tends to be progressive and unrelenting. Accordingly, the actual pathogens and patterns of infection can vary between children with cancer versus those with HIV infection. For example, the child with HIV infection is at increased risk for developing bacterial infections with encapsulated organisms such as *Streptococcus pneumoniae* or *Haemophilus influenzae*. This is most likely consequent to the antibody dysfunction and defective neutrophil chemotaxis that occur in children with HIV infection. Unless they have indwelling catheters in place or are hospitalized, children with HIV infection are less commonly infected with the bacteria that predominate in pediatric cancer patients. Fungi also can cause significant infections in children with HIV disease; the major pathogen is *Candida*, and the major site of infection tends to be the oral cavity (manifested as thrush) or the esophagus (manifested as an esophagitis with retrosternal burning pain). It is rare for the child with HIV infection to develop invasive fungal disease because quantitative impairments of neutrophils are much less common in these children than in children with cancer. Parasitic infections do occur in children with HIV disease, most notably *P. carinii*, although this again represents a reactivation infection consequent to the degree of immunosuppression that has occurred in the child with HIV. In infants, however, *Pneumocystis* pneumonia can occur as a primary infection and is associated with considerable morbidity and mortality. This underscores the importance for early diagnosis and for surveillance to define high-risk children. To date, it has been infrequent for children with HIV infection to develop some of the other opportunistic infections that have been so common in adults, such as toxoplasmosis or cryptococcosis. However, children with HIV disease are subject to viral infections including the respiratory viruses (which can be associated with chronic shedding of respiratory syncytial virus or parainfluenza), the herpesvirus, cytomegalovirus, and, of course, the varicella-zoster virus. These are the same organisms that can infect normal healthy children, but for the child with HIV disease, the consequences of infection can be considerably greater. Indeed, children with HIV can develop chronic infection, with varicella-zoster virus, and severe infections, including blindness, with cytomegalovirus. Children with HIV infection can also develop chronic infections with organisms such as cryptosporidia, salmonellae, or mycobacteria. Although the atypical mycobacteria (e.g., *Mycobacterium avium-intracellulare*) predominate in children, like adults with HIV disease, *Mycobacterium tuberculosis* is another likely cause of infection, and the increased frequency of this infection in high-risk children, along with the burgeoning problem of drug-resistant strains, is of considerable concern.

In summary, children with immunodeficiencies are subject to a wide array of pathogens. Many of these organisms are part of the normal flora of patients and do not cause infection when the immune system is intact. Thus, for example, the child with cancer is more susceptible to infections that arise from within his or her own body than from those that occur as a consequence of exposure to others. To a large degree this is also true of children with HIV infection, although they have a heightened susceptibility to the common bacterial organisms that occur throughout childhood, particularly *S. pneumoniae* and *H. influenzae*. Although children with immunodeficiency are more vulnerable to these infections, were they to share these same organisms with children who were immunocompetent, either no infection would occur, or if infection did occur, it would be no more serious than had it been acquired from a child who had no known immunodeficiency state.

INFECTION CONTROL

There are both similarities and differences in the infection control measures that should be considered and applied to children with cancer, acquired immunodeficiency syndrome (AIDS), or other immunodeficiency states. Because they will represent the majority of the children at risk, the recommendations that follow will be categorized according to (a) whether the underlying disease is cancer and treatment is with immunosuppressive therapies and (b) whether these children have AIDS. The single overriding principle that applies to the care of immunocompromised children (as well as healthy children) is careful handwashing, especially following diaper changes or assisting with toileting procedures. Second, adherence to the principles of standard precautions when handling blood should always be followed. It is more likely that a child (or staff member) in a child care center or preschool will not be diagnosed or recognized as being immunocompromised. Thus, staff education and adherence to simple infection control principles and procedures should be followed at all times and by everyone to keep the child care center or preschool safe for both children and staff members.

Special Infection Control Needs.

Children with Cancer, Transplants, or Those Receiving Immunosuppressive Therapy.   Since the majority of infections that arise in children who are immunocompromised because of cancer or its therapy are from organisms that are already part of those normally found in the patient's own body, they generally do not require special infection control procedures. Indeed, the majority of these organisms (gram-positive and gram-negative bacteria, *Candida, P. carinii,* and even herpesviruses) are widespread and generally are not causes of infection in immunocompetent individuals. Thus, these patients are at risk for infection from microorganisms that they already carry within them rather than from organisms that they might acquire from other children or from their environment. At the same time, the microorganisms responsible for causing infection in neutropenic children or in children who are receiving immunosuppressive therapy do not represent a particular hazard for children who are immunocompetent (i.e., whose immune systems are normal). There are, however, some exceptions, the most notable of which are viruses such as the varicella-zoster virus and measles. Children with cancer or those receiving immunosuppressive therapy who have not had a prior history of chickenpox or who have not been immunized prior to the onset of their disease and are exposed to an individual with chickenpox or with dermatomal zoster are at risk to develop primary varicella. Untreated, this infection can be extremely serious in the immunosuppressed child and carries a significant risk of morbidity or even mortality. Fortunately, the advent of antiviral therapy with acyclovir has significantly reduced the serious morbidity and mortality associated with primary varicella in an immunosuppressed individual. As the varicella-zoster vaccine becomes more widely used, it may also decrease the risk for infection. Although the varicella-zoster vaccine is NOT currently recommended for use in immunocompromised children, it is anticipated that herd immunity (i.e., immunity in large numbers of children, resulting in decreased risk for infection for those who are not immunized) could decrease the overall risk for this infection. Nonetheless, the major current objective is to attempt to prevent

varicella by recognizing when an exposure has occurred and administering immunoprophylaxis to the immunosuppressed child. Thus, if there are active cases of chickenpox in the child care center, children who are immunosuppressed should not be in attendance, since it is unlikely that they would be able to remain separated enough to offer protection. Chickenpox is, of course, one of the most contagious illnesses, and individuals who are seronegative are at high risk for developing infection through close contact with an infected individual. Should an exposure occur in the child care center, it is imperative that the physician of the child with cancer or those receiving immunosuppressive therapy be notified immediately. In almost all instances, the recommendation will be for the child to receive varicella zoster immune globulin, as this has been shown to either attenuate or prevent entirely the risk for developing an infection following exposure. However, to be successful, varicella-zoster immunoglobulin must be administered within 72 hours from the time of exposure. If an immune-compromised child has received intravenous immunoglobulin (IVIG) within 2 weeks of the exposure, it is not necessary to administer zoster immune globulin. Similarly, children who are immunosuppressed and who are exposed to a youngster who has developed measles should also receive immunoprophylaxis with gamma globulin in order to attempt to attenuate or prevent infection.

For the child with cancer, two additional infection control issues apply. First, although it is acceptable for children with low blood counts to attend child care or preschool, it must be noted that when their neutrophil count is low, they are at risk for developing an infectious complication, primarily with organisms that arise from within their own body. Fever is the major predictor of infection in patients with neutropenia. Consequently, if a child with cancer who is neutropenic becomes flushed and appears febrile or has lethargy or lassitude, his or her temperature should be taken. This should be done by the oral or axillary route but never with a rectal thermometer. This is because the use of a rectal thermometer in a child who is neutropenic can lead to erosions around the anus that could become a site of serious infection. If the temperature is elevated above 38°C, the child's parents or caretakers should be notified, and most likely, the child will need to be admitted to the hospital to receive antibiotic therapy until the source of the fever is determined or the period of risk (low neutrophil count) has passed. The second specific consideration applies to children who have indwelling Hickman-Broviac–type catheters. Of course, these catheters should not be manipulated in the child care or preschool environment, but if the child complains of tenderness around the skin or on the chest wall or along the abdomen where the catheter is placed, visual inspection to determine whether there is redness or tenderness should be undertaken. If this is the case, immediate medical attention is necessary, since an infection along the catheter tunnel is likely. Similarly, if the child develops a fever, even in the absence of low blood counts, and has an indwelling catheter, it is important that the child's parents and physician be notified, since, again, antibiotic therapy is likely to be necessary. However, in neither of these cases do the infections that arise represent hazards for other children.

Children with HIV Infection.   Children with HIV infection also are at risk for infections that arise from both their own indigenous flora and those that can be acquired from sources outside their own body. Since the predominant bacterial infections that occur in children with HIV infection are due to encapsulated bacteria such as *S. pneumoniae* or *H. influenzae*, it is quite possible that these organisms might be acquired from other children in a child care setting. However, since these organisms are ubiquitous, it is not reasonable to impose any particular isolation or restriction that would exclude children with HIV disease. Importantly, the advent of immunization against *S. pneumoniae* may decrease the risk for such infections in the future.

Even if they were immunized in the past, children with HIV may develop pertussis, making it important to consider this possibility in a child with a persistent or whooping-like cough. As with a child with cancer, most opportunistic infections (oral, pharyngeal, or esophageal candidiasis, *P. carinii* pneumonia) represent reactivation infections and are not ones that could be altered by special isolation or protection systems. Also similar to the child with cancer or to those receiving immunosuppressive therapy, children with HIV infection are at heightened risk for complications related to varicella-zoster virus or measles virus. Consequently, the same isolation and immunoprophylactic procedures described above for children with cancer should be applied to those with HIV infection. Although data are anecdotal, there is the suggestion that certain respiratory viral infections such as those due to the respiratory syncytial virus may be more serious in children with HIV infection or that symptoms and virus excretion may be more prolonged. However, because these organisms are also ubiquitous and because they could not be easily differentiated on clinical grounds from other upper or even lower respiratory tract infections occurring in immunocompetent children, it is not possible to recommend specific preventive strategies that might protect the child from acquiring this particular organism.

For both children with cancer and children with HIV infection, there are few data regarding the hazards of exposure to immunocompetent individuals who have been recently vaccinated. Although it appears likely that most vaccinations with attenuated or killed viruses or organisms are not likely to cause problems, it is possible that excretion of certain viruses such as oral poliovirus might represent a hazard for the child who is severely immunosuppressed. There is at least the theoretical possibility that excretion of poliovirus following administration of the live oral polio vaccine in an immunocompetent child might contribute to transmissibility. The live varicella vaccine has recently been approved for normal healthy children, and since a small percentage of children who receive this viral vaccine may develop a rash with vesicles that contain virus, it is possible that contact with these children may represent a hazard. However, since this same live vaccine has been tested in children undergoing cancer therapy and has not been associated with significant morbidity, the severity of infection associated with such contacts is likely to be minimal.

Risks to Healthy Children.

Children with Cancer, Transplants, or Those Receiving Immunosuppressive Therapy. Since the vast majority of infections that occur in children undergoing cancer therapy are with organisms that are not likely to be pathogenic to an immunocompetent child, normal healthy children are not at increased risk for infectious complications simply by having close contact with children with cancer. Moreover, those organisms that are potential infectious hazards are not associated with any increase in morbidity because they were acquired from a child who had cancer or who was receiving immunosuppressive therapy. Again, the major organisms of concern are likely to be viral and include in particular the varicella-zoster virus. It should be noted that children receiving immunosuppressive therapy may have a longer incubation period for varicella-zoster virus than do immunocompetent children, and rather than considering their period at risk as being from days 10 to 21 after exposure, most authorities would recommend that they be considered at risk for infection from days 10 to 28 after exposure to a child who had active varicella. There are no data to support that children with cancer have an increased likelihood for transmitting other common viral or bacterial pathogens as compared with those who are immunocompetent, and, therefore, no special precautions or recommendations are necessary.

Children with HIV Infection.   Although children with HIV infection do have an increased rate of infection with common bacterial organisms such as *S. pneumoniae* and *H. influenzae*, they are as likely to acquire as to transmit these organisms, and there are no data to support that children with HIV infection are more contagious or that the organisms are more virulent. However, it must be noted that among the bacteria are two organisms that could represent infectious hazards in healthy children. The first is *Salmonella*, since children with HIV infection can develop chronic infections with this organism. It has been generally recommended that HIV-infected children who are not toilet-trained be excluded from child care settings. While on the surface this advice seems reasonable, it is still possible for fecal-oral transmission to occur. Of course, the most important infection control measure that can be executed in any setting is careful handwashing. If both children and staff are instructed about the importance of this practice, especially after toileting or changing diapers, it seems likely that the risks for infection transmission can be well controlled. The second bacterial infection that deserves mentioning is mycobacteria. Although the majority of mycobacterial infections that occur in children and adults with HIV infection are due to atypical organisms, there has been an increase in the incidence of tuberculosis in urban areas, particularly with drug-resistant strains, that has been particularly associated with individuals infected with HIV. Although children who develop primary tuberculosis infections are usually not contagious, if a child with HIV disease has active tuberculosis, the child could pose a hazard to other children and would need to be excluded until the infection was cleared. Importantly, parents of children with HIV are vulnerable to acquisition or reactivation of tuberculosis and, if they are infected and contagious, they pose a threat to other children as well as personnel.

Most of the fungal organisms that occur in children with HIV do not represent infectious hazards for healthy children. *Candida* is a ubiquitous organism and most immunocompetent children are already colonized with it. *Cryptococcus* occurs only rarely in children with HIV infection, and person-to-person spread with this organism does not occur. Although *Histoplasma* can occur in children with HIV infection, in endemic areas this organism is ubiquitous, children are at risk for acquiring it in their home and environment, and the risk would not be increased by contact with children with HIV infection. Similarly, most of the parasitic infections that might occur in children with HIV disease are not likely to represent infectious hazards to immunocompetent or healthy children. *P. carinii* represents a reactivation infection, and virtually 100% of children who are immunocompetent have already acquired this organism by the time they are 2 years of age. Thus, exposure to a child with *P. carinii* pneumonia does not represent a hazard to the healthy child. Infants less than 2 years of age with HIV infection are susceptible to *P. carinii* pneumonia if their CD4 count declines and they are not receiving prophylaxis. Gastrointestinal infections associated with cryptosporidia or *Isospora belli* can be a significant cause of diarrhea in the HIV-infected child. These organisms can cause transient infection in other immunosuppressed children as well as in immunocompetent individuals. However, in healthy children, symptoms are transient and chronic infection does not occur. Thus, exposure to an HIV-infected child with cryptosporidia diarrhea does not represent a hazard to the healthy child in the child care or preschool setting.

Similar to children with cancer or those receiving immunosuppressive therapy, varicella can be a more significant infection in children with HIV disease. In addition, chronic or persistent cutaneous infections with the varicella-zoster virus can occur in HIV-infected children. Of course, if the HIV-infected child does develop active varicella, he or she should not be in a child care or preschool setting until the infection is resolved. Should a healthy child acquire the varicella-zoster virus from an HIV-infected child, there is no likelihood that the infection will be more serious than if it had been acquired from another healthy individual. Children with chronic skin lesions, whether due to the varicella-zoster virus or bacteria or other organisms, represent a risk when those lesions are active or draining. In general, if lesions are draining and cannot otherwise be covered, it is recommended that the HIV-infected child not have contact with other children in the child care or preschool setting.

The major concern, of course, centers around the possible transmission of HIV itself within the child care or preschool setting. Fortunately, this is an extremely difficult virus to transmit, and transmission can only occur by direct contact with blood or through sexual activities. Casual contact such as is incurred by playing or interacting in a normal family setting is not associated with the transmission of HIV infection. Indeed, a number of studies have demonstrated that even close contact, including kissing and sharing of food and eating utensils, toothbrushes, and other supplies, does not contribute to a risk for transmission of this virus. Much has been made about the possibility of transmission of HIV by biting. However, likelihood for this route of transmission is remote. At this time, the American Academy of Pediatrics recommends that only children who engage in repetitive biting behavior be excluded from child care or school. Thus, the only concerns that require attention for transmission of HIV should center on either blood transmission or sexual activity. Should the child with HIV infection have an injury that bleeds, or have a bloody nose, or have a cutaneous lesion that is oozing blood, care should be taken in assisting or helping the child. The use of standard precautions is recommended because in many settings it is possible that a child may be unrecognized as being infected with the virus. Accordingly, children and staff should be educated that whenever there is a youngster or an individual who has a bleeding lesion, gloves should be worn when offering assistance, and bloody fluids that may have spilled onto the floor, toys, or surfaces should be cleaned with a dilute (1:10 to 1:100) solution of bleach and water. Of course, such a solution should not be used to clean the child, since it can be caustic to body surfaces.

Should there be a question of sexual abuse within the child care or preschool setting, the possibility for HIV transmission must be considered, and testing may be appropriate and necessary.

Hepatitis B virus is transmitted in a similar way to HIV but is far more contagious, presumably because the inoculum size in blood or body fluids is much higher for hepatitis B virus than for HIV. The most effective precautions that could be used to curtail transmission of hepatitis B are those of standard precautions and universal immunization. Thus, if standard precautions are exercised, they will be effective against both hepatitis B virus and HIV. While hepatitis B is not found in the stool, hepatitis A can be transmitted by the fecal-oral route and underscores the importance of handwashing. Cytomegalovirus is also a ubiquitous organism in immunocompromised children and can be acquired by seronegative women. Urine or secretions are the likely sources for infection and again focus on the need for handwashing when body secretions and excretions are handled.

While precautions are easier to employ when the child is known to be infected or immunodeficient, it must be underscored that within a child care center, it is likely that the diagnosis will be unrecognized or that information may be withheld. Thus, especially in areas of the country where the rate of HIV is highest (i.e., large urban areas), it is likely that children with HIV will be found in child care centers and preschools.

Exclusion from Child Care or Preschool Attendance.

Children with Cancer, Transplants, or Those Receiving Immunosuppressive Therapy.   The major reasons for exclusion are when the child requires medical care or has an infection that is clearly transmissible to healthy children or staff members. As noted above, if the child with cancer has a low neutrophil count and develops a fever, he or she should be referred to a medical care system for antibiotic therapy. Similarly, if the child has an infection around an indwelling catheter or develops a fever and has a catheter, he or she must be referred to medical care for immediate intervention. Relatively few infections that occur in the child with cancer or those receiving immunosuppressive therapy represent hazards to other children and thus criteria for exclusion from the child care center.

Those that would include infections with varicella-zoster virus manifested either as chickenpox or dermatomal zoster or as infection with the measles virus. Although the immunocompetent child who has a negative history for varicella and who has contact and exposure with an infected child is at risk to develop chickenpox 10 to 21 days after the exposure, the child with cancer or who is receiving immunosuppressive therapy has a somewhat longer period of risk that might extend up to 28 days after the infectious exposure. Thus, a child with cancer may need to be excluded from the child care center or preschool from day 10 to 28 after an exposure if he or she is at risk to develop primary varicella. Risk is defined as a negative history of infection or a negative antibody titer against the varicella-zoster virus. Should the child have another potentially communicable disease, such as tuberculosis, exclusion from the center is necessary until adequate therapy has been delivered. It should be noted, however, that similar precautions would pertain to immunocompetent children who might acquire a similar infection.

Children with HIV Infection.   Similar to the child with cancer, only rarely is it necessary to exclude the child with HIV infection from the care center. Indeed, the major infectious hazards that would represent a source of concern would be if the child had an infection with tuberculosis, varicella, or measles. Similar guidelines and durations of exclusion would be followed for the child with HIV infection, as was noted for children with cancer or who were immunocompetent.

Recommendations for Personnel.   The most important practice that personnel can follow in caring for any child is careful handwashing. Indeed, whether the child is immunocompetent or immunosuppressed, the transmission of a variety of common infections, including respiratory viruses and gastrointestinal viruses (including hepatitis), could be reduced if careful handwashing is practiced. Furthermore, staff members should instruct children to wash their hands, particularly after toileting. Staff, of course, should always wash their hands between diaper changes or when assisting children with their toileting activities. When there is a known infectious hazard and staff must come in contact with soiled diapers, disposable gloves should be worn by the staff member. It must be underscored that wearing gloves is not a substitute for careful handwashing, since this practice must still be followed and adhered to as carefully as possible.

In urban areas where the risk for having a child with either HIV disease, tuberculosis, or hepatitis B is higher than in rural areas, staff should be informed about the potential infectious hazards as well as their routes of transmission. To that regard, staff must also be comfortable with the reality that the transmission of HIV virus by the kinds of contact that take place in a care setting is virtually impossible. Nonetheless, staff should exercise the principles of standard precautions when handling bloody secretions or a bleeding lesion. As noted above, spilled blood should be cleaned with a dilute solution of bleach and water.

Parental Advice. Parents should be reassured that the presence of a child who has cancer, who is receiving immunosuppressive therapy, or who has HIV does not represent a threat to the health of their child. Education is the best way to provide assurance. The now-vast experience of household contacts, as well as those in various school settings, should provide reassurance that contact with children with AIDS or those who are severely immunosuppressed because of cancer treatment will not result in transmission of diseases beyond those that could be acquired from otherwise healthy children. Any time children are in a closed setting, the likelihood for transmission of a variety of common infectious diseases is increased. However, children with AIDS or those receiving immunosuppressive therapy are not more likely to transmit infection but indeed are more likely to acquire certain of these infections. Thus, the parent of the healthy child can be reassured that his or her child will not be exposed to undue hazard by having contact with a child with cancer or with a child who is immunosuppressed because of a variety of therapies or because of HIV.

Children with Chronic Lung Disease

Leigh B. Grossman

INFECTIOUS RISKS

Children with cystic fibrosis (CF), asthma, bronchopulmonary dysplasia, or other chronic pulmonary disease are not at increased risk of acquiring infection. However, they are at marked risk of developing severe and life-threatening infection with pathogens that ordinarily cause mild upper respiratory infection, bronchitis, flu, and pneumonia in the healthy child.

COMMON INFECTIONS

Unless there are other aspects to their disease that make them immunocompromised (e.g., corticosteroid therapy, asplenia, acquired immunodeficiency syndrome, transplantation, or cancer therapy), the causes of infection in children with chronic lung disease do not differ from those of their family or other children in the child care center or preschool.

INFECTION CONTROL

Special Infection Control Needs. Preventing infection is the hallmark of effective infection control for this population. Vaccine prevention of preventable causes of infection is imperative, and this specifically includes pneumococcal vaccine, *Haemophilus influenzae* type b vaccine, and yearly immunization with influenza vaccine.

Respiratory syncytial virus infection is common in the day care setting and is a very high-risk pathogen for the infant with chronic lung disease. Preventive immunotherapies should be discussed with the child's physician. If possible, the infant with chronic lung disease should have a limited number of caretakers who thus minimize the child's exposure to a large number of pathogens. Consideration should be given to avoiding group child care during the times when many children at the center or school have upper respiratory illness (e.g., influenza season). In the case of the child with CF who is infected with *Burkholderia cepacia*, other children with CF are at risk of becoming infected with this pathogen and thus should not be in contact with the infected child.

Risks to Healthy Children. There are no unusual infectious risks caused by children with chronic pulmonary disease. These children may have unusual pulmonary and upper respiratory flora, but these organisms are not causative of disease in healthy children.

Exclusion from Child Care or Preschool Attendance. Children with pulmonary disease who have worsening of their pulmonary symptoms (cyanosis, grunting, altered breathing, increase in cough, vomiting) should be evaluated promptly by their physician. They should not be monitored in the child care or preschool setting.

Exclusion for infectious diseases should be guided by the recommendations for all children (note Chapter 4 and the specific infection in Section IV), realizing that children with chronic pulmonary problems may have a prolonged and more serious course.

Recommendations for Personnel. All personnel should receive annual influenza immunization to minimize their likelihood of developing infection and then spreading infection to high-risk infants and children. Personnel should be extremely cautious in caring for the child with chronic lung disease to ensure that mild infection in themselves or other attendees is not spread to these children. This is best effected through careful handwashing, particularly after handling children with other viral respiratory illnesses.

Parental Advice. Parents of healthy children should be told that children with chronic lung disease pose no unusual infectious risks to healthy children.

Parents of a child with chronic pulmonary disease should monitor their child for signs and symptoms of increased respiratory distress, particularly during seasons of increased viral respiratory illnesses. Parents should consider alternate child care situations where their child avoids group child care during times when many children at the center have upper respiratory illnesses. Parents should ideally have their child with chronic pulmonary disease cared for by a limited number of caregivers who receive annual influenza vaccination.

8

Children with Cardiac Disease

Karen S. Rheuban

INFECTIOUS RISKS

Children with congenital heart disease often do not tolerate significant lower respiratory tract illness. The mortality rate of patients with respiratory syncytial virus and coexisting congenital heart disease is high. Because pulmonary compliance is already reduced in the baseline state, patients with large left-to-right shunts and pulmonary edema do not tolerate acute pneumonitis and other lower respiratory tract infections.

COMMON INFECTIONS

The infections of children with heart disease do not differ from those of the surrounding family members. The exceptions include the child known to have asplenia, in which case overwhelming bacterial infection may occur (bacteremia and meningitis), and the patient who has been immunosuppressed following heart transplantation.

INFECTION CONTROL

Special Infection Control Needs. Prevention of infection is key to the management of children with heart disease in the day care setting. Immunization against such common infectious agents as influenza, *Haemophilus influenzae* type b, and pneumococcus will prevent a significant number of infections known to worsen the course of children with congestive heart failure and will help prevent overwhelming infection in children with asplenia. Respiratory syncytial virus infection is common in the day care setting and is a very high-risk pathogen for the infant with congenital and, particularly, cyanotic congenital cardiac disease. Preventive immunotherapies should be discussed with the child's physician. Immunosuppressed patients are at particular risk when exposed to the varicella virus and may not be immunized with live viral vaccines. Children with a history of rheumatic fever with cardiac involvement are at risk of recurrence of rheumatic fever when reinfected with group A beta hemolytic streptococci and should, therefore, receive prophylaxis in the form of oral or intramuscular penicillin. Patients with congenital and acquired heart disease should receive antibiotic prophylaxis against bacterial endocarditis for dental and other invasive procedures, most of which would not be relevant to the child care setting unless in an emergency.

Careful handwashing should be practiced when a viral illness is prevalent in the child care center or the preschool. If at all possible, the infant with significant heart disease should receive care from a limited number of caretakers during outbreaks of upper and lower respiratory viral infections.

9

The Child with Disabilities

Susan M. Anderson

Children with physical disabilities, cognitive disabilities, or sensory impairments all may be provided care within a child care or preschool setting.

The etiology of motor impairment in children with physical disabilities is varied; the majority are children with encephalopathies. Children with static encephalopathies include those with cerebral palsy, a nonprogressive disorder of movement, tone, and posture, and those with Down syndrome who have hypotonia and motor delays. Children may have progressive encephalopathies from either infectious etiologies such as acquired immunodeficiency syndrome (AIDS) or metabolic disease such as nonketotic hyperglycinemia. Children with static encephalopathy have a nonprogressive disorder and will continue to gain skills but at a slower than expected pace; in contrast, children with progressive encephalopathies will continue to have motor deterioration and lose previously acquired abilities. Children who have an acquired physical disability secondary to a closed head injury may have an evolving motor exam with improvement noted over time. Children with spinal cord injuries or myelomeningocele have paralysis below the motor level of the lesion. Children with neuromuscular disease include children with anterior horn cell disease (e.g., Werdnig-Hoffmann), myopathies, and Duchenne's muscular dystrophy. Neuromuscular disease, most commonly, has a progressive course, but may be static. Children with physical disabilities may also include children with congenital or acquired amputations and children with burn injuries.

Children with static or progressive encephalopathies may also have cognitive impairments. Children with static encephalopathies include those with mental retardation, developmental delay, and Down syndrome; these children continue to learn new skills, but do so at a slower than expected rate. Children with cognitive disabilities secondary to progressive encephalopathies will have deterioration of their language and problem-solving abilities, whereas children with closed head injuries may have an evolving picture with improvement noted over time. Children with learning disabilities are rarely identified before school age; however, the hallmark of the learning disabled child is discrepancy between language-based and problem-solving abilities. Autism is a non-progressive disorder of both verbal and non-verbal communication that has dramatically increased over the past 20 years. Children with minimal brain dysfunction or attention deficit disorder may be included among those with nonprogressive cognitive disabilities.

Children with sensory impairments include those who are blind or deaf.

INFECTIOUS RISKS

Children with disabilities are at increased risk of infection for several reasons. Children with severe motor impairment may be at increased risk secondary to both immobility and ineffective neurologic control of critical musculature. A child who is both immobile and has impaired control of pharyngeal musculature may be less able to clear respiratory secretions and thus be at risk of pulmonary infection. Children with severe immobility may be more prone to otitis media, particularly if their head is frequently in a dependent position and they are not able to clear oral secretions. Children with spinal cord injuries or myelomeningocele, because they have neurogenic bladders, are at increased risk of bladder colonization and symptomatic urinary tract infection.

Children with disabilities may also have reduced ability to manifest their symptoms. Some children may be unable to communicate symptoms effectively because of oral motor dysfunction or language delay. In addition, there may be the loss of physical ability to demonstrate specific symptoms. Children with neurogenic bladders, despite having an increased incidence of urinary tract infections, often do not have classic symptoms of urinary tract infection, such as frequency, urgency, and dysuria. Children with specific brain injury or cervical level spinal cord injury may have ineffective temperature control and may not demonstrate fever. In addition, children with disabilities may be less likely to receive well child care or be completely immunized.

COMMON INFECTIONS

There is no increased incidence of upper respiratory infections in children with disabilities. The occurrence of an upper respiratory infection in a child with oral motor dysfunction may compound the difficulty the child already has in handling secretions. There is an increased incidence of otitis media in children with cleft palate, secondary to palatal insufficiency. There is also an increased incidence of otitis media in children with Down syndrome, secondary to shortened and relatively horizontal eustachian tubes. There is an increased incidence of otitis media in children with oral motor dysfunction related to the inability to handle oral secretions.

As for lower respiratory infections, there is an increased incidence of aspiration pneumonia in some children with motor disabilities, secondary to both oral motor dysfunction and the increased incidence of gastroesophageal reflux. Many of these children have a disordered swallow secondary to oral motor dysfunction and are unable to protect their airway. Children with oral motor dysfunction may include those with motor disability such as cerebral palsy, myopathy, or anterior horn cell disease and those with Arnold-Chiari malformation, which may be seen as a single malformation or in combination with myelomeningocele. Children with impaired function of respiratory musculature such as those with neuromuscular disease or cervical-thoracic spinal cord injury are more likely to develop pneumonia and debilitating lung disease if they acquire any respiratory tract infection. Therefore, yearly vaccination for influenza and routine immunization for *Haemophilus influenzae* type b, pertussis, and pneumococcus are important preventive measures in this high-risk population.

Children with disabilities are just as likely as other children to get viral gastroenteritis, but they are more likely than other children to have complications such as dehydration secondary to inadequate oral intake.

In children with neurogenic bladders (commonly seen with myelomeningocele or spinal cord injury), there is an increased incidence of significant bacterial colonization of the urinary tract. Due to lack of sensation, children with neurogenic bladders are often not symptomatic with lower urinary tract disease in terms of classic symptoms of dysuria, frequency, and urgency but may present with the history of a change in color or odor of their urine or symptoms of fever, vomiting, or abdominal pain. There is an increased incidence of urinary tract infection with significant immobility, as might be seen with severe cerebral palsy or prolonged casting for immobility (e.g., spica cast).

Children with disabilities are just as likely as other children to have childhood meningitis. Children with shunted hydrocephalus have an increased incidence of bacterial meningitis or ventriculitis (often with skin flora or unusual organisms) secondary to the presence of the foreign body.

Skin infections may be more common in certain subgroups of disabled children. Decubitus ulcers may develop in children with spinal cord injury or myelomeningocele secondary to the loss of sensation. Cellulitis and impetigo may be more likely in children who are mentally retarded or have severe autism because of repeated self-stimulatory or self-injurious behavior.

INFECTION CONTROL

Special Infection Control Needs.   For children who have disabilities, the most important infection control procedures are those that apply to any child, such as good handwashing. In addition, there should be appropriate education of all child care providers regarding those signs and symptoms of infection to which any particular child in their care is prone. For example, those who are caring for a child with myelomeningocele should be aware of the signs of infection of the urinary tract and meningitis/ventriculitis and should provide vigilant skin care, particularly in the diaper region.

Children with AIDS may have cognitive or motor disabilities, which are most often progressive in nature. The child with AIDS, because he or she is immunocompromised, is at risk of acquiring infection from other children in the child care setting. There is no risk to other children or child care providers who have casual contact with the child with AIDS. As with all children, handwashing is recommended after diaper changes. It has been suggested that children with AIDS who are frequent biters of other children or those who may have open or oozing sores may put others in the child care setting at risk; however, this has not been proven.

Children with congenital cytomegalovirus (CMV) may have motor, cognitive, or sensory disabilities. Because CMV is such a ubiquitous virus, 1% of all infants are infected in utero. However, only 5% of these have severe manifestations of prenatal infection. Children with congenital CMV may excrete virus for some time following their birth. However, the majority of children in child care settings who excrete CMV are those who acquire the infection postnatally. For this reason, children with congenital CMV should not be singled out for isolation or exclusion. No special measures are indicated except good handwashing.

Children with congenital rubella most commonly have visual, hearing, or cognitive impairments. Children with congenital rubella are able to transmit the disease to susceptible contacts until they are 12 months of age or until they have documented negative nasopharyngeal and urine cultures after 3 months of age. Although other infants in a child care environment may have acquired passive immunity from their mother, older infants, unimmunized children, children of unimmunized mothers, and child care providers may be included among susceptible contacts. Because 10 to 15% of the adult population is rubella-susceptible, susceptible child care providers and preschool staff should be immunized.

Children with congenital herpes may have recurrent cutaneous or oral herpes lesions but do not need to be excluded from child care or preschool settings. Cutaneous herpetic lesions should be covered with a dressing. Because oral herpes is extremely common and those who are infected may shed between recurrence of their fever blisters, there is no need to exclude these children.

Risks to Healthy Children.   Healthy children are only at risk of acquiring infection from children with disabilities in those special circumstances that have been described in which the disability is of an infectious etiology. Be careful, however, not to assume that all children whose disability is of an infectious etiology necessarily put other children at risk. For example, a child who has cerebral palsy resulting from an episode of *H. influenzae* meningitis at 9 months of age does not impart any increased infectious risk to healthy children.

Exclusion from Child Care or Preschool Attendance.   A child should be excluded from a child care center or preschool if the treatment of the disease is not consistent with normal setting functioning. For example, a child with pyelonephritis may require hospitalization and intravenous antibiotic therapy. If a child care center or preschool is unable to provide the environment and resources to maintain this intravenous access, then this child should be excluded from the child care setting until this special medical treatment is no longer needed.

A child should be excluded from a child care or preschool setting if that individual child's health is at significant risk secondary to his or her presence in that setting. For example, a child with AIDS who is immunocompromised may himself be at risk by being in close proximity to other children.

A child should be excluded from attendance at a child care center or preschool if the child's presence in the center places other children at risk for infection. A child who both is a chronic biter and has hepatitis B may infect other children through biting. Children who are actively shedding rubella virus in an environment where there are many susceptible individuals may infect others through secretion exposure; however, susceptible individuals may protect themselves through immunization.

Recommendations for Personnel.   Routine health care maintenance is of primary importance in a child care center or preschool that provides care to disabled children. Personnel should ascertain for each child all pertinent diagnoses in language understandable to all caretakers.

Child care providers should have an understanding of each disability and all associated complications such that the signs and symptoms of infection in each individual child will be recognized. Emergency phone numbers should be maintained for primary physicians and other subspecialty physicians, if appropriate, for all children in a child care and preschool setting. As with all children, the immunization status of each child with disabilities should be determined.

Personnel in the child care or preschool setting should monitor routine safety. Play areas, both inside and outside, should be accessible and safe for all children in the care of that center. The surfaces should be appropriate for mobility. If the center transports children, car seats and child restraints should be available and adapted for all children in the care of that center.

The most important factor in the prevention of infection in children both with and without disabilities is good handwashing.

Parental Advice. Children with disabilities are no more likely to transmit infections to other children than are children without disabilities; a child cannot catch a disability from another child. Parents should be aware of the health, safety, and illness policies of the center and should make certain that their own child and all children in the center are fully immunized.

Children with Chronic Skin Disease (Eczema)

Kenneth E. Greer

INFECTIOUS RISKS

Although the cause of atopic eczema is unknown, there are several important known factors that probably account for the increased risk for cutaneous infection. These patients have deficiencies in their immune system. Most notable is the deficient chemotactic responsiveness of white blood cells, making these children unusually susceptible to cutaneous viral, bacterial, and certain fungal infections. In addition, eczematous skin appears to be especially prone to colonization with certain infectious organisms.

COMMON INFECTIONS

Atopic eczema patients are markedly susceptible to cutaneous infections with viruses, such as herpes simplex (eczema herpeticum or Kaposi's varicelliform eruption when it becomes widespread), varicella-zoster virus, molluscum contagiosum, warts, and vaccinia (eczema vaccinatum). Eczema vaccinatum occurred when children or their families were vaccinated for smallpox, and it may still occur in children of military personnel who receive smallpox vaccination. Eczema patients also are unusually susceptible to bacterial infection or colonization with *Staphylococcus aureus,* and they may be more prone to develop superficial fungal infections with *Trichophyton rubrum.*

INFECTION CONTROL

Special Infection Control Needs. The varicella vaccine should be provided to all atopic children who have not had chickenpox because the likelihood of exposure to chickenpox is high in this setting and the complications in this population can be severe. When the child with chronic skin disease is infected with certain organisms, special precautions may be necessary to prevent the spread to other children. Conversely, when nonatopic children or other personnel in the center have certain cutaneous infections, especially fever blisters (herpes simplex, cold sores), varicella, and impetigo, the child with atopic eczema should be protected from close contact with these individuals who are infected. Medical treatment is available for these infections, but in specific instances, such as with eczema herpeticum, the child with chronic skin disease may have to be excluded from the center temporarily. The primary physician would be the best person to make this decision.

Risks to Healthy Children. If the viral infection is widespread and uncovered (molluscum contagiosum, herpes simplex, etc.), there is a potential risk of spread. However, these situations have not been reported and are more theoretical than real. Atopic children who are being medically treated for heavy bacterial colonization or infection present no significant risk for infection to the other children.

Exclusion from Child Care or Preschool Attendance. Children are excluded from the center or preschool only when they are considered to be contagious. This is usually the case when they have herpes simplex infection. In addition, if the child has serious bacterial infection with *S. aureus* and the child is not being adequately treated, temporary removal from the child care or preschool setting would be appropriate. In general, atopic children should be treated as are other children at the center.

Recommendations for Personnel. The personnel need to be aware of the special needs of the atopic child, which often include needs not necessarily related to infection (dietary, exercise, clothing) but which may exacerbate the skin condition, allowing for an increased risk of infection. In addition, the personnel need to be aware of what types of infections these children may develop.

Parental Advice.   Advise parents of well children that eczema in and of itself is not contagious. If the atopic eczema child requires therapy for an intercurrent infection, like any other child at the center or school, the child will receive treatment and return only when there is no longer an infection risk to the other children.

Children from Developing Nations

Ross A. Pennie

INFECTIOUS RISKS

Children from developing nations often come from regions where sanitation is poor and diseases are transmitted by food and drink contaminated by pathogenic organisms. Overcrowding and malnutrition may lead to increased incidence of other diseases, such as tuberculosis. In many developing countries, low immunization rates result in increased incidence of polio, measles, and diphtheria. Because these diseases are highly contagious during their acute stages and may be imported by visitors and immigrants, it is important to protect children in child care settings by ensuring they receive all of their routinely recommended vaccines.

There are several organisms that a previously infected child can continue to carry and excrete for some time after the acute symptoms have resolved. In a child care center or preschool, it is these organisms, excreted for relatively long periods, that pose the most risk of child-to-child transmission.

COMMON INFECTIONS

Pathogenic organisms potentially carried for prolonged periods by children from developing nations are:

Bacteria
   Salmonella
   Shigella

   Campylobacter jejuni
   Mycobacterium tuberculosis
Viruses
  Hepatitis A virus
  Hepatitis B virus
  Hepatitis C virus
  Cytomegalovirus
  Human immunodeficiency virus
  Poliovirus
  Enteroviruses
Parasites
  Protozoa
    Cryptosporidium
    Cyclospora cayetanensis
    Giardia lamblia
    Entamoeba histolytica
    Dientamoeba fragilis
    Plasmodia (malaria)
  Worms
    Hymenolepis nana (dwarf tapeworm)
    Trichuris trichiura
    Hookworm
    Ascaris lumbricoides
    Strongyloides stercoralis
    Schistosoma
    Taenia solium (cysticercosis agent)

However, many of the organisms listed above are not transmissible directly from one child to another. The reason varies with the organism but may be because the life cycle requires an intermediate animal host, the eggs must mature in the soil before they are contagious, or the organism must be transferred very directly through sexual activity or infected blood or needles.

Therefore, common tropical organisms readily transmissible in a child care center or preschool are:

  Bacteria
   Salmonella
   Shigella

Campylobacter jejuni
Mycobacterium tuberculosis
Parasites
  Protozoa
    Cryptosporidium
    Cyclospora
    Giardia lamblia
    Entamoeba histolytica
  Worms
    Hymenolepis nana (dwarf tapeworm)
    Taenia solium (cysticercosis)
  Viruses
    Cytomegalovirus
    Hepatitis A
    Enteroviruses
    Poliovirus

INFECTION CONTROL

Special Infection Control Needs. The organisms of concern are all transmissible by the fecal-oral route (except for cytomegalovirus and *M. tuberculosis*). Therefore, infection control should focus on good personal hygiene, good handwashing, the preparation of food by staff who do not care for children in diapers, and the exclusion of children with diarrhea that is not manageable and/or is associated with fever. These measures are not special and are recommended for every child care center or preschool, regardless of whether it is attended by children from developing nations.

Children with tuberculosis are not contagious unless they are obviously ill with symptoms such as chronic cough and weight loss. A chronically ill child from a developing country should therefore be evaluated by a physician before the child enters the care center or school.

Risks to Healthy Children. Healthy children are at theoretical risk of infection from the shorter list of enteric pathogens listed above. Practically speaking, the organisms most commonly transmitted are *Salmonella, Shigella, Cryptosporidium, Giardia lamblia,* and hepatitis A. The risk of infection can be reduced by the routine use of good personal hygiene as discussed above.

Exclusion from Child Care or Preschool Attendance. Children from developing nations should be excluded from child care or preschool attendance when they have an unexplained chronic illness or when they have acute diarrhea. A child who repeatedly bites should be excluded until it is certain that he or she carries neither hepatitis B virus nor human immunodeficiency virus.

Recommendations for Personnel. Child care and preschool personnel should understand that there is little likelihood that a child from a developing country will pass along a dangerous disease to other children. Routines of good personal hygiene and the exclusion of children with diarrhea that is not manageable and/or is associated with fever should be established to minimize the transmission of gastrointestinal disease.

Any child who appears to be chronically unwell should be evaluated by a doctor who has been informed that the child may have a disease endemic to the tropics and be investigated accordingly.

Because hepatitis A is a more serious disease in adults than young children, personnel should receive the hepatitis A vaccine. Personnel should also ensure that they are fully immunized against polio.

Parental Advice. Parents may find the following information helpful:

- Children get diarrhea in child care centers and preschools regardless of whether there are children there from developing nations.

- Parents should make certain that there is good personal hygiene practiced in the child care center or preschool before enrolling their child.

- Foreign children in the child care or preschool setting are at minimal risk of spreading serious disease to other children.

- Parents should ensure that their children have received all the routine vaccines according to the schedule recommended by their jurisdiction.

Section IV

Specific Infections

Adenovirus

Scott A. Halperin

CLINICAL MANIFESTATIONS

Adenovirus is a common viral infection with diverse clinical manifestations. Occasionally, these manifestations may be so distinct that a clinical diagnosis can be made with assurance. In most cases, however, adenovirus causes an illness indistinguishable from that caused by a variety of other pathogens. Adenovirus most frequently causes infection of the respiratory and gastrointestinal tracts. It is an unusual cause of the common cold but a very common cause of upper respiratory infection with pharyngitis and fever. Adenovirus causes conjunctivitis, exudative tonsillitis, laryngotracheitis (croup), bronchitis, bronchiolitis, and pneumonia. Adenovirus also is the cause of a characteristic syndrome called pharyngoconjunctival fever, which occurs in epidemics most commonly associated with contaminated swimming pool water.

In addition to these infections of the upper respiratory tract, adenovirus is a major cause of childhood diarrhea. The so-called enteric adenoviruses are not cultivatable in routine tissue culture and are identified by electron microscopy of the stool. Upper respiratory symptoms also may occur in children with enteric adenovirus infection.

ETIOLOGIC AGENT

Adenoviruses are nonenveloped, double-stranded DNA viruses. In humans, 51 distinct serotypes have been identified; additional serotypes have been isolated from other species. Adenoviruses attach to target cells, and the viral DNA enters the nucleus. Viral DNA replication occurs in the nucleus, giving rise to the characteristic inclusions. Adenovirus infection of a cell can result in a lytic infection where there is rapid proliferation of the virus, which results in cell death. Adenovirus can also cause latent infection, usually of lymphoid cells such as those of the tonsils. Finally, adenovirus is capable of oncogenic transformation. The importance of this final adenovirus-cell interaction in human disease is not clear.

EPIDEMIOLOGY

Source of the Organism.   Adenovirus can be found in the respiratory secretions, conjunctiva, and stool of infected individuals.

High-Risk Populations.   Adenovirus infection occurs most often and is more severe in young infants and children. Outbreaks occur commonly in situations where close contact is common, including child care centers, schools, and hospitals. Particularly severe epidemics occur in military recruit populations. Infections in immunocompromised patients are increasing, particularly in bone marrow and solid organ transplant recipients and patients with acquired immunodeficiency syndrome.

Mode of Spread.   Spread of adenovirus infection is by small-droplet aerosols. Infection is initiated when virus-containing particles come in contact with the nose, throat, or conjunctival mucosa of susceptible individuals. Adenovirus is also spread by the fecal-oral route.

Incubation Period.   Two to 14 days.

DIAGNOSIS

In most situations, an etiologic diagnosis of adenovirus infection is not made. Typically, a clinical syndrome such as conjunctivitis, croup, bronchiolitis, pneumonia, or gastroenteritis is made without identifying the specific pathogen. A definitive diagnosis can be made through viral culture or through direct detection of the virus in clinical specimens using electron microscopy, radioimmunoassay, immunofluorescence, enzyme-linked immunosorbent assay

(ELISA), or polymerase chain reaction (PCR). Increasingly, real time PCR is being used for rapid diagnosis of adenovirus infection. Specific diagnosis can also be accomplished by demonstration of an antibody rise to adenovirus in paired serum specimens. Enteric adenoviruses are noncultivatable in routine tissue culture and are detected through use of specialized cell cultures, electron microscopy, antigen detection assays, or nucleic acid detection systems such as PCR.

THERAPY

No specific therapy is available for the treatment of adenovirus infections although some successes with the use of cidofovir in immunocompromised patients with adenovirus infection have been reported. Most infections are not severe and do not require hospitalization; however, in the very young or immunocompromised patients, the infection may be severe and require hospitalization for supportive care.

INFECTIOUS PERIOD

Adenovirus can be isolated in respiratory secretions from 2 days prior to symptoms to 8 days after the onset of symptoms. Enteric adenoviruses have been identified in the stool from a mean of 3 days before diarrhea began to 5 days after diarrhea stopped, although excretion can occur for 2 to 3 months. Adenovirus can be cultured from the conjunctiva for 2 weeks after the onset of symptoms.

INFECTION CONTROL

Vaccine. There is no commercially manufactured adenovirus vaccine. Vaccines for certain adenovirus types, which were not used in children but were routinely used in military recruits, are no longer available.

Exclusion from Child Care or Preschool Attendance. No exclusion is required for respiratory infection due to adenovirus. The child's own condition should determine continued participation in child care. Children with enteric adenovirus infection should be excluded from child care until they are no longer having diarrhea. Adenoviral conjunctivitis often occurs in epidemics that are difficult to control; therefore, if an epidemic of keratoconjunctivitis is present, children should be excluded until purulent conjunctival secretions have resolved.

Recommendations for Other Children.   Since exposure has already occurred before onset of symptoms, no specific steps need be taken once adenovirus infection has occurred. Each child should be monitored for any symptoms suggestive of more serious disease that may require a visit to the child's physician. The possibility of a more severe disease in immunocompromised children should be remembered.

Recommendations for Personnel.   There is no increased risk for adult caretakers due to adenovirus infection. Particular attention to handwashing and care with infected secretions, particularly stool, will prevent continued spread within the center.

Parental Advice.   Adenovirus infections are usually mild and self-limited. However, parents should be aware that complications such as otitis media, dehydration, and pneumonia may occur, which would require a visit to the family physician.

13

Amebiasis

William J. Rodriguez*
Barbara A. Jantausch

CLINICAL MANIFESTATIONS

Most amebic infections are asymptomatic. Some persons in whom a chronic state of intestinal amebiasis develops may experience intermittent diarrhea, constipation, flatulence, vague abdominal complaints, cramps, and tiredness. Those persons in whom diarrhea develops usually have cramps.

Acute amebic dysentery occurs less frequently. The patient may have fever and dysentery (i.e., stools that are liquid and mixed with blood or mucus), abdominal pain, and chills. Headache, tenesmus, and leukocytosis may be present.

Ulcerative lesions in the gastrointestinal tract can lead to metastases of the parasite to the liver through the portal vein (1 to 5% of patients), resulting in *hepatic abscess*. In approximately one-fourth of instances, enlargement of the liver with pain occurs. Jaundice is rare, but leukocytosis and elevated alkaline phosphatase are common. A radiograph may show elevation of the right hemidiaphragm. Metastases can occur to the lung, brain, and skin. On rare occasions, perforation of the colon, peritonitis, and death can occur.

---

*No official support or endorsement of any product or study or the content of these chapters by the U.S. Food and Drug Administration is provided or should be inferred. No commercial interest or other conflict of interest exists between Dr. Rodriguez and the manufacturers of any of the products mentioned.

ETIOLOGIC AGENT

Entamoeba histolytica is a protozoan parasite that has a global distribution. *E. histolytica* is now recognized as being two distinct species that are identical morphologically: *E. histolytica* and *E. dispar*. *E. histolytica* causes local and invasive disease, whereas *E. dispar* is nonpathogenic. The cyst is the infectious particle and is usually found in formed stool. After ingestion, cysts mature into active trophozoites that primarily remain in the liquid portion of the bowel contents.

EPIDEMIOLOGY

Source of the Organism.   Humans and primates are the reservoirs of *E. histolytica* and transmit the infection to animals including dogs, cats, and pigs. Food and water can be contaminated with amebic cysts, such that raw fruits and vegetables washed in contaminated water become additional sources of infection.

High-Risk Populations.   Distribution is worldwide but more prevalent in lower socioeconomic groups in developing countries. Travelers to endemic areas and children in day care centers have potential for acquisition of disease.

Mode of Spread.   Fecal-oral transmission, person-to-person transmission, and ingestion of contaminated food and drink result in infection. Infection is transmitted by the ingestion of amebic cysts. Reservoirs of infection are those infected with no symptoms who may be shedding millions of cysts. Cysts are resistant to chlorination and can survive for several weeks in a moist environment.

Incubation Period.   The incubation period is usually 1 to 4 weeks but may range from just a few days to several months.

DIAGNOSIS

Intestinal Amebiasis.   The diagnosis is made on finding cysts or trophozoites in fresh stool or bowel wall scrapings. Three stool specimens should be submitted 24 hours apart for evaluation, because cyst shedding may be intermittent. Cysts are more likely to be found in formed stool and trophozoites in liquid stool. Trophozoites may lose viability and morphology quickly, hence a *fresh stool* specimen should be examined within 30 minutes. Preserved samples in PVA (polyvinyl alcohol) should be used if no fresh samples are available. *E. histolytica* and *E. dispar* have a similar appearance on stool examination. They may be differentiated by stool antigen detection assays, isoenzyme analysis, and polymerase chain reaction (PCR).

Acute Dysentery.   Mobile trophozoites with ingested red cells may be seen in dysenteric stools. Amebic ulcers may be seen on sigmoidoscopy. Serologic testing, specifically the indirect hemagglutination assay (IHA) with a titer of 1:128 or greater, is helpful in the diagnosis of acute dysentery or hepatic abscess. The IHA is not positive in patients with *E. dispar* infection. Also available are enzyme-linked immunosorbent assay, immunofluorescence, and counterimmunoelectrophoresis. Serology is helpful in the dysenteric phase as well as the extraintestinal phase.

Hepatic Abscess.   Serology is very helpful (*E. histolytica*–specific IgG and IgA titers). In addition to serology, imaging results provide useful diagnostic information. Elevation of the right hemidiaphragm may be seen in 50% of patients on chest x-ray. Ultrasound of the abdomen and computed tomography can confirm the presence of a hepatic lesion.

THERAPY

No treatment is necessary for *E. dispar* infection. Asymptomatic excretors with *E. histolytica* intraluminal infection should be treated with iodoquinol, 30 mg/kg/day (maximum, 2 g/day) orally, divided every 8 hours for 20 days. Alternative therapy includes diloxanide furoate, 20 mg/kg/day divided every 8 hours for 10 days, or paromomycin, 30 mg/kg/day orally, divided every 8 hours for 7 days. Diloxanide furoate is not commercially available in the United States, but information may be obtained from the Centers for Disease Control and Prevention. For intestinal amebiasis, liver abscess, or other invasive forms of disease caused by *E. histolytica*, a tissue amebicide such as metronidazole, 35 mg/kg/day (maximum, 2250 mg/day) orally, divided every 8 hours for 10 days, should be used in conjunction with iodoquinol or paromomycin in the dose above for 20 days. Corticosteroids and antimotility drugs should be avoided. Percutaneous or surgical drainage may be prudent in the case of a large liver abscess.

INFECTIOUS PERIOD

Individuals are infectious for as long as cysts are being shed in the stool. Untreated patients may excrete cysts for years.

INFECTION CONTROL

Vaccine.   None available.

Exclusion from Child Care or Preschool Attendance.   Infected children should be kept out of the child care or preschool setting until they are treated and asymptomatic and their stools are free of oocysts.

Recommendations for Other Children.   Children who develop gastrointestinal symptoms should be removed from the setting, and their stools examined for *E. histolytica*.

Recommendations for Personnel.   Personnel should practice good handwashing, especially after using the toilet and handling diapers. Personnel who become symptomatic with gastrointestinal symptoms should remain at home and have their stool examined for oocysts. New children should not be admitted to the center during an outbreak.

Parental Advice.   Parents should observe their children for gastrointestinal symptoms. Symptomatic children should be kept at home and be seen by their pediatrician, and their stool should be submitted for ova and parasite evaluation.

Ancylostoma duodenale (Hookworm)

Jonathan P. Moorman

CLINICAL MANIFESTATIONS

The initial manifestation may consist of pruritus and a papular or vesicular rash at the site of larval penetration into the skin. While light infections often are asymptomatic, heavy infections may be associated with the development of abdominal pain, anorexia, diarrhea, and weight loss. Gastrointestinal symptoms appear to be more common in *Ancylostoma duodenale* infections than in infections caused by the other human hookworm, *Necator americanus*. The most significant consequence of hookworm infection is the development of iron-deficiency anemia due to gastrointestinal blood loss. The average daily blood loss for this worm is 0.2 ml/day, with the severity of the anemia depending on the parasite burden and dietary iron intake. It may be associated with pallor, listlessness, dyspnea, palpitations, cardiomegaly, and stunted growth. Other findings in hookworm infections may include hypoalbuminemia, peripheral eosinophilia, and occult blood in the stool.

ETIOLOGIC AGENT

A. duodenale is one of two species of hookworms that cause widespread human infection. Humans acquire hookworm infection by coming into contact with infective larvae present in contaminated soil. The larvae penetrate the skin or gut, pass into the circulation, and are carried to the lungs. They then penetrate the alveolar walls, ascend the trachea, and are swallowed, ending up in the small intestine where they attach to the duodenal or jejunal mucosa and mature into adult worms. The adult worms produce thousands of eggs that are passed in the stools, completing their development in soil. Under suitable conditions, the larvae will hatch and molt, becoming infective for humans. This process generally requires 5 to 10 days, during which time the eggs and larvae are not infective for humans.

EPIDEMIOLOGY

Source of the Organism.   Hookworms are found predominantly in tropical and subtropical zones, with *A. duodenale* predominating in southern Europe, northern Africa, northern Asia, and parts of South America. These areas provide appropriate environmental conditions for the development of hookworm eggs. The infective larvae are found in soil contaminated with human feces, and most infections result from direct contact with the soil, generally through bare feet. Rarely, food contaminated with *A. duodenale* larvae can serve as the source of the infection. The possibility of transmammary transmission of *A. duodenale* also has been considered, although to date the larvae have not been demonstrated in breast milk.

High-Risk Populations.   Individuals who have direct contact with fecally polluted soil in endemic areas will have a significant risk of acquiring hookworm infections. Children's propensity to play in dirt and to be barefoot increases their risk of infection. However, since effective transmission requires development of the larvae in soil, direct person-to-person spread of hookworm infection does not occur. Therefore, institutional or child care settings should not increase a child's risk of infection.

Mode of Spread.   Transmission occurs through skin contact with soil containing infective larvae. In a few instances, food contaminated with larvae has been implicated in the transmission of *A. duodenale.*

Incubation Period.   The time interval between acquisition of *A. duodenale* and the appearance of eggs in the feces has been reported to range from 43 to 105 days. The longer intervals reflect a period of interrupted development that some larvae undergo after infecting humans. Considerable variability is also observed in the time between infection and the development of symptoms; individuals may develop gastrointestinal symptoms approximately 20 to 38 days following an acute hookworm infection.

DIAGNOSIS

The diagnosis is established by identifying characteristic hookworm eggs in the feces; *A. duodenale* eggs cannot be distinguished from those of *N. americanus*. Although direct microscopic examination of a fecal smear will generally be adequate for the detection of moderate and severe infections, concentration techniques may be required to demonstrate eggs in light infections. Either the zinc sulfate flotation technique or the formalin-ether technique may be used. The larvae or adult worms are rarely seen in stool specimens, and although larvae can be grown from specimens by using Harada-Mori fecal cultures, this technique is rarely used diagnostically.

THERAPY

In countries where hookworms are endemic and reinfection is common, light infections often are not treated. In this country, hookworm infections are generally treated with either mebendazole, albendazole, or pyrantel pamoate. Mebendazole is given in a dose of 100 mg twice a day for 3 days or 500 mg once. Albendazole is given in a single 400 mg dose. Pyrantel pamoate is given as a single daily dose of 11 mg/kg (maximum, 1 g), repeated for 3 days. Although pyrantel pamoate and albendazole are approved drugs, the U.S. Food and Drug Administration considers them investigational for this condition. Although these regimens appear to be well tolerated, experience with them in children less than 2 years of age is limited; the decision to treat a child in this age group should be made on an individual basis after determining the potential risks and benefits of therapy. A repeat stool examination should be performed 1 to 2 weeks following therapy, and retreatment should be undertaken if hookworm infection is persistent.

In addition to the use of antihelmintic drugs, iron supplementation should be provided to individuals with significant anemia.

INFECTIOUS PERIOD

Without therapy, hookworm infections may persist for many years, although egg production tends to decrease over time.

INFECTION CONTROL

Vaccine.   None is available although several candidates are currently being studied.

Exclusion from Child Care or Preschool Attendance.   Isolation is not indicated for children infected with hookworms. Since human-to-human transmission does not occur and the eggs passed in feces are not infectious, an infected child does not need to be kept out of any child care or preschool setting.

Recommendations for Other Children.   Other children are not at risk of acquiring hookworm infection unless they are exposed to soil with infective larvae. Unlike the situation with many other enteric pathogens, children should not acquire the infection if they inadvertently ingest fecal material contaminated with hookworm eggs. Therefore, no additional precautions need to be undertaken for children in a center when one child is found to have hookworm infection.

Recommendations for Personnel.   Personnel should be instructed to continue techniques that decrease fecal-oral transmission of pathogens, including good handwashing and appropriate disposal of fecal material. In areas of the country where fecal contamination of the soil may be a problem, children in the child care or preschool setting should not be allowed to wander barefoot or play in the soil.

Parental Advice.   Parents should be told that the risk of person-to-person transmission is minimal. If the attendee appears to have acquired the hookworm infection locally, the need for sanitary disposal of feces and the potential for spread through contaminated soil should be reviewed with all of the parents.

Ascaris lumbricoides
(Roundworm)

Jonathan P. Moorman

CLINICAL MANIFESTATIONS

The majority of *Ascaris* infections are asymptomatic, and overt disease is proportional to the intensity of the infection. During the initial phases of infection with *Ascaris lumbricoides*, larvae migrate through the lungs. Infected individuals may be asymptomatic or have symptoms ranging from a mild transient cough to severe pneumonitis. In heavy infections, fever, eosinophilia, and pulmonary infiltrates may occur transiently with the pneumonitis. Once the larvae have passed into the small intestine and have matured into adult worms, ascariasis is generally asymptomatic. Spontaneous passage of the worms from the rectum, mouth, or nares may be the first indication of infection. Some individuals with ascariasis complain of vague abdominal discomfort, and a small number develop intestinal obstruction due to the adult worms. Migration of adult worms may occasionally be associated with intestinal perforation or blockage of the bile duct. Chronic ascariasis probably contributes to impaired nutrition and school performance.

ETIOLOGIC AGENT

A. lumbricoides is the largest intestinal roundworm parasitizing humans. Infection is acquired through the ingestion of eggs containing infective larvae. After ingestion, the larvae hatch, penetrate the intestinal wall, and migrate via venules or lymphatics, passing through the liver and heart to the lungs. They then penetrate the alveolar walls, migrate through the upper respiratory tract, enter the esophagus, and pass into the small intestine, where they mature into adult worms. Female worms pass 200,000 eggs daily in the feces; these eggs under appropriate environmental conditions can develop into infective-stage larvae within 5 to 10 days. Unfertilized eggs or eggs that have not embryonated are not infectious.

EPIDEMIOLOGY

Source of the Organism.   Although *A. lumbricoides* has a cosmopolitan distribution, it is most prevalent in areas with poor socioeconomic standards. Inadequate sanitation and the use of human feces as fertilizer contribute to the prevalence of ascariasis by maintaining infective eggs in the soil. Transmission of the infection results from direct ingestion of soil, as in the case of some children, or indirectly through contaminated hands or food.

High-Risk Populations.   Preschool- and young school-age children are at risk of acquiring ascariasis primarily because of their extended contact with soil and ingestion of soil either directly or indirectly through unwashed hands and food. This is reflected in the age distribution of ascariasis in endemic areas, where the prevalence increases sharply during the first 2 to 3 years of life.

Mode of Spread.   Transmission occurs through ingestion of *A. lumbricoides* eggs containing infective larvae. Since the eggs passed in human feces are not infectious until they have matured for several days to weeks, person-to-person transmission does not occur.

Incubation Period.   The interval between acquisition of infection and the development of adult worms capable of passing eggs is approximately 8 to 12 weeks. Individuals who develop pulmonary symptoms do so approximately 5 to 14 days after infection, during which time the larvae are migrating through lung tissue.

DIAGNOSIS

During early stages of the infection, when the larvae have not matured into adult worms, the diagnosis may occasionally be established by finding larvae in sputum or gastric washings. Once adult worms are present, the diagnosis is readily established by finding *A. lumbricoides* eggs in fecal specimens. Occasionally, the diagnosis is made after the infected individual passes adult worms by mouth or rectum. Eosinophilia may be seen in pulmonary syndromes.

THERAPY

Several relatively nontoxic drugs are now available for the treatment of ascariasis. Mebendazole is effective at a dose of 100 mg twice daily over 3 days or 500 mg once. Pyrantel pamoate can be given as a single oral dose of 11 mg/kg (maximum, 1 g), and albendazole can be given in a single 400-mg dose, but these are considered investigational for treatment of ascariasis. None of these drugs has been used extensively in children less than 2 years old; therefore, the decision to treat a child of that age group should be made on an individual basis. In cases of intestinal obstruction due to ascariasis, piperazine citrate may be effective; the drug paralyzes adult worms, which may then be evacuated by the intestinal peristalsis.

INFECTIOUS PERIOD

In untreated individuals, *A. lumbricoides* adults may survive for 12 to 18 months. Individuals may asymptomatically shed eggs for years.

INFECTION CONTROL

Vaccine.   None available.

Exclusion from Child Care or Preschool Attendance.   Children with ascariasis are not at risk of directly transmitting the infection to other children, and they therefore do not need to be kept out of the child care setting.

Recommendations for Other Children.   Feces passed by a child with ascariasis will not be directly infectious to other children. Therefore, other children in the center are at risk of acquiring ascariasis only if they ingest soil containing eggs that have developed infective larvae. To prevent potential transmission of a number of intestinal parasites, children should be kept from eating dirt, and good hygiene with handwashing should be emphasized.

Recommendations for Personnel.   Prevention of spread through the maintenance of good hygiene and appropriate disposal of all fecal material should be emphasized. Personnel should specifically be cautioned to avoid inadvertent contamination of hands, food, and utensils with soil potentially containing infective eggs.

Parental Advice.   The means of transmission, including the absence of person-to-person spread, should be discussed with parents. The need to prevent geophagia and to maintain good hygiene among their children also should be emphasized.

Campylobacter

Marian G. Michaels

CLINICAL MANIFESTATIONS

Campylobacter jejuni is a major cause of gastrointestinal infection in both children and adults. The infection it causes presents in a similar fashion to many of the other enteric infections. Usually, infected individuals have acute onset of diarrhea and abdominal discomfort of variable severity. A febrile prodrome can occur, and malaise, headache, and nausea often accompany or just precede the diarrhea. Frank blood in the stool is somewhat more common in *Campylobacter* enteritis than in infections caused by *Shigella* or *Salmonella*, while vomiting appears to be a slightly less frequent finding.

Most often the disease is self-limited, usually lasting less than a week. However, even when clinical symptoms have disappeared, patients can continue to shed bacteria for up to 7 weeks. This prolonged shedding is the rationale for antibiotic treatment of children in day care or preschool.

Though complications are unusual, a protracted, relapsing course occasionally develops that can be confused with inflammatory bowel disease. Also, bacteremia, postinfectious arthritis, Guillain-Barré syndrome, carditis, megacolon, cholecystitis, and meningitis have been reported, albeit rarely.

ETIOLOGIC AGENT

Campylobacter is a microaerophilic, motile, spiral-shaped gram-negative rod. There are several different species, but the most common one to cause enteritis is *C. jejuni*. In addition, *C. upsaliensis* has caused outbreaks of diarrhea in day care centers in Brussels. *C. fetus* occasionally causes systemic disease in premature infants and other immunocompromised hosts.

EPIDEMIOLOGY

C. jejuni has worldwide distribution. In recent times, it has been more common than *Shigella* and *Salmonella* as a cause of bacterial diarrhea in children. In the United States, infection occurs throughout the year, with peaks in the summer and early fall. The actual prevalence of *C. jejuni* in a community is difficult to ascertain, as most people, even those with diarrhea, do not have stool cultured. In patients with diarrhea in developing countries who have had cultures obtained, the rate of isolation ranges from 4 to 45%. *C. jejuni* is not commonly found in the stool of asymptomatic people in the United States.

Source of the Organism.   Animal and bird species are common reservoirs for *Campylobacter*. Feces of migratory birds have a high prevalence of *Campylobacter* spp. Commercial chicken carcasses have often been found to be contaminated, as well as the carcasses of sheep, cattle, and swine. *Campylobacter* species have been found in surface water. In addition, *C. jejuni* can infect household pets and cause diarrhea in these animals, especially while they are young. Another source associated with outbreaks of *C. jejuni* enteritis is the consumption of unpasteurized milk or untreated water.

High-Risk Populations.   Day care centers with children who are not toilet-trained are predisposed to transmitting *Campylobacter* infections in similar fashion to the transmission of other infectious diarrheal diseases. Children drinking unpasteurized milk or untreated water or those eating undercooked meat are at increased risk, as are those who have new puppies or kittens that have diarrheal illnesses. There is also an increased risk in people traveling to developing countries.

Mode of Spread.   Ingestion of contaminated foods or water and fecal-oral spread are the primary modes of transmission. Direct contact with infected animal or bird feces is also a method of spread. Maternal transmission of the bacteria to the newborn at the time of delivery has been reported.

Incubation Period. Incubation is between 1 and 7 days, with most illness occurring 2 to 4 days after exposure, but can be variable, depending on the size of the inoculum.

DIAGNOSIS

Diagnosis is made either by direct microscopy of fecal material using special stains or by isolation of *C. jejuni* in stool culture. Special isolation techniques are required. These include using either blood-based media containing antibiotics or a filtration system and then incubating the media at 42°C in an atmosphere containing 5% oxygen, 10% carbon dioxide, and 85% nitrogen. Specimens should be inoculated with minimal delay. If more than a 2-hour delay is anticipated, specimens should be stored at 5°C in Cary and Blair transport media.

THERAPY

The enteritis caused by *C. jejuni* is, in general, a self-limited disease often requiring only symptomatic treatment with oral rehydration fluids. The value of antibiotic treatment is controversial, as it does not appear to alter the course of the disease. However, many researchers have demonstrated that despite continued symptoms, the shedding of *C. jejuni* is halted within 72 hours of administering antibiotics. Thus, in the child care setting where children are not toilet-trained, it is prudent to treat with antibiotics.

Erythromycin remains the drug of choice. Doses for children are 30 to 50 mg/kg/day given orally in four divided doses for 5 to 7 days. The dose for older children and adults is 250 mg four times a day orally, again for 5 to 7 days. Newer macrolide antibiotics such as clarithromycin and azithromycin have activity against *C. jejuni* and, therefore, are alternate drugs that could be used to halt the shedding of bacteria.

Systemic infections usually require hospitalization and administration of parenteral antibiotics. In vitro testing shows that *C. jejuni* is usually resistant to the penicillins and cephalosporins but is normally sensitive to many other antimicrobial agents, including erythromycin (as mentioned above, this is the drug of choice in patients treated orally), the nitrofurans, the aminoglycosides, chloramphenicol, clindamycin, the quinolones, and the tetracyclines. Typically, the latter two types of drugs are contraindicated in young children. In addition, resistance to fluoroquinolones has been increasingly reported.

INFECTIOUS PERIOD

Children are contagious 2 to 3 days after appropriate antibiotics are begun. Those who have not been treated can continue to shed organisms in their stool for 5 to 7 weeks. Adults who have not had gastrointestinal symptoms have rarely, if ever, been implicated in the spread of *C. jejuni.*

INFECTION CONTROL

Vaccine.   None available.

Exclusion from Child Care or Preschool Attendance.   Two days after beginning antibiotics or until the child is asymptomatic, whichever is the shorter period of time.

Recommendations for Other Children.   Good hygiene.

Recommendations for Personnel.   Extra-careful attention should be paid to handwashing after changing diapers and before food preparation. Toys and countertops should be cleaned more frequently, especially if used by children with diarrhea.

Parental Advice.   Parents should enforce good personal hygiene in their toilet-trained child. They can be reassured that their child does NOT require a stool culture unless he or she becomes symptomatic.

17

Candida
(Thrush, Diaper Dermatitis)

Charles M. Ginsburg

CLINICAL MANIFESTATIONS

The skin and the mucous membranes are the most common sites of involvement in infections caused by the various species of *Candida*. In most instances, the infection is superficial and acute; however, in neonates and immunocompromised patients of all ages, the pathogen may be invasive and has the potential to cause disseminated or chronic disease.

Oral candidiasis (thrush), the most common infection caused by *Candida* species, is an acute inflammation of the tongue and oral mucous membranes that is manifested as white or grayish-white focal or diffuse plaques on the mucous membranes. In severe disease, the lesions may extend to the angles of the mouth (perlèche), where fissuring and cracking may occur. The plaques are tightly adherent to the mucosa, and attempts to remove them generally produce bleeding and result in a tender erosion in the mucosa.

The diaper area and the intertriginous areas of the axillae, groin, and intergluteal fold are the most common sites for candidal invasion of the skin. Regardless of the area involved, the clinical appearance is similar; the affected skin is fiery red and, depending on the duration of infection, contains lesions that range from slightly raised red papules to discrete eroded lesions with a red raised border.

Often, there are also discrete macular or papular satellite lesions in areas that are separated from the primary site of involvement by

111

normal skin. *Candida* also may infect the skin surrounding the nails of the hands and feet, particularly in infants and children who suck their thumbs or other digits. The paronychial lesions are similar to those that occur on other areas of the skin; however, the lesions are generally more edematous than those that occur on glabrous skin, and, often, there is purulent drainage from the lesions as a result of secondary bacterial infection caused by strains of staphylococci.

ETIOLOGIC AGENT

Although there are multiple species of *Candida*, one species, *Candida albicans*, is responsible for the majority of infections in normal hosts.

EPIDEMIOLOGY

Source of the Organism.   *Candida* species are ubiquitous in the environment, largely as the result of human-to-human transmission. The digestive tract, the vagina, and, less commonly, the skin are the principal reservoirs for the organism.

High-Risk Populations.   Neonates, immunocompromised patients, and those with chronic endocrine disorders such as diabetes mellitus are predisposed to infection with species of *Candida*. In normal hosts, the organism has a proclivity to invade traumatized skin or mucous membranes or those areas of the skin that become macerated as a result of excess moisture.

Mode of Spread.   The mode of spread of *Candida* is dependent on the age of the patient. Newborns generally acquire the organism from their mother's colonized vagina during the birth process. By contrast, infants and older children acquire the organism from their mother's skin or hands or from unsterilized nipples or bottles. Additionally, in situations where there are breaks in the mucosal or epidermal barrier, children may acquire the organism from infected individuals.

Incubation Period.   The incubation period for *Candida* infections is not known.

DIAGNOSIS

The presumptive diagnosis of most superficial *Candida* infections can be made on clinical grounds. In instances where the diagnosis is unclear, a definitive diagnosis can be made by obtaining scrapings from the surface of the infected lesions for microscopic examination and for culture on Sabouraud agar. The material obtained from scrapings can be stained with Calcofluor or with potassium hydroxide and then examined under the microscope. Although round thin-walled cells may be visualized, they are not indicative of tissue invasion; segmented mycelia are the only forms that are routinely associated with tissue invasion.

THERAPY

Oral or superficial cutaneous *Candida* infections may be treated with nystatin suspension administered three to four times daily for 5 to 7 days. Additional important ancillary measures for treatment of cutaneous disease consist of keeping the affected area dry and, possibly, administering a corticosteroid cream to patients with severe, highly inflammatory cutaneous lesions. Caretakers of diapered infants should be reminded to change the diapers frequently, clean the skin with soap and water, and avoid occlusive pants, cornstarch, and baby powders.

INFECTIOUS PERIOD

Patients are infective while active lesions are present.

INFECTION CONTROL

Vaccine.   None available.

Exclusion from Child Care or Preschool Attendance.   Since most children with candidiasis do not have systemic symptoms and their activities of daily living are not compromised, they may attend day care or preschool without limitation.

Recommendations for Other Children.   If careful hygienic procedures are followed by the adult personnel in the center and the infected patient is on effective therapy, there is little risk to the other children in the center.

Recommendations for Personnel.   Normal hosts who work in the center are at little risk for acquisition of the pathogen, provided that careful handwashing techniques are utilized. This latter aspect is particularly important for personnel caring for children with oral or cutaneous candidal infections. Immunosuppressed hosts who work in the center should avoid direct contact with infected children but may work with uninfected children, since the risk for aerosol transmission of the organism is small.

Parental Advice.   Since this agent is ubiquitous and the pathogenicity of the organism for normal hosts is small, it is probably unnecessary to inform parents of normal children that there are cases of *Candida* infection at the center. Parents of children who are immunocompromised should be informed of cases of *Candida* so that they can consult their child's physician to obtain recommendations about management of their child.

Chlamydia

Margaret R. Hammerschlag

CLINICAL MANIFESTATIONS

Chlamydia trachomatis: Major clinical manifestations of *C. trachomatis* infection are conjunctivitis and pneumonia. The conjunctivitis may present unilaterally or bilaterally. The clinical presentation is extremely variable, ranging from mild conjunctival infection and discharge to severe inflammation with chemosis, pseudomembrane formation, and copious mucopurulent discharge. The conjunctivae may be very friable and may bleed when stroked with a swab.

The clinical presentation of pneumonia due to *C. trachomatis* is very characteristic. The onset is gradual with rhinitis and cough. The infants are usually afebrile. Physical examination reveals tachypnea and the presence of rales. Wheezing is distinctly uncommon. Chest radiographs demonstrate hyperexpansion and variable infiltrates. A very suggestive laboratory finding is peripheral eosinophilia (>400 cells/mm^3).

Chlamydia pneumoniae: This *Chlamydia* species is a frequent cause of atypical pneumonia that is very similar in presentation to *Mycoplasma* pneumonia. Clinical manifestations include coryza, fever, development of cough, sore throat, pleuritic chest pain, and, possibly, pleural effusions. *C. pneumoniae* also has been associated with otitis media and exacerbations of asthma.

ETIOLOGIC AGENT

C. trachomatis: An obligate intracellular bacterium. All members of the genus have a unique developmental cycle including a 48- to 72-hour life cycle and distinct infectious and reproductive forms (elementary body and reticulate body). The organisms form characteristic intracytoplasmic inclusions that can be detected by staining with Giemsa stain, iodine, or specific fluorescein-conjugated monoclonal antibodies in tissue culture. McCoy cells, a murine-derived fibroblast line, or HeLa 229 cells are the cell lines frequently used in clinical laboratories for *C. trachomatis* culture.

C. pneumoniae: Shares the same lipopolysaccharide antigen as other members of the genus. It also forms inclusions that do not stain with iodine, unlike those of *C. trachomatis*. Cell lines used for isolation of *C. pneumoniae* are HEp-2 or HL.

EPIDEMIOLOGY

Source of the Organism.   *C. trachomatis*: Among adults, *C. trachomatis* is primarily a sexually transmitted disease. The adult genital tract is the major reservoir. In many adults, especially women, the infection is frequently asymptomatic and may persist for years if not treated. Newborn infants acquire the infection from their mother's birth canal during delivery.

C. pneumoniae: Believed to be a primary human respiratory pathogen. The upper respiratory tract may be the primary reservoir. Preliminary clinical data suggest that *C. pneumoniae* may cause prolonged asymptomatic infection of the respiratory tract. Asymptomatic nasopharyngeal infection may occur in 2 to 5% of adults and children, but the role in spread of infection is unknown.

High-Risk Populations.   *C. trachomatis*: Since infection is acquired from an infected mother at delivery, risk factors are those for infection in the mother: young age, early sexual activity, and multiple sexual partners. The institution of routine prenatal screening and treatment of pregnant women has resulted in a dramatic decrease in perinatal *C. trachomatis* infection among infants in the United States.

C. pneumoniae: Not known.

Mode of Spread.   *C. trachomatis*: Vertical transmission from infected mother to infant during passage through an infected birth canal. If delivery has been by cesarean section without rupture of membranes, transmission is unlikely to occur. There are no data supporting any form of horizontal transmission postnatally.

C. pneumoniae: Believed to be person-to-person by aerosol droplet or respiratory secretions. Outbreaks have been described in institutional settings, including military barracks and nursing homes. Spread within households has also been described.

Incubation Period. *C. trachomatis*: Conjunctivitis—5 to 14 days; pneumonia—14 days to 2 months.

C. pneumoniae: Not known. Some preliminary data suggest 3 to 4 days.

DIAGNOSIS

C. trachomatis: Conjunctivitis—determined by isolation of the organism from conjunctival culture or demonstration of chlamydial antigen by either direct fluorescent antibody test, enzyme immunoassay, or nucleic acid amplification test on conjunctival smears or secretions; pneumonia—determined by isolation of the organism from nasopharyngeal secretions obtained by swab or nasopharyngeal aspirate or by antigen detection or nucleic acid amplification methods as described above. Serology is not useful.

C. pneumoniae: Culture of *C. pneumoniae* is performed in only a few laboratories. There are no commercially available U.S. Food and Drug Administration–approved serologic tests or nucleic acid amplification tests. Serology is of limited value in children.

THERAPY

C. trachomatis: Conjunctivitis—oral erythromycin suspension, 50 mg/kg/day in four divided doses for 14 days. Additional topical therapy is not necessary; pneumonia—same dose as for conjunctivitis. Azithromycin suspension, 20 mg/kg, once a day for 3 days appears to be as effective as erythromycin, although data are limited.

C. pneumoniae: Oral erythromycin at the same dose as for *C. trachomatis* infection for 10 days. Alternatives include clarithromycin, 20 mg/kg/day in two divided doses for 10 days, and azithromycin, 5 to 10 mg/kg/day every day for 5 days. The optimum dose and duration of therapy are not known.

INFECTIOUS PERIOD

C. trachomatis: Not applicable, as horizontal transmission does not appear to occur.

C. pneumoniae: Not known.

INFECTION CONTROL

Vaccine.   *C. trachomatis*: None available.

C. pneumoniae: None available.

Exclusion from Child Care or Preschool Attendance.   *C. trachomatis*: It is not necessary to keep the child home, since horizontal transmission (child to child) appears to be very unlikely.

C. pneumoniae: Until asymptomatic and on appropriate therapy.

Recommendations for Other Children.   *C. trachomatis*: None.

C. pneumoniae: If infection is symptomatic, children should be taken to their physician.

Recommendations for Personnel.   *C. trachomatis*: None.

C. pneumoniae: If infection is symptomatic, personnel should seek medical attention.

Parental Advice.   *C. trachomatis*: None for parents of other children. Parents of infected children should be advised to seek treatment for themselves.

C. pneumoniae: Inform parents that this infection can progress to pneumonia. Children should be watched closely and brought to medical attention if symptomatic.

19

Coronaviruses
(Common Cold)

Ronald B. Turner

CLINICAL MANIFESTATIONS

The spectrum of clinical illness produced by the coronavirus infection is not clearly defined. The major clinical syndrome caused by these viruses seems to be the common cold. Colds produced by coronaviruses are similar to rhinovirus colds. Some volunteers with coronavirus colds complain of mild gastrointestinal symptoms.

Gastroenteritis has been suggested to be a symptom of coronavirus infection; however, this association has not been clearly established. Necrotizing enterocolitis has been reported in association with coronavirus infection of newborn infants.

ETIOLOGIC AGENT

The coronaviruses are RNA viruses not closely related to other human viral pathogens. Four distinct human coronaviruses are recognized; 229E, OC43, NL63, and SARS. The antigenic interrelationships between different strains of virus within these major groups are complex and poorly understood. Experiments in humans inoculated with 229E indicate that solid immunity to reinfection is produced against the infecting strain of virus, but protection does not extend to other 229E strains.

EPIDEMIOLOGY

Source of the Organism. Infection with the human strains of coronavirus is limited to humans, and no animal or inanimate reservoir of infection has been identified.

119

High-Risk Populations.   No populations have been identified that are at high risk for acquisition of infection. Newborn infants may be at increased risk of severe disease once infected. The factors that predispose to infection are not known.

Mode of Spread.   The limited data available suggest that coronaviruses may spread by small-particle aerosols. Further study is necessary to confirm this observation.

Incubation Period.   The incubation period for coronavirus colds is 48 to 72 hours.

DIAGNOSIS

Reliable methods are not available for the routine diagnosis of coronavirus infections. Both serologic assays and polymerase chain reaction have been used for the diagnosis of these infections in the research setting.

THERAPY

There is no specific therapy available for treatment of coronavirus infection.

INFECTIOUS PERIOD

The period of infectivity is not known.

INFECTION CONTROL

Vaccine.   None available.

Exclusion from Child Care or Preschool Attendance.   Exclusion from child care or preschool settings is not necessary for children infected with coronavirus.

Recommendations for Other Children.   No special precautions are indicated.

Recommendations for Personnel.   No special precautions are indicated.

Parental Advice.   Coronavirus colds generally are mild upper respiratory illnesses, and no special precautions are necessary.

20

Coxsackievirus A16
(Hand, Foot, and Mouth Syndrome)

Ziad M. Shehab

CLINICAL MANIFESTATIONS

Hand, foot, and mouth syndrome is an illness characterized by the development of an enanthem consisting of ulcers usually located on the buccal mucosa, tongue, or gums. About 2 days after the onset of the enanthem, an exanthem develops that is characterized by a vesicular eruption over the hands and/or the feet. In addition, the buttocks are sometimes involved, but the rash there tends not to be vesicular. Resolution is usually complete within 1 week.

ETIOLOGIC AGENT

Hand, foot, and mouth syndrome is usually caused by coxsackievirus A16. Other types of coxsackieviruses have also been associated with this syndrome, such as coxsackievirus A4, A5, A9, A10, B2, B5, and enterovirus 71.

EPIDEMIOLOGY

Source of the Organism.   Humans are the only natural host for enteroviruses.

High-Risk Populations.   Young children are particularly susceptible to this infection because of their immunologic innocence. Household members are also at increased risk.

Mode of Spread.   The virus is transmitted by the fecal-oral or oral-oral routes.

Incubation Period.   Usually 4 to 6 days.

DIAGNOSIS

The infection is diagnosed based on the typical course and manifestations of the illness. It can be confirmed by viral cultures of the throat and rectal swabs.

THERAPY

No specific therapy is available. Treatment is entirely symptomatic. Hospitalization is not required.

INFECTIOUS PERIOD

The infectivity of patients with hand, foot, and mouth syndrome is prolonged, spanning from before the onset of the enanthem to weeks following resolution of the illness. Keep in mind that most infections are entirely asymptomatic.

INFECTION CONTROL

Vaccine.   None available.

Exclusion from Child Care or Preschool Attendance.   Excretion of the virus in hand, foot, and mouth syndrome is prolonged, and most infections are asymptomatic. Therefore, removal of the child from day care or preschool is not warranted and would have little to no impact on the spread of the infection.

Recommendations for Other Children.   Emphasize basic hygiene regarding handwashing.

Recommendations for Personnel.   Emphasize basic hygienic measures (e.g., handwashing) with all children and staff in the center.

Parental Advice.   Reassure parents that this is a self-limited, mild, and, in most instances, asymptomatic infection with no serious sequelae.

21

 Cryptosporidia

William J. Rodriguez*
Barbara A. Jantausch

CLINICAL MANIFESTATIONS

Cryptosporidium causes severe diarrhea in immunocompromised patients and self-limited disease in immunocompetent hosts. *Cryptosporidium* is recognized as a common enteric pathogen throughout the world, being more common in developing countries, and as a cause of diarrheal outbreaks in child care centers and preschools in the United States.

Immunocompetent patients experience self-limited disease and have watery nonbloody stools, abdominal pain, and weight loss for approximately 10 to 14 days. Vomiting and cough can also occur. Fever can occur as well, particularly among children. Rarely, patients may be asymptomatic carriers. Immunocompromised patients may have severe, protracted, or voluminous diarrhea resulting in dehydration and malnutrition; they may experience disseminated infection.

ETIOLOGIC AGENT

Cryptosporidium, meaning "hidden spore" in Greek, is a coccidial protozoan parasite belonging to the class Sporozoa and the order

*No official support or endorsement of any product or study or the content of these chapters by the U.S. Food and Drug Administration is provided or should be inferred. No commercial interest or other conflict of interest exists between Dr. Rodriguez and the manufacturers of any of the products mentioned.

Eucoccidida, which also includes *Toxoplasma gondii*, *Isospora*, and *Plasmodium* species. The organism has a monoxenous life cycle similar to *Isospora* and passes through sporozoite, trophozoite, merozoite, and gametocyte stages within the same host. The oocyst is the infective particle. Seventeen species of *Cryptosporidium* have been identified; *Cryptosporidium parvum* and *Cryptosporidium muris* have been associated with mammalian infection.

EPIDEMIOLOGY

Source of the Organism.   The organism is found in the gastrointestinal tract of infected humans and animals, such as those in petting zoos, as well as reptiles, birds, and mammals, and in contaminated food and water and on fomites. Community outbreaks have occurred as a result of contamination of municipal water supplies and swimming pools.

High-Risk Populations.   Immunocompromised persons; healthy homosexual men; travelers, especially to developing countries; animal handlers; household contacts of infected persons; hospitalized persons; children in child care centers, preschools, and hospitals; and child care personnel with exposure to infected persons are at greatest risk for acquiring disease.

Mode of Spread.   Spread occurs through fecal-oral transmission, person-to-person transmission, and direct and indirect contact of infected feces, contaminated food, water, and surfaces. The diaper changing area and mouthing of shared objects by infants and toddlers can be sources of the organism.

Incubation Period.   The incubation period is estimated to be between 2 and 14 days, with a median of 7 days.

DIAGNOSIS

Diagnosis is made by detection of *Cryptosporidium* oocysts in stool by using special staining techniques including modified Kinyoun acid-fast and fluorescein-conjugated monoclonal antibody stain. An enzyme immunoassay test for stool antigen is also commercially available. False negatives and false positives may occur, and thus microscopic confirmation should be performed. At least three stool specimens collected on different days should be submitted for examination. The organism can also be identified by light and electron microscopy of intestinal biopsy samples. Fecal examinations may rarely show leukocytes or blood.

THERAPY

As the disease is self-limited in the immunocompetent host, hospitalization is usually not necessary but may be required in severe cases. There is a U.S. Food and Drug Administration–approved antiparasitic drug, nitazoxanide, indicated for the treatment of *Cryptosporidium* infection. There have been reports of success with paromomycin alone or in combination with azithromycin. Antiperistaltic agents have not been found to be beneficial and have been noted to worsen abdominal cramping.

INFECTIOUS PERIOD

Oocysts may be shed in the stool of immunocompetent patients for 2 to 5 weeks, although in most cases this stops within 2 weeks after resolution of symptoms. Immunocompromised patients usually shed oocysts forever.

INFECTION CONTROL

Vaccine.   None available.

Exclusion from Child Care or Preschool Attendance.   Children should be kept out of the child care or preschool setting until they are asymptomatic. They should refrain from recreational swimming and/or bathing for 2 weeks after symptoms resolve.

Recommendations for Other Children.   Children who develop diarrhea should have their stools evaluated for oocysts. Good handwashing, proper disposal of stools, and cohorting of children with similar symptoms should be practiced.

Recommendations for Personnel.   Personnel should practice good handwashing, especially after using the toilet and handling diapers. The organism is resistant to chlorine. Use of an ammonia solution to decontaminate the environment may inactivate cysts. Personnel who become symptomatic should remain at home and have their stools evaluated for oocysts. During an outbreak no new enrollees should be accepted, and children with similar symptoms should be cohorted.

Parental Advice.   Parents should monitor their children for symptoms of diarrhea. Symptomatic children should be removed from the child care or preschool setting, be seen by their pediatrician, and have three stool specimens evaluated for oocysts.

22

Cytomegalovirus

Stuart P. Adler

CLINICAL MANIFESTATIONS

The majority of children with infections due to cytomegalovirus (CMV) acquired after birth have no symptoms. Occasionally, particularly in older children and adults, CMV will cause infectious mononucleosis with sore throat, swollen lymph nodes in the neck, enlarged liver, rash, and atypical white cells in the blood. However, this is very rare, especially in young children in day care or preschool.

ETIOLOGIC AGENT

CMV infects only humans. CMV is the largest and most complex virus that infects humans. Only one major serotype exists.

EPIDEMIOLOGY

Source of the Organism. The virus is acquired by transmission from human to human, and nearly all humans eventually become infected. Infections occur more frequently when there is crowding and intimate contact.

High-Risk Populations. Everyone in the population eventually acquires an infection with CMV. In immunocompromised patients, infection can be severe and/or prolonged. Infection in susceptible pregnant women can result in fetal infection.

Mode of Spread. The exact mode of spread of the virus is unknown, although we assume that intimate contact (e.g., diaper changing, kissing, feeding, bathing, and other activities that result in contact with infected urine or saliva) is important for spread. The virus will remain alive on surfaces and diapers for several hours.

Incubation Period.   The incubation period for this infection is approximately 1 month.

DIAGNOSIS

CMV infection is best diagnosed by obtaining a sample of urine for culture. Seroconversion is also possible but requires a serum obtained before infection and one obtained after infection.

THERAPY

No therapy is available.

INFECTIOUS PERIOD

Most children who acquire CMV infections shed the virus for many months, with a range of 6 months to 2 years. Adults shed for a shorter period, probably less than 6 months.

INFECTION CONTROL

Vaccine.   None available.

Exclusion from Child Care or Preschool Attendance.   Children excreting CMV should not be kept out of day care.

Recommendations for Other Children.   No attempts should be made to prevent children from spreading CMV from child to child in the child care center or preschool, as many children will naturally be infected with this virus.

Recommendations for Personnel.   Pregnant personnel should assume that all children are excreting the virus. If possible, at least 6 months before pregnancy, women should be tested to determine whether they have immunoglobulin G (IgG) antibodies to CMV (immunity) and therefore are unlikely to give birth to a child affected by this virus. If a pregnant woman lacks immunity (tests seronegative) and is pregnant or attempting to become pregnant, it is suggested that she be assigned to work with children older than 2 years of age. If or when contact with children younger than 2 years of age is necessary, avoidance of contact with urine and saliva, avoidance of intimate contact (e.g., kissing, snuggling) is suggested. Use of standard precautions, including scrupulous handwashing technique and glove use, is required.

Parental Advice.   Pregnant women with a child younger than 2 years of age in group child care or preschool should assume their child is shedding the virus and thus exercise careful handwashing and scrupulous control of secretions and excretions. Routine testing of serum for IgG antibodies for pregnant mothers is not currently advised.

Diphtheria

Moses Grossman

CLINICAL MANIFESTATIONS

Diphtheria may be nasal, tonsillopharyngeal, laryngotracheobronchial, or limited to the skin. Diphtheria toxin produces serious damage to the myocardium, the nervous system, and the kidney, resulting in life-threatening complications.

Tonsillopharyngeal diphtheria, the most common form, is manifested by a febrile illness with a severe sore throat, systemic toxicity, and the presence of a yellowish, white exudate over the pharynx, tonsils, or uvula. The exudate becomes organized into a pseudomembrane and may spread to a considerable extent.

In laryngotracheobronchial diphtheria, the exudate involves the larynx and produces life-threatening airway obstruction.

Nasal diphtheria is a mild form of the disease, often devoid of toxic manifestations, and is more likely to affect very young children.

Skin or mucous membrane diphtheria may be found in warm climates presenting as a shallow ulcer, often coated with a pseudomembrane.

ETIOLOGIC AGENT

The causative organism is *Corynebacterium diphtheriae*, a gram-positive, non–sporeforming, slender rod with a tendency to branch, which sometimes gives a palisade-like appearance on gram stain. *C. diphtheriae* has been divided into gravis, mitis, and intermedius types. All are capable of producing a potent toxin when induced by a lysogenic bacteriophage.

EPIDEMIOLOGY

Source of the Organism. Infection is limited to humans. Infected persons as well as carriers may spread the organisms. Carriers are usually contacts of infected individuals.

High-Risk Populations. Crowding, which generally occurs in low socioeconomic settings, facilitates the spread of the organism. Unimmunized or partially immunized individuals are particularly susceptible to the disease, though immunization does not provide 100% protection.

Mode of Spread. The organism is spread by intimate contact through nasal or oral secretion or contact with infected skin.

Incubation Period. The incubation period for diphtheria is usually 2 to 6 days.

DIAGNOSIS

The diagnosis is based entirely on isolation of the organism from culture obtained from the infected site. Isolation requires the use of special media both for transport and for growth; thus, the laboratory needs to know that it is *C. diphtheriae* that is suspected. The final step in diagnosis is the demonstration of toxigenicity of the isolated organism.

THERAPY

The cornerstone of therapy is the early administration of diphtheria antitoxin in order to neutralize the circulating diphtheria toxin. The antitoxin is prepared from horse serum; tests for sensitivity must be done prior to initiating therapy with antitoxin. The administration is intravenous, and the dose is empiric, based on the extent of involvement. Antimicrobial therapy is important because it shortens the duration of communicability. Erythromycin is the preferred antimicrobial; penicillin is also effective.

The child always needs to be hospitalized and may require extensive support measures and monitoring of vital functions, depending on the degree of involvement. Cardiac function and paralysis, particularly cranial nerve involvement, may present serious management problems.

INFECTIOUS PERIOD

Untreated, patients are usually infectious up to 2 weeks but occasionally may harbor organisms for months. Treatment usually eradicates organisms after 4 days.

INFECTION CONTROL

Vaccine.   All children attending day care must be fully immunized against diphtheria. All previously immunized individuals who are exposed to a child with diphtheria should receive a booster of toxoid if their last dose of toxoid was 5 or more years before exposure.

Exclusion from Child Care or Preschool Attendance.   The infected child should be kept out of the child care or preschool setting for at least 1 week after initiation of antibiotic therapy. A negative culture should be documented before returning the child to the center.

Recommendations for Other Children.   An outbreak of diphtheria in a child care or preschool setting would be most unusual. It would certainly create a panic among parents and providers and should bring in public health authorities at a very early stage. It would be wise to have a meeting of all concerned to explain the issue and answer questions.

Children, providers, and the family of the index case must be cultured and placed under clinical surveillance for a week.

Those who have been immunized but have not had a booster during the preceding 5 years require a booster dose of diphtheria toxoid. Care must be taken to give only the adult type of toxoid to adults. Immunization should be given to those who have not been previously immunized.

Additionally, all close contacts of the index case should receive antimicrobial prophylaxis—oral erythromycin (40 to 50 mg/kg/day for 7 days; maximum, 2 g/day). Intramuscular benzathine penicillin G (600,000 to 1.2 million units) is an alternative to erythromycin.

Recommendations for Personnel.   Personnel should be cultured and placed under clinical surveillance for 1 week. Those who have not been immunized should be immunized. Those who were immunized more than 5 years before exposure should receive a booster dose of diphtheria toxoid. Culture-positive individuals or very close contacts should receive 1 week of prophylactic antibiotic therapy with either oral erythromycin or injectable penicillin.

Parental Advice.   All parents should be notified in writing of the occurrence of diphtheria in the center. Written recommendations as outlined above should be distributed to all parents, and documented compliance should be required for return to the child care center or preschool.

24

Enterobius vermicularis
(Pinworm)

Jonathan P. Moorman

CLINICAL MANIFESTATIONS

Most *Enterobius vermicularis* infections are asymptomatic. Pruritus ani is the most common symptom associated with enterobiasis and usually occurs at night, leading to restless sleep. Symptoms may recur every 6 to 8 weeks, corresponding to the life cycle of the parasite. Much less often, pruritus vulvae may be associated with infection. In rare cases, aberrant migration of the adult worm from the perineum has been associated with vaginitis, salpingitis, and peritonitis. Although a number of other manifestations, such as anorexia, weight loss, abdominal pain, enuresis, and teeth grinding, have been attributed to enterobiasis, no controlled studies have indicated a causal relationship between those symptoms and *E. vermicularis* infections.

ETIOLOGIC AGENT

E. vermicularis, the human pinworm, is an intestinal nematode. Humans acquire enterobiasis by ingesting infective eggs. The larvae hatch in the intestines, developing into adult worms that live in the cecum and surrounding colon. Gravid female worms migrate to the anus usually at night and deposit their eggs on the perianal and perineal skin. The females die after laying their eggs. Within a few hours, the deposited eggs are mature and capable of transmitting infection if they are ingested.

EPIDEMIOLOGY

Source of the Organism.   Enterobiasis, the most common human helminth infection, occurs worldwide. The infective eggs, which are transmitted from person to person or indirectly through contaminated objects, appear to be relatively resistant to disinfectants and under optimal environmental conditions may remain viable for up to 13 days.

High-Risk Populations.   Due to their lack of hygiene, children are more likely to ingest *E. vermicularis* eggs and become infected than are adults. Therefore, enterobiasis tends to be prevalent in almost any setting where groups of children can be found. This includes large families, schools, child care centers, and mental institutions. In these settings the infection is often ubiquitous with continuous transmission and reinfection of the children. Good personal hygiene can diminish the risk of enterobiasis, and if bathing and changes of undergarments are infrequent within a population, infection is even more likely to be a significant problem.

Mode of Spread.   Transmission occurs through ingestion of *E. vermicularis* eggs with spread of the organisms via the patient's hands, especially the fingernails. Persons with enterobiasis may be reinfected if they scratch themselves and transfer eggs from their anal area to their mouth. Those in close contact with an infected individual may be exposed to contaminated fomites. Transmission of *E. vermicularis* eggs can also occur through contact with soiled clothing or bed linens or through ingestion of eggs in house dust.

Incubation Period.   The time period between acquisition of infection and the deposition of eggs by the female worm has not been well established. Estimates range from 2 weeks to 2 months.

DIAGNOSIS

The diagnosis is established by detecting the eggs deposited in the perianal region. This is best done by applying transparent adhesive tape to the perianal region in the morning before a stool is passed or before a bath. After mounting the tape on a glass slide, it can be examined for the presence of *E. vermicularis* eggs. The test may need to be repeated one or more times to rule out enterobiasis, with three tests detecting 90% of infestations. Less often, the characteristic eggs may be identified in a stool specimen, or the female worm may be observed in the perianal area at night. Eosinophilia does not occur with pinworm infection.

THERAPY

Several effective and reasonably nontoxic drugs are available for the treatment of enterobiasis. Pyrantel pamoate can be given as a single oral dose of 11 mg/kg (maximum, 1 g). Mebendazole can also be given as a single oral dose of 100 mg. Albendazole can be given in a single oral dose of 400 mg but is considered investigational therapy. It is generally recommended that treatment with these agents be repeated in 2 weeks to eliminate any remaining adult worms. Some authorities recommend treating all individuals in the household of an infected child, while others recommend treating only those who are symptomatic or known to be infected. Limited data are available regarding the use of these therapies in children less than 2 years old; therefore, the risks and benefits of therapy should be carefully considered, and a decision to treat a child in this age group should be made on an individual basis.

INFECTIOUS PERIOD

Individuals will have the potential of transmitting *E. vermicularis* as long as they harbor adult male and female worms; although the female worm dies after laying her eggs, reinfection of the host is common, providing an ongoing source of adult worms.

INFECTION CONTROL

Vaccine.   None available.

Exclusion from Child Care or Preschool Attendance.   Once the diagnosis of enterobiasis has been made, the child should be treated with one of the recommended regimens. After appropriate treatment, the child does not need to be kept out of the child care center or preschool.

Recommendations for Other Children.   Given the prevalence of enterobiasis, particularly within groups of children, it is highly likely that other children will also be infected. Any children noted by parents or center personnel to have pruritus ani should be checked for *E. vermicularis* and treated appropriately if the infection is present.

Recommendations for Personnel.   Personnel should be made aware of the means of transmission and of the potential for them to be infected by the children. Good hygiene among the children and personnel with washing of hands, bedclothes, and toys should be emphasized. It should, however, also be understood that total prevention within a child care center or preschool is very unlikely, if not impossible.

Parental Advice.   Parents should understand that enterobiasis is ubiquitous and often unavoidable among children in any group setting. They should be educated regarding the mode of transmission, clinical manifestations, means of diagnosis, and therapeutic options. Lastly, they should be reassured that the diagnosis of enterobiasis in their child or in another attendee is not necessarily an indication of poor hygienic conditions.

Enteroviruses

Ziad M. Shehab

CLINICAL MANIFESTATIONS

Enteroviral infections are relatively widespread and include infections with polioviruses, coxsackieviruses, echoviruses, and enteroviruses. They are divided into polio and nonpolio enteroviruses.

Infection with polioviruses results in an asymptomatic infection in 90 to 95% of cases. In addition, a minor illness may result. Occasionally, an aseptic meningitis can ensue. The most dramatic result of poliovirus infection is paralytic poliomyelitis.

The majority of infections with nonpolio enteroviruses also are asymptomatic. The spectrum of illnesses caused by these viruses spans from asymptomatic to life-threatening. Of the symptomatic infections, most are nonspecific febrile illnesses. Some specific enanthems and exanthems have been associated with them, such as herpangina, a febrile illness with papulovesicular enanthem of the palate and tonsillar pillars, and hand, foot, and mouth syndrome. Other diseases caused by enteroviruses include exanthems with or without meningitis, aseptic meningitis, epidemic pleurodynia, respiratory diseases, gastroenteritis, hemorrhagic conjunctivitis, and, rarely, myocarditis, pericarditis, or paralytic disease.

ETIOLOGIC AGENT

Enteroviruses are single-stranded RNA viruses that are ubiquitous. They are prevalent during the summer and fall.

Enteroviruses of humans consist of the following antigenic types:

Poliomyelitis
    Polioviruses 1, 2, 3

Coxsackie A viruses
    A1 to A22 and A24

Coxsackie B viruses
    1 to 6

Echoviruses
    1 to 7, 9, 11 to 22, 25 to 27, 29 to 33

Enteroviruses
    68 to 71, 73

EPIDEMIOLOGY

Source of the Organism.   The only known reservoir of human enteroviruses is the human being.

High-Risk Populations.   Young children are especially susceptible to these infections because of lack of prior exposure. In immunocompromised hosts, enteroviruses can establish persistent infections.

Mode of Spread.   The virus is transmitted via a fecal-oral or oral-oral route.

Incubation Period.   The incubation period is usually 7 to 14 days, although incubation periods of 2 to 35 days are not uncommon.

DIAGNOSIS

The diagnosis is established by virus isolation from a throat swab, stool specimen, and, occasionally, cerebrospinal fluid or blood, or rarely by demonstration of a rise in specific antibody titer. Detection of viral RNA by the polymerase chain reaction has resulted in a more rapid and sensitive diagnostic method for meningitis and infections in the neonate using cerebrospinal fluid, serum, or urine.

THERAPY

No specific therapy is available for enteroviral infection. The treatment is supportive. In the more severe illnesses, such as meningoencephalitis, myocarditis, or poliomyelitis, hospitalization is often required. Bed rest and support for respiratory failure may be required in cases of poliomyelitis.

INFECTIOUS PERIOD

The infectivity of patients with enteroviral infections is prolonged, spanning from before the onset of the clinical illness to weeks following its resolution. Note that most infections are entirely asymptomatic.

INFECTION CONTROL

Vaccine.   No vaccines are available for nonpolio enteroviruses. As of January 2000, only the inactivated poliovirus vaccine (IPV) is available in the United States. The recommended regimen consists of 4 doses administered at 2, 4, 6 to 18 months, and 4 to 6 years of age.

Exclusion from Child Care or Preschool Attendance.   Excretion of the virus in nonpolio enteroviral infections is prolonged, and most infections are asymptomatic. Therefore, removal of the child from day care is not warranted and would have little to no impact on the spread of the infection. Children with nonvaccine poliovirus infections should be kept out of child care or preschool until shedding of poliovirus has resolved.

Recommendations for Other Children.   Emphasize basic hygiene regarding handwashing. In the care of poliomyelitis, children whose immunizations are incomplete should receive polio vaccine.

Recommendations for Personnel.   Emphasize basic hygiene measures (e.g., handwashing) with all children and staff in the day care center. A booster dose of inactivated polio vaccine should be considered.

Parental Advice.   Emphasize basic hygiene regarding handwashing. In the case of poliomyelitis, children whose immunizations are incomplete should receive polio vaccine, and inactivated polio vaccine should be given to all household contacts.

Escherichia coli
(Diarrhea)

William J. Rodriguez*
Barbara A. Jantausch

CLINICAL MANIFESTATIONS

Disease caused by the various types of *Escherichia coli* is not very prevalent in the United States. Five major mechanisms of disease are postulated: enterotoxigenic strains (ETEC), enteropathogenic strains (EPEC), enteroinvasive strains (EIEC), Shiga toxin producers, formerly called enterohemorrhagic strains (EHEC), and enteroaggregative strains (EAEC).

ETIOLOGIC AGENT

ETEC: These produce either heat-labile, heat-stable, or both kinds of enterotoxins, causing disease by affecting the small bowel absorptive mechanism. This results in loss of electrolytes and water. Cramps, watery diarrhea, some vomiting, and very little if any fever are the hallmarks. Disease is self-limited and usually lasts 5 days. Enterotoxigenic strains are a common cause of traveler's diarrhea and diarrhea in infants in developing countries.

EPEC: These *E. coli* strains are serotypeable but not enterotoxigenic or invasive. Those strains that destroy the villi in the small intestine cause lowering of disaccharidases and may cause malabsorption.

*No official support or endorsement of any product or study or the content of these chapters by the U.S. Food and Drug Administration is provided or should be inferred. No commercial interest or other conflict of interest exists between Dr. Rodriguez and the manufacturers of any of the products mentioned.

Although they usually cause self-limited disease in older children and adults, younger children and infants may have prolonged diarrhea lasting 2 weeks or longer. These latter patients may experience voluminous watery diarrhea without blood or mucus. These strains produce outbreaks of diarrhea in infants in the United States.

EIEC: These strains belong to restricted serotypes and cause disease with a clinical picture comparable to that seen with *Shigella*. These strains affect the colon and distal small bowel. Affected patients usually have fever, headache, and stool that may contain leukocytes and, less commonly, blood.

STEC: These strains, common in Argentina and South Africa, are represented in the United States in *E. coli* O157:H7. They produce Shiga toxin and create a syndrome characterized by severe abdominal cramps with a predominantly afebrile state accompanied by grossly bloody diarrhea and occasional chills. Hemolytic uremic syndrome (HUS) has been found to be associated with these strains that were previously called enterohemorrhagic *E. coli*. Gastrointestinal symptoms are usually self-limited and last about 5 days.

EAEC: These strains have been postulated to be a cause of protracted (exceeding 14 days) watery diarrhea in the infant and young child (which may exceed 14 days) and an infrequent cause of traveler's diarrhea in adults.

EPIDEMIOLOGY

Source of the Organism.   Infected persons and food or water contaminated with feces are sources of the organism. *E. coli* O157:H7, which is the most common of these *E. coli* strains in the United States, can be transmitted by undercooked ground beef and other products such as unpasteurized milk, contaminated apple cider, raw vegetables, and drinking water. Person-to-person transmission can occur during outbreaks. Hemolytic uremic syndrome can occur as a complication in 5 to 10% of children with *E. coli* O157:H7 infection; it can occur in higher proportions during outbreaks of *E. coli* O157:H7 infection.

High-Risk Populations.   *ETEC*: Newborns, travelers.

EPEC: Newborns (uncommon), children in day care centers.

EIEC: Those exposed to contaminated food.

STEC: Those exposed to infected persons, such as children in day care centers, contaminated food, or water.

EAEC: Infants and young children.

Mode of Spread.   The organism is spread via fecal-oral transmission and person to person: caregiver to infant, patient to patient.

Incubation Period.   The incubation period is 10 hours to 6 days.

DIAGNOSIS

ETEC: The diagnosis is made by detecting heat-labile or heat-stable enterotoxin in an animal system, by cell culture, or through immunoassay. Tissue culture (Chinese hamster ovarian or y-1 mouse adrenal Ca line) or immunoassay will detect heat-labile toxin.

EPEC: There is no generally reliable commercially available system. Specialized immunologic methods are available in a limited number of laboratories.

EIEC: The organism is identified by demonstrating invasiveness in tissue culture or the conjunctival sac of animals or by identification of specific serotypes.

STEC: Strains are first identified by demonstrating the presence of a sorbitol nonfermenter on sorbitol McConkey agar (SMAC). The sorbitol-negative *E. coli* strain is next tested for agglutination with O:157 antiserum, and its identity as an *E. coli* is then verified. DNA probes and polymerase chain reaction (PCR) are also available. Cultures for these microbes should be requested early in the illness (first 7 days). Identified strains should be sent to the state health laboratory.

EAEC: Strains of *E. coli* negative for heat-labile and heat-stable enterotoxin are tested for the presence of adherence to HEp-2 cells. A rise in titer of the O antigen of the specific strain is then sought.

THERAPY

ETEC: This is the only *E. coli* that is treatable early because diagnosis of the others is usually difficult. Trimethoprim-sulfamethoxazole (TMP-SMX) is given empirically.

EPEC: Neomycin or TMP-SMX. Antimicrobial therapy should not be given to infants with inflammatory or bloody diarrhea.

EIEC: TMP.

EHEC: No antibiotic.

EAEC: No general treatment is available.

Fluid and electrolyte supplementation is of paramount importance in treating any of these infections.

INFECTIOUS PERIOD

The infectious period occurs while the person is shedding the organism; it is generally considered to be while the person is symptomatic. The degree and extent of shedding may vary beyond that time.

INFECTION CONTROL

Vaccine.   None available.

Exclusion from Child Care or Preschool Attendance.   The child should be kept out of the child care or preschool setting until he or she is asymptomatic and has negative stool cultures. In the case of STEC O157:H7, the child should remain out of the child care setting until the child is asymptomatic and at least two serial stool cultures are negative for EHEC O157:H7 or until 10 days after cessation of symptoms in the case of other *E. coli* organisms.

Recommendations for Other Children.   Close contacts of a symptomatic child with an enteroinvasive strain may need to be cultured and, if their stool is positive, should be considered for treatment even if asymptomatic. In the event of an outbreak of STEC O157:H7, the public health authorities should be notified immediately and the child care center closed to new admissions.

Recommendations for Personnel.   Personnel should be cohorted, practice good handwashing, and stay at home and be cultured if symptomatic. If initial contact measures are not successful, it may be necessary to close the center temporarily (see Recommendations for Other Children).

Parental Advice.   Parents should report even mild gastroenteritis symptoms in their child. Symptomatic children should be removed from day care, seen by their pediatrician, and have their stool examined.

Giardia lamblia

Theresa A. Schlager

CLINICAL MANIFESTATIONS

Infants and children infected with *Giardia lamblia* can be asymptomatic or can be symptomatic with either a brief episode of diarrhea or a chronic illness with multiple symptoms. Asymptomatic infection may be seen in as many as 50% of the infected children. Surveys of the prevalence of *G. lamblia* in stool reveal rates ranging from 1 to 26%. An increased rate of asymptomatic infection has been seen in day care settings during outbreaks of diarrhea due to *G. lamblia*. Symptomatic infants and children with a brief illness will usually have diarrhea that is profuse and watery but unassociated with significant fever, toxicity, or dehydration and that usually resolves without specific dietary alteration or drug therapy. Symptomatic patients who develop a chronic illness ordinarily have protracted, intermittent symptoms including watery diarrhea, abdominal cramps, a protuberant abdomen, wasted extremities, edema, significant weight loss, retarded growth, and anemia. Their stools contain an increased amount of fat but do not usually contain visible blood, pus, or mucus.

ETIOLOGIC AGENT

G. lamblia is a flagellated protozoan type of parasite. Only two species appear to infect humans. The protozoan exists in two forms: a trophozoite form that inhabits the lumen of the upper small intestine where it can cause symptoms, and a cyst form that inhabits the lower small intestine and the large intestine and that when excreted in stool is infectious. When cysts are ingested by a susceptible host, trophozoites are released following the exposure of the cysts to the acidity of the stomach. The trophozoites can then inhabit the intestine, sometimes in very large numbers.

EPIDEMIOLOGY

Source of the Organism. *G. lamblia* is distributed throughout the world and is the most common parasitic infection in the United States. Humans are the principal reservoir of infection, but dogs and beavers are other sources of infection. Feces or objects (toys, diaper-changing tables, eating utensils) soiled with feces or water or food contaminated with cysts are infectious by the oral route even if only small numbers of cysts are ingested. Most epidemics result from contaminated water. Prevention of waterborne outbreaks requires adequate filtration of municipal water obtained from surface water sources, because concentrations of chlorine used to disinfect drinking water are not effective against the cysts.

High-Risk Populations. High-risk populations include the following:

- Infants and children in day care centers or preschools. In some areas, *G. lamblia* is the most common cause of diarrhea in child care centers and preschool—both in outbreaks and in sporadic cases. The children most frequently infected are non–toilet-trained toddlers. Following child care center or preschool outbreaks, 12 to 25% of family members of children (especially non–toilet-trained children) attending the center have become infected. There is increasing evidence that children in day care centers are a common source for spread of *G. lamblia* to the surrounding community.

- Infants and children exposed to unprocessed water sources.

- Patients with acquired immunodeficiency syndrome.

- Patients with hypogammaglobulinemia.

- Malnourished children.

- Children who have had previous stomach surgery with removal of part of the stomach wall.

- Children with reduced gastric acidity.

Mode of Spread. Infection is spread via the fecal-oral route. This requires the ingestion of cysts contained in feces, water, or food or on shared objects (toys, diaper-changing tables, eating utensils) contaminated with infested feces.

Incubation Period. The incubation period is 1 to 4 weeks.

DIAGNOSIS

The traditional diagnosis of giardiasis has been by microscopic examination of the stool for trophozoites or cysts. Recently, rapid diagnostic tests that use antigen detection methods have been widely employed. Direct immunofluorescence assay (using monoclonal antibodies against cell wall antigens) and enzyme immunoassay (using monoclonal antibody against soluble stool antigen) are highly sensitive and specific. In addition, these tests are more sensitive than microscopy in detection of *Giardia* in stool samples. Polymerase chain reaction has been used to detect *Giardia* in water systems and for rapid source tracking in epidemiologic studies.

THERAPY

At present, only symptomatic infections are treated; the benefits and risks of treating asymptomatic patients have not been characterized. Several pharmaceutical agents available in the United States are effective therapy for giardiasis: metronidazole, furazolidone, albendazole, and newly approved nitazoxanide (Alinia; Romark Laboratories). Reported cure rates with metronidazole are 90% or higher after a 5- to 7-day course. Metronidazole can be formulated into liquid preparation by special request. Patients should be warned not to ingest ethanol while taking metronidazole. Furazolidone is somewhat less effective, with an 85% cure rate after a 7- to 10 day course, but has the advantage of liquid formulation. Furazolidone may cause nausea, vomiting, brown discoloration of urine, and occasional hemolysis in children with glucose-6-phosphate dehydrogenase deficiency. Although animal data have suggested that both metronidazole and furazolidone may be carcinogenic, there is no clinical evidence that short-term therapy in humans is carcinogenic. Albendazole has been shown to be as effective as metronidazole for treating giardiasis in children. In addition, albendazole is effective against many helminths and is suggested for treatment when multiple intestinal parasites are suspected.

Paromomycin, a nonabsorbable aminoglycoside, is less effective than other agents but is commonly used for treatment in pregnant women because of theoretical concerns regarding potential teratogenic effects with the other available agents.

Nitazoxanide has been recently approved in the United States for treatment of diarrhea caused by *Giardia* and *Cryptosporidium* in children aged 1 to 11 years.

If relapse occurs, therapy with any of the available agents can be repeated. Relapse is particularly common in immunocompromised patients who may require prolonged or combination therapy.

INFECTIOUS PERIOD

Patients are infectious as long as they excrete cysts, and they may excrete cysts in their stools for prolonged periods (12 to 14 months). Excreted cysts may remain infectious for months if they remain in a moist environment.

INFECTION CONTROL

Vaccine.   A vaccine is not presently available.

Exclusion from Child Care or Preschool Attendance.   Children who have had symptomatic giardiasis who have completed a course of therapy should be allowed to return to the child care or preschool setting when diarrhea is no longer present. The local health department should be notified.

Recommendations for Other Children.   Symptomatic infected children should be treated. Routine testing is not recommended for children exposed to a child with *G. lamblia*. Washing of children's hands on arrival at the center, after a diaper change or use of the toilet, and before meals and snacks should be consistently practiced. Use of liquid soap in a dispenser along with disposable paper towels is recommended. Shared surfaces and toys should be disinfected on a daily basis with a freshly prepared solution of commercially available cleanser (detergents, disinfectant detergents, or chemical germicides).

Recommendations for Personnel. Symptomatic infected staff members should be treated. Without failure, staff members should practice careful handwashing (10 seconds with soap and warm running water) upon arrival at the center, after changing a child's diaper, after using the toilet or providing assistance to a child using the toilet, and before food handling. Disinfecting diaper-changing surfaces along with proper disposal of diapers is recommended.

Parental Advice. A child care center or preschool should notify parents of children who have been in direct contact with a child who has diarrhea and from whom G. *lamblia* has been identified. Parents should contact their physician for advice if their child develops diarrhea or signs of chronic illness. Parents should encourage children to avoid swallowing recreational water and should avoid drinking untreated water during community outbreaks.

Gonorrhea
(*Neisseria gonorrhoeae*)

Michael F. Rein

CLINICAL MANIFESTATIONS

In neonates, the most common presentation of gonorrhea is purulent conjunctivitis, which is often accompanied by asymptomatic infection of the nasopharynx. One may also see vaginitis, rhinitis, urethritis, or involvement of the sites of fetal monitoring. Among older prepubertal girls, vaginitis is the most common infection and presents as vaginal itching and discharge, both of which may be relatively mild. Infection may spread to the fallopian tubes, where it mimics lower abdominal pain of other etiologies. For prepubertal boys, as in adult men, the most common infection is acute urethritis, presenting as urethral discharge and dysuria. At any age, the organism rarely spreads to the joints, skin, meninges, or cardiac valves. Pharyngitis results from direct inoculation.

ETIOLOGIC AGENT

Neisseria gonorrhoeae is a gram-negative coccus. The organism has become increasingly resistant to a variety of antimicrobial agents, and older treatments, such as penicillin, can no longer be used. Approximately 200 auxotype/serovar phenotypes have been described. Strains also vary by susceptibility to antimicrobials and plasmid content. Determination of the phenotype may be useful for epidemiologic and forensic purposes, and, thus, the organism should always be cultured in pediatric cases.

EPIDEMIOLOGY

Source of the Organism.   *Neisseria gonorrhoeae* is characterized by poor environmental survival, limited range of susceptible anatomic sites (in pediatric gonorrhea: the urethra, vagina, cervix, rectum, throat, and conjunctiva), and presence of the organism at only these sites in those infected. Thus, an infected individual is by far the most common source of a new infection.

High-Risk Populations.   Older children with gonorrhea tend to come from family backgrounds of poverty and psychosocial problems, conditions that increase the risk of sexual abuse by infected persons.

Mode of Spread.   Contamination of a susceptible site by an infected discharge is required for transmission, and thus, in adults and children outside the neonatal period, sexual contact is the only plausible means of transmission. Newborns may acquire the organism from their mothers, either during delivery or, more rarely, in utero. The age beyond which the presence of the organism indicates sexual transmission instead of persistent perinatal infection is unknown. Transmission by rectal thermometers, bedding, or the much-maligned toilet seat is highly questionable, and acquisition by kissing is so rare that its occurrence is reportable. In theory, purulent conjunctival discharge could be infectious, but such transmission is extremely rare. Urine from an infected person has caused disease when used as a folk remedy for conjunctivitis.

Incubation Period.   The incubation period is usually only 2 to 5 days, and thus gonococcal conjunctivitis is actually rare in day care populations; however, several months' incubation of perinatally acquired infection has been reported.

DIAGNOSIS

The organism may be presumptively diagnosed by a gram-stained smear. Culture is accomplished on digested sheep blood ("chocolate") agar, which is incubated in an atmosphere enriched with carbon dioxide. Isolation should be undertaken by inoculating suspected discharge onto two plates, one with and one without antimicrobials to inhibit commensal flora. Isolation of the organism is mandatory in almost any case, since only culture permits subsequent subspecies definition of the individual organism and possible pinpointing of the source. The identity of isolates from children should be confirmed by at least two tests that detect different properties of the organism, such as its pattern of fermenting sugars and its antigenic structure. Nonculture methods (e.g., enzyme-linked immunosorbent assay [ELISA], DNA probe, DNA amplification tests) for identifying *N. gonorrhoeae* have not been adequately studied in pediatric populations. Because pediatric cases almost always involve forensic considerations, careful attention to the chain of custody of the specimen is essential.

THERAPY

Children over 45 kg are most easily treated for anogenital gonorrhea with cefixime in a dose of 400 mg given orally once. Younger or smaller children (arguably all children) should be treated with a single intramuscular administration of 25 mg/kg of ceftriaxone, up to a maximal dose of 125 mg. Hospitalization is required only for management of complications such as severe conjunctivitis or disseminated infections, or for management of the social situation in sexually abused children. The possibility of simultaneous infection with *Chlamydia trachomatis* should always be considered, as coinfection is common in adults.

INFECTIOUS PERIOD

The infected person is no longer contagious within 24 hours of receiving effective treatment. Without therapy, the period of contagiousness may last for months.

INFECTION CONTROL

Vaccine.   None available.

Exclusion from Child Care or Preschool Attendance.   The child may return to day care the day after effective treatment.

Recommendations for Other Children.   The risk of nonsexual transmission to other children is inconsequential. If the child was infected elsewhere, no further measures for control of infection are necessary, but the child may develop emotional and behavioral problems.

Recommendations for Personnel.   Handwashing is always important, but the risk of transmission to the conjunctivae of personnel is small, and the risk of transmission to the genitals is inconsequential.

Parental Advice.   If the infection was not acquired at the child care center or preschool, other parents should not be informed, because the infection is stigmatizing, and the risk of transmission is negligible. Detection of the infection may have forensic implications for the child care center or preschool.

29

Haemophilus influenzae
(Meningitis, Cellulitis, Epiglottitis, Pneumonia, Arthritis)

Trudy V. Murphy

CLINICAL MANIFESTATIONS

Before the introduction of universal vaccination, strains of *Haemophilus influenzae* that elaborate the type b polysaccharide capsule were responsible for 97% of the serious invasive infections in children caused by *H. influenzae*. These infections require public health intervention when the patient has been attending a child care or preschool facility.

Systemic or invasive infection begins when *H. influenzae* type b reaches the bloodstream, providing access to many body sites. Invasion is accompanied by a worsening in the child's condition and rapid development of fever. The most common infections are meningitis, cellulitis, epiglottitis, pneumonia, and arthritis. All sites of invasive infection have the same importance for public health purposes. Although *H. influenzae* type b is isolated from the middle ear in a small percentage of cases, otitis media is not considered a systemic or an invasive infection.

H. influenzae that elaborate a polysaccharide capsule other than type b (a, c–f) or that do not elaborate a capsule (nontypeable strains) are a rare cause of invasive infection in children. Nontypeable strains are isolated from the middle ear in about 20% of children with acute

155

otitis media. They also cause sinusitis. Infections caused by nontypeable strains of *H. influenzae* and strains with capsular types other than type b do not require public health intervention and will not be covered further.

ETIOLOGIC AGENT

The bacterium *H. influenzae* is a small, pleomorphic, gram-negative rod. Strains are classified based on the presence of a serologically distinct polysaccharide capsule (capsular types a–f) or on the absence of capsule (nontypeable strains).

EPIDEMIOLOGY

Source of the Organism.   Infection with *H. influenzae*, in the absence of disease, is called colonization or carrier state. Before universal use of the conjugated *H. influenzae* type b vaccine in infants, up to 5% of healthy preschool children were colonized in the nose and throat with type b *H. influenzae*. Older children and adults had rates of colonization of about 0.1%. Colonization persists for a few weeks or for several months and contributes to the natural acquisition of antibody that protects against systemic infection. Before universal vaccination in the United States, at least a third of all children became carriers at some time before 5 years of age; 1 in 200 to 250 children developed invasive infection. Since 1993, invasive infections have been uncommon in the United States.

High-Risk Populations.   Serious, invasive infections with *H. influenzae* type b occur primarily in young children and in the elderly. In the United States, 75 to 90% of systemic infections in children occur before 2 years of age. Among young children attending child care centers or preschools, those who are immunodeficient or immunocompromised, those who have abnormal or no splenic function (e.g., sickle cell disease) and those who are unimmunized, have increased rates of infection caused by *H. influenzae* type b.

Unimmunized children who are younger than 4 years of age and who are siblings or household contacts exposed to a case of invasive *H. influenzae* type b infection are at increased risk of (secondary) invasive infection. Unimmunized children who are younger than 24 months of age and who are classmates of a case in day care also may be at slightly increased risk of invasive infection.

Mode of Spread.   *H. influenzae* type b bacteria are found in high concentrations in nasal secretions and occasionally in low concentrations in saliva of healthy children who are carriers. In nasal secretions, some bacteria live for several hours on nonabsorbent surfaces (e.g., plastic). Spread probably occurs after infected secretions reach the mucous membranes of the nose, eye, or mouth either after coughing or sneezing. Spread also occurs when contaminated face cloths or nose wipes, food, toys, or hands, etc. come in contact with the mucous membranes. Spread is usually "slow," compared with that of other infections (e.g., chickenpox).

Incubation Period.   No incubation period for invasive infection with *H. influenzae* type b has been determined. Clusters of cases occur rarely, and usually within a 60-day period. The long and variable interval between "primary" and "subsequent" cases in both households and day care suggests they arise more commonly after exposure to children who are carriers than after direct exposure to the primary case patient.

DIAGNOSIS

The only certain method of diagnosing invasive *H. influenzae* type b infection is by isolation of the bacterium from a normally sterile body fluid or tissue (e.g., blood and cerebrospinal, pleural, or joint fluid), or from the aspirate of an area of cellulitis. Positive cultures obtained from the throat, ear, or eye (conjunctiva) indicate local, not invasive infection. *H. influenzae* type b, if present, can be missed unless special culture medium is used. The capsular serotype should be determined for all *H. influenzae* isolated from normally sterile body fluids.

Urine or cerebrospinal fluid can be tested for the presence of type b capsular antigen by latex or other antigen detection tests. A positive result suggests invasive infection but must be interpreted within the context of the clinical findings since these tests have a high rate of false results. False-positive results arise from vaccine capsular antigen eliminated in urine during the first few days following vaccination and from "over reading" the test. False-negative results occur early in infection, when capsular antigen is in small concentration, or when the sample is dilute or contaminated with other bacteria (e.g., urine).

THERAPY

Treatment of invasive *H. influenzae* type b infections is usually started in the hospital in order to monitor for complications of the infection. Antibiotic treatment for 10 days is recommended; treatment is started by using intravenous antibiotics (e.g., a third-generation cephalosporin such as cefotaxime or ceftriaxone). Children who have had meningitis should have their hearing tested.

INFECTIOUS PERIOD

Parenteral antibiotic therapy of invasive *H. influenzae* type b infection usually suppresses or eradicates colonization in less than 24 hours, rendering the child noncontagious during therapy. After treatment, *H. influenzae* type b has been recovered again from the nasopharynx of some patients. Children and patients who are carriers of *H. influenzae* type b can transmit the bacterium.

INFECTION CONTROL

Vaccine.   *Routine Use.* To prevent invasive *H. influenzae* type b infections, three or four doses of a conjugate vaccine are strongly recommended for all children starting at 2 months of age, including children attending day care. Children 15 months to 5 years of age require one dose of conjugate vaccine.

Exclusion from Child Care or Preschool Attendance.   Children who have invasive *H. influenzae* type b infection may return to the child care or preschool as soon as they are well enough to participate in the program. A few patients will be carriers after treatment of the invasive infection depending on the type of antibiotic given. Prophylactic treatment with oral rifampin should be considered before the patient returns. Most children receiving prophylaxis will not be contagious after taking the second dose of rifampin. Children younger than 2 years of age who are not fully vaccinated should also complete an age-appropriate schedule of *H. influenzae* type b conjugate vaccine starting 1 month after recovery from the invasive infection.

Recommendations for Other Children.   When a primary (first) case of invasive *H. influenzae* type b infection occurs in a child attending a child care center or preschool, the patient could have acquired the infection from siblings, playmates, or other contacts and may not have transmitted the bacteria to classmates in the child care center or preschool. The patient also could have acquired the infection at the child care center or preschool from classmates who are healthy carriers. Before universal vaccination, the risk of a second case in the same group of children was estimated to be 0 to 1.3% during 1 to 60 days after the primary case among children younger than 24 months of age. Since the risk of a second case is variable, children should be carefully monitored for the occurrence of disease. In addition, general measures as outlined above are warranted to reduce the spread of infected secretions from child to child. The following are recommendations that apply to children and adult care providers in the same classroom or care group as the child with invasive *H. influenzae* type b infection:

- Confirm that the ill child's infection is invasive, such as meningitis, epiglottitis, pneumonia, cellulitis, or bacteremia (but not ear, sinus, or conjunctival infection), and that the infection is caused by *H. influenzae* type b.

- Report confirmed cases to appropriate health department officials (required by law in many states).

- Consult with local health officials, the facility medical advisor, or the patient's physician to develop a recommendation for managing contacts at the facility.

- If all classmates of the case patient are 24 months of age or older, notifying parents of the illness is sufficient intervention. The risk of another case among contacts is not significantly increased. Parents should assure that their child is vaccinated.

- If classmates of the patient are younger than 24 months of age and unvaccinated, parents should be notified of the illness and they should check their child's vaccination status to ensure that the child has been fully vaccinated against *H. influenzae* type b. Rifampin prophylaxis can be considered.

Rifampin prophylaxis of classmates and adult caretakers in child care or preschool is advocated by some authorities after a single (first) case. The decision to give rifampin prophylaxis should take into account the following: (a) the availability of resources to prescribe, purchase, and administer rifampin in an effective manner; (b) the potential side effects; (c) the risk of subsequent infection; (d) that rifampin prophylaxis is not uniformly effective in preventing subsequent cases; and (e) that some children younger than 1 year of age may be protected against invasive infection after receiving two doses of conjugate vaccine, and most older children are protected within 2 to 3 weeks after a single dose of vaccine.

A second case in a classroom group is more likely than a single case to indicate the presence of *H. influenzae* type b colonization among children in the classroom group. If a second case occurs within 1 to 60 days and incompletely vaccinated children remain in the group, carefully supervised administration of rifampin prophylaxis is recommended by most authorities. Unimmunized children should receive the *H. influenzae* type b conjugate vaccine according to age-appropriate recommendations.

- Rifampin prophylaxis. The common oral antibiotics used to treat pharyngitis or ear infections have low rates of success in eradicating colonization with *H. influenzae* type b. Rifampin is the only antibiotic that is 90 to 95% effective in temporarily eradicating *H. influenzae* type b from the nasopharynx. *H. influenzae* type b bacteria resistant to rifampin are uncommon. The efficacy of rifampin prophylaxis in preventing subsequent cases in day care is unknown. Failures are reported.

  Prophylaxis should be given as soon as possible after diagnosis of the case. Prophylaxis is most likely to be effective if given to all children at the same time. This prevents reacquisition from untreated children. All members of the classroom or group are candidates for prophylaxis, including vaccinated children, those older than 24 months, those unexposed or enrolled after the case-patient's illness, and adult care providers.

Rifampin is a prescription antibiotic that should be given only with sufficient knowledge of the child's or the adult's health to exclude allergy and conditions that might preclude its use. Consider possible contraindications (e.g., pregnancy, liver disease) and drug interactions (e.g., lowered efficacy of birth control pills, displacing protein-bound drugs, increased hepatic metabolism). Rifampin turns urine, saliva, and tears an orange color, which can stain clothing and soft contact lenses. Some individuals experience nausea or vomiting or rash while taking rifampin.

Rifampin is taken orally at a dosage of 20 mg/kg/day (maximum dose, 600 mg/day), once a day for 4 days. Infants younger than 2 months of age are not given rifampin, or they are given a lower dosage of 10 mg/kg/day. Rifampin is available in 150-mg and 300-mg capsules, which can be cut to provide a dose to the nearest 75 mg. The powder is removed from the capsule and dispensed in a teaspoon of ice cream or applesauce. Rifampin also can be mixed by the pharmacist in a suspension of 85% flavored sucrose solution, but this must be shaken well before measuring and can give wide fluctuations in the dispensed dose. For adequate absorption, rifampin should be given when the stomach is empty.

- There are no specific recommendations regarding enrollment of new children at a facility after a case of invasive *H. influenzae* type b infection. Children who are eligible for vaccine (2 months of age or older) should have had at least one dose of *H. influenzae* type b conjugate vaccine before starting to attend the facility. If rifampin prophylaxis is to be given, new children who will be assigned to a classroom where there was a case should wait to attend the facility until prophylactic treatment is completed.

Recommendations for Personnel.   Care providers of children in classroom groups with a case of invasive *H. influenzae* type b infection are at extremely low risk of infection. However, up to 7% are carriers when two or more cases occur in a day care center or preschool classroom. Thus, when rifampin prophylaxis is given to children, it should also be given to care providers of the children.

Parental Advice.   The parents of children who are in the classroom or group of any child who has invasive *H. influenzae* type b infection should be notified in writing. The notification letter should inform them of (a) the date of the infection, (b) the classroom or group assignment of the case child, (c) the correct name of the germ, and (d) the recommendations for children at the facility. Parents should also be informed of the signs of infection, and the importance of prompt medical attention and notification of the child care provider in the event their child becomes ill. Parents should be encouraged to make sure their child is fully immunized with the *H. influenzae* type b conjugate vaccine.

Hepatitis A

Timothy R. Townsend

CLINICAL MANIFESTATIONS

Only about one quarter of children infected with the hepatitis A virus (HAV) have any symptoms, as opposed to infections among adults in which three quarters are symptomatic. Often, the initial clue that HAV transmission is occurring in a group child care setting is the occurrence of clinical illness among the adults, either caretakers or family members of the children, who are in contact with the children. Typical signs and symptoms found among symptomatic children are jaundice, dark urine, malaise, and light-colored stools. Diarrhea is a common finding among children but is rare among adults. There is no evidence that HAV causes a persistent infection and progressive liver damage.

ETIOLOGIC AGENT

The HAV is a small, nonenveloped RNA virus in the same family, Picornaviridae, as the rhinoviruses and the enteroviruses. There is a single antigenic strain found worldwide.

EPIDEMIOLOGY

Source of the Organism.   Humans are the only source of the HAV. There is no evidence for an animal or inanimate reservoir of the virus.

High-Risk Populations.   There are no markers such as age, race, or gender that place a person at higher susceptibility to infection. Exposure, primarily through oral ingestion, to fecally contaminated objects defines the risk of infection. Child care centers and preschools that have children who are not toilet-trained are at higher risk of having HAV transmission than those where only toilet-trained children are clients. Among centers with non–toilet-trained children, those that have poor infection control practices that permit greater fecal contamination associated with diaper changing are at greater risk for having HAV transmission than those with good infection control practices.

Since the institution of the hepatitis A vaccination programs in 1999 for children ages 2 to 18 years living in states with a high incidence of disease, there has been a dramatic decrease in the number of reported cases in all ages. In 2005, the Advisory Committee on Immunization Practices recommended routine hepatitis A vaccination for all children.

Mode of Spread.   Hepatitis A is transmitted primarily by the fecal-oral route, although there have been a few transfusion-associated cases reported.

Incubation Period.   The incubation period is 15 to 50 days.

DIAGNOSIS

Since most infections among children are asymptomatic, serologic testing is the most reliable means of diagnosing HAV infection. A single-serum specimen tested for immunoglobulin M (IgM) anti-HAV and immunoglobulin G (IgG) anti-HAV can indicate that an IgM-negative, IgG-negative person is susceptible and not currently infected; an IgM-positive, IgG-negative person is currently infected or was infected within the past few months; an IgM-positive, IgG-positive person was infected approximately 2 to 6 months ago; and an IgM-negative, IgG-positive person was infected more than 6 months ago.

THERAPY

There is no known effective therapy for HAV infection. Supportive therapy to maintain fluid and caloric intake is usually sufficient, and hospitalization is rarely required.

INFECTIOUS PERIOD

Among symptomatic persons 10 days after the onset of dark urine, viral particles are no longer detectable in stool, and epidemiologic evidence supports the concept that by the time a person is ill enough to seek treatment, infectivity has waned.

INFECTION CONTROL

Vaccine.   An inactivated HAV vaccine was licensed in 1995. In the summer of 2005, the U.S. Food and Drug Administration licensed the vaccine to be used in children starting at 1 year of age. The second dose should be given 6 months after the first dose. In the fall of 2005, the Advisory Committee on Immunization Practices recommended that all children be vaccinated starting at 1 year of age and that the vaccine be accepted into the "Vaccines for Children" program. The duration of protection is unknown, but the vaccine efficacy in the first year or two following vaccination has ranged from 85 to 95%. The vaccine's indications list several other populations in which the vaccine should be used: the vaccine is indicated for high-risk groups (travelers, illicit drug users, men who have sex with men, patients with underlying liver disease) and is recommended for all employees in child day care centers and preschools.

A new combined hepatitis A and hepatitis B vaccine has been licensed and is equally efficacious when compared to either the hepatitis A or hepatitis B vaccine alone. In previously unimmunized children older than 12 years of age and in all unimmunized child care personnel, this combination vaccine is an ideal method of providing excellent protection against both the hepatitis A and B viruses.

Exclusion from Child Care or Preschool Attendance.   Symptomatic children could return to a child care or preschool setting 10 days after onset of symptoms. Asymptomatic children will be identified in the context of an outbreak, and the epidemiologic circumstances will determine when it is safe for them to return. (The outbreak investigators, usually health authorities, are in the best position to make this decision.)

Recommendations for Other Children and Personnel/Parental Advice. Since hepatitis A is a reportable disease and the occurrence of a single symptomatic child, family member of a child in day care, or adult caretaker often means an outbreak is occurring at the child care center and preschool, it is important to notify the local health authority. The health authorities are the only ones with the expertise to investigate the situation and make recommendations concerning other children, personnel, and parents of children at the center. Issues such as serotesting, use of immune serum globulin, and vaccine and/or closure of the center involve considerable expense and should be approached judiciously. Until the proper authorities can investigate and recommend control measures, parents of children can be taught simple infection control measures to minimize fecal-oral transmission so as to protect family members from further spread; personnel can examine diaper-changing and handwashing practices so as to prevent further spread; and other children can be carefully observed for onset of illness. Finally, the child care center or preschool must communicate with each family it serves, both to transmit information from the health authorities and to assist the authorities with their investigation. Closing the center as the initial response to an outbreak will force infected children to other child care centers and preschools, thereby worsening the situation.

31

Hepatitis B

Timothy R. Townsend

CLINICAL MANIFESTATIONS

Hepatitis B virus (HBV) infection in children is symptomatic in less than 10% of cases. When it is symptomatic, the typical signs and symptoms of fatigue, anorexia, jaundice, dark urine, light stools, nausea, vomiting, and abdominal pain are indistinguishable from other causes of hepatitis. The younger a person is at the time of infection, the greater the risk of becoming a chronic HBV carrier, which is associated with a greater risk of developing chronic active hepatitis, cirrhosis, and hepatocellular carcinoma later in life.

ETIOLOGIC AGENT

HBV is an incompletely double-stranded DNA virus that is coated with a surface protein (hepatitis B surface antigen [HBsAg]) and has a central core (hepatitis B core antigen [HBcAg]) containing the DNA and a protein, the hepatitis e antigen. A group-specific genetic determinant "a" and two pairs of genetic subdeterminants, "d" "y" and "w" "r," make for different strains, but in a given geographic location a single strain predominates. Immunity is group-specific, so infection with one subtype usually confers immunity to other subtypes.

EPIDEMIOLOGY

Source of the Organism.   The source of infection is a person either acutely infected or a chronic carrier of HBV. The virus is found in highest concentrations in blood or bloody body fluids and in much lower concentration in other body fluids such as saliva, urine, or stool.

High-Risk Populations. In the United States, infection among pre-adolescents is very uncommon, since HBV is a behaviorally associated infection (sexual activity, parenteral drug abuse). Those preadolescents who are infected are those born to acutely infected or chronic carrier women. Now that universal screening for HBsAg of pregnant women is recommended and widely practiced, identification of at-risk and infected infants should be facilitated. For those infants or children whose mothers were not screened during pregnancy, reliance on maternal risk history (immigrant from Asia, Africa, or the Middle East; parenteral drug use; sexual activity with multiple partners) is relatively poor in accurately identifying infected women.

Mode of Spread. HBV is transmitted via percutaneous or per-mucosal exposure to infective blood or other infectious body fluids from a person who is HBsAg-positive. Transmission can occur in household settings or in institutions for persons with mental retardation, but the risk of transmission in these settings only becomes significant over time with repeated exposures. These exposures usually consist of sharing toothbrushes or razors or aggressive behavior such as biting. When institutionalized children with mental retardation have been placed in normal school classrooms, the risk of transmission has been less than 1% per year even with the children with disabilities showing aggressive or self-mutilative behavior and sharing food, eating utensils, and toys they put in their mouths. There has been only one reported instance where transmission occurred in a child care setting. In this report, the infected child was engaging in unusually aggressive behavior. In another reported instance a known chronic carrier with severe eczema who had been documented to have transmitted HBV to a household member did not transmit the infection to others in a child care setting despite being in that setting a number of months.

Incubation Period. The incubation period ranges from 6 weeks to 6 months.

DIAGNOSIS

Since most infections are asymptomatic, serologic testing is the most accurate means to diagnose HBV infection. A person with a positive HBsAg and positive immunoglobulin M (IgM) anti-HBc is acutely infected. A person with a positive HBsAg and a positive IgG anti-HBc is a chronic carrier (must be positive for HBsAg 6 months later to confirm this). A person who is anti-HBs-positive has been infected in the past or has been vaccinated and is now immune. A person who is negative for HBsAg, anti-HBc, and anti-HBs is not and has not been infected but is susceptible to infection.

THERAPY

Interferon-alpha and nucleoside analogs such as lamivudine both singly and in combination have been used with some success in treating chronic carrier individuals. Drug resistance and low virological cure rates have been problematic.

INFECTIOUS PERIOD

Persons are considered infectious if their HBsAg test is positive. There have been rare reports of persons who have a negative HBsAg test but a positive anti-HBc test who have transmitted HBV, but most persons with this serologic profile are noninfectious.

INFECTION CONTROL

Vaccine.   A very effective vaccine is available and is recommended for children attending child care centers and preschools. It should be a requirement for child care center or preschool entry. Now that universal immunization of infants for hepatitis B is taking place, hepatitis B has become less of an issue. A combined hepatitis A and hepatitis B vaccine is now available. In previously unimmunized children older than 12 years of age and in all unimmunized child care personnel, this combination vaccine is an ideal method of providing excellent protection against both the hepatitis A and B viruses.

Exclusion from Child Care or Preschool Attendance.   HBV-infected children need not be excluded from the child care or preschool setting. Other than the single instance of transmission described earlier, there have been no reported outbreaks of HBV in child care settings. As noted above, in transmission studies of deinstitutionalized children with mental retardation, whose behaviors are more likely to transmit HBV than children in the noninstitutional child care setting, the risk was extremely low. Exclusion should only be considered after education of parents, personnel, and children on ways to prevent transmission has failed and universal vaccination has not yet occurred. If a child is excluded, then exclusion should last only as long as the child tests positive for HBsAg.

Recommendations for Other Children.   Children should be taught how to minimize the risk of transmission: Don't bite, put a bandage on cuts and scrapes, and don't share toothbrushes.

Recommendations for Personnel.   It should be required that all personnel receive the hepatitis B vaccine. Personnel are at very low risk of becoming infected by a child. Personnel should be instructed to observe the children for biting or other aggressive behavior, uncovered cuts or scrapes, and toothbrush sharing. If universal vaccination has not occurred and the behavior continues to be a problem, then the use of vaccine or exclusion of the infected child should be reconsidered by the management of the center.

Parental Advice.   Parents should be informed of the very low risk and the steps being taken to minimize the risk. They should be told of the recommended option of vaccination and exclusion of the infected child and what events or situations will cause the child care center or preschool to choose either of those options. Finally, they should be told that exclusion would be the option of last resort and that in the case of deinstitutionalized retarded children in school classrooms, exclusion is legally indefensible when transmission cannot be demonstrated.

32

Hepatitis C

Timothy R. Townsend

CLINICAL MANIFESTATIONS

Hepatitis C virus (HCV) is clinically indistinguishable from hepatitis due to hepatitis A virus or hepatitis B virus, although in most cases the signs, symptoms, and biochemical abnormalities are not as severe. Posttransfusion HCV infection is symptomatic in about 25% of cases. Persistent infection develops in approximately 85% of patients with HCV infection. Chronic active hepatitis develops in 60 to 70% and cirrhosis in approximately 20% of those patients.

ETIOLOGIC AGENT

HCV is a single-stranded RNA virus classified as a separate genus in the Flaviviridae genus.

EPIDEMIOLOGY

Source of the Organism. The reservoir for HCV is the chronic HCV carrier.

High-Risk Populations. The highest rates of infection occur in persons with large and repeated percutaneous exposure to blood or blood products. Intravenous drug users and hemophiliacs have a seroprevalence rate of 60 to 90%. Hemodialysis patients have a 20% seroprevalence, household and sexual contacts of infected persons a 1 to 10% rate, and health care workers a 1% rate. Perinatal transmission has been documented at 5% (range, 0 to 25%). For most infected children, no source of infection is identified.

Mode of Spread.   Infection is spread primarily by parenteral exposure to blood and blood products from a person with HCV infection. For most infected children, no specific source for their infection is identified. There have been no reports of transmission of HCV in child care settings.

Incubation Period.   The incubation period of HCV averages 7 to 9 weeks (range, 2 to 24 weeks).

DIAGNOSIS

A diagnostic serologic test for anti-HCV has been available since 1990. This is a two-stage test: an enzyme-linked immunosorbent assay which, if positive, is confirmed by a recombinant immunoblot. Within 5 to 6 weeks after the onset of disease, 80% of patients will have detectable antibody.

Tests that document the presence of HCV RNA by polymerase chain reaction are new, and no standards for clinical use have been established. However, these tests are highly sensitive and important adjunctive studies to be used in early diagnosis, infant diagnosis, and in patients receiving antiviral therapy.

THERAPY

Recombinant interferon-alpha alone and combined with ribavirin are currently available and have been licensed for treatment of chronically infected patients. However, interferon-alpha therapy appears to have a sustained therapeutic response in less than 20% of patients and up to 50% with combination therapy. Several recent trials of pegylated interferon combined with ribavirin have shown improved response rates, up to 80%. All patients with hepatitis C should receive hepatitis A and B vaccines to prevent other and compounding sources of hepatic damage.

INFECTIOUS PERIOD

All persons with antibody to HCV or HCV RNA in the blood are considered infectious.

INFECTION CONTROL

Vaccine.   None available.

Exclusion from Child Care or Preschool Attendance, Recommendations for Other Children and Personnel, and Parental Advice.   Until there are data demonstrating that transmission of HCV occurs in a child care or preschool setting, no exclusion of children with HCV infection is indicated. To date, no outbreaks of HCV have been reported in these settings, nor have there been case reports suggesting possible disease transmission in a child care or preschool setting. Adherence to scrupulous standard precautions in this setting should prevent transmission of HCV.

Hepatitis D

Timothy R. Townsend

CLINICAL MANIFESTATIONS

Infection with hepatitis D virus (HDV) can occur only in a person with an active (acute or chronic carrier) hepatitis B virus (HBV) infection. Infection can occur simultaneously with infection with HBV (coinfection), in which case the clinical manifestations of both infections are the same as those of HBV alone except that the risk of fulminant hepatitis is greater with coinfection. Infection can occur in a person who is a chronic HBV carrier (superinfection). This super-infection can be asymptomatic or symptomatic and indistinguish-able from a symptomatic HBV infection. Both coinfection and superinfection can lead to a chronic HDV carrier state associated with chronic active hepatitis and cirrhosis.

ETIOLOGIC AGENT

HDV is considered a defective virus in that its ability to infect and cause hepatitis is dependent on the presence of active HBV infec-tion. The virus consists of an outer coat of hepatitis B surface antigen and an internal protein antigen, the delta antigen, containing a very-low-molecular-weight single strand of RNA.

EPIDEMIOLOGY

Source of the Organism.   The reservoir for HDV is the chronic HDV-HBV carrier.

High-Risk Populations.   In the United States, approximately 6% of chronic HBV carriers have antibody to HDV, suggesting HDV is much less of a problem than in endemic areas such as southern Italy. Higher prevalences have been found in some intravenous drug abuser populations and hemophiliacs.

Mode of Spread.   HDV is spread the same way HBV is spread.

Incubation Period.   The incubation period for coinfection is the same as that for HBV, 6 weeks to 6 months. For superinfection the incubation period may be shorter.

DIAGNOSIS

The diagnosis should be suspected in any fulminant HBV infection. Serologic testing using immunoglobulins G and M, anti-HDV, and delta antigen will confirm the diagnosis and permit an estimate of the recency of infection.

THERAPY

There is no known therapy for HDV.

INFECTIOUS PERIOD

In an acutely coinfected person when there is evidence that active HBV infection is over (disappearance of the hepatitis B surface antigen), HDV should no longer be able to be transmitted. A superinfected person who is a chronic carrier of both HBV and HDV is infectious for as long as the HBV carrier state lasts.

INFECTION CONTROL

Vaccine.   There is no vaccine available against HDV. However, since HDV can only be spread in the presence of HBV, vaccination against HBV is protective against HDV; therefore, all recommendations for HBV should be followed.

Exclusion from Child Care or Preschool Attendance, Recommendations for Other Children and Personnel, and Parental Advice.   Recommendations concerning HDV infection in a child care setting should be no different from those for HBV infection.

Hepatitis E

Timothy R. Townsend

CLINICAL MANIFESTATIONS

Hepatitis E virus (HEV) is the enterically transmitted non-A, non-B hepatitis virus. Clinical disease is similar to that of the other viral hepatitides and includes jaundice, fever, anorexia, malaise, and arthralgia. Chronic infection does not occur with HEV infection. Illness is both more severe among pregnant women and more often fatal, with case fatality rates as high as 25%.

ETIOLOGIC AGENT

HEV is a single-stranded RNA virus. Hepatitis E–like viruses are found in a number of animal species, but it is unclear whether human hepatitis E can be acquired from animals.

EPIDEMIOLOGY

Source of the Organism.   The reservoirs of HEV are infected humans and fecally contaminated food and water.

High-Risk Populations.   Adults are more commonly infected than children. Endemic and epidemic disease is present in Mexico, Asia, and Africa. Infection of travelers to endemic areas has been reported.

Mode of Spread.   The most common modes of transmission are fecal-oral, associated with person-to-person spread, and ingestion of contaminated water.

Incubation Period.   The incubation period is approximately 6 weeks (range, 2 to 9 weeks).

DIAGNOSIS

The diagnosis of HEV infection is made by excluding the other acute viral hepatitides (A, B, C, D) and hepatitis associated with cytomegalovirus and Epstein-Barr virus infection. No test is commercially available, but persons requiring information about serologic and polymerase chain reaction testing for non-A, non-B, non-C hepatitis should contact the Centers for Disease Control and Prevention.

THERAPY

There is no proven therapy for HEV infection.

INFECTIOUS PERIOD

The infectious period for HEV infection is not known. More than 95% of those who have biochemical resolution of their hepatitis have no viral particles in their stools or HEV RNA detectable in sera. There is not a chronic carrier state associated with HEV infection.

INFECTION CONTROL

Vaccine.   Passive immunization has not been shown to be effective, and recombinant vaccines are being developed.

Exclusion from Child Care or Preschool Attendance.   The child should not attend day care or preschool until symptoms have resolved.

Recommendations for Other Children.   Adherence to careful sanitation and handwashing.

Recommendations for Personnel.   Strict adherence to sanitation practices and handwashing.

Parental Advice.   Until there are data demonstrating that transmission of HEV occurs in a child care or preschool setting, firm recommendations concerning exclusion of the infected child or management of children, personnel, or parents are not possible. However, given the epidemiology of this pathogen, children should be monitored for signs and symptoms of hepatitis and brought to their primary care provider, if symptomatic.

Herpes Simplex Virus
(Gingivostomatitis)

Richard J. Whitley

CLINICAL MANIFESTATIONS

Herpes simplex virus infections cause a wide spectrum of diseases ranging from asymptomatic and benign infections, such as fever blisters, to life-threatening diseases, such as neonatal herpes and herpes simplex encephalitis. Infections caused by herpes simplex virus in individuals who are immunocompromised can be severe. The most common childhood manifestation of herpes simplex infections are herpes simplex gingivostomatitis, a disease of the oropharynx characterized by vesicular ulcerative lesions in association with fever and a painful mouth. The oral pain can lead to hospitalization because of inadequate oral fluid intake.

Other childhood manifestations of herpes simplex infections include herpes simplex keratoconjunctivitis, neonatal herpes simplex virus infection presenting within the first 4 weeks of life, and herpes simplex encephalitis. Children who are immunocompromised can reactivate a latent infection that results in severe and progressive orofacial disease.

Patients with herpes simplex infections are most contagious to other individuals when skin vesicles are present.

ETIOLOGIC AGENT

Herpes simplex virus consists of two serotypes: herpes simplex type 1, which generally causes infections above the belt, and herpes simplex type 2, which generally causes infections below the belt, although this distinction is becoming less common. Herpes simplex types 1 and 2 are members of the herpesvirus family. Other members of this family include: cytomegalovirus, Epstein-Barr virus, varicella-zoster virus, human herpesvirus 6, human herpesvirus 7, and Kaposi sarcoma herpesvirus. All members of the herpesvirus family are large DNA viruses containing double-stranded DNA that resides in the core of the virus.

EPIDEMIOLOGY

Source of the Organism.   The virus is only found in infectious secretions of individuals actively replicating herpes simplex virus. Sites from which herpes simplex virus can be retrieved are vesicular lesions, the oropharynx during gingivostomatitis, tissue obtained at biopsy of individuals with severely progressive disease, and from the genital tract during episodes of recurrent genital herpes. Recently, herpes simplex virus DNA has been detected by polymerase chain reaction (PCR) in the saliva in 1% of the asymptomatic population and in genital secretions in the absence of detectable lesions.

High-Risk Populations.   High-risk populations include individuals who are immunocompromised or babies born to women who have genital herpetic infection at delivery.

Mode of Spread.   Transmission of herpes simplex virus is by direct and intimate personal contact. Virus has not been known to be transmitted from inanimate objects to human beings. Intimate personal human contact is the only mechanism known today for transmission of this infection.

Incubation Period.   The incubation period is from 3 to 5 days.

DIAGNOSIS

Infections caused by herpes simplex virus are usually diagnosed by clinical manifestations. In most individuals the vesicular rash is diagnostic; however, virus can be isolated in cell culture systems. Under unusual circumstances, the diagnosis of neonatal herpes simplex infection and herpes simplex encephalitis is often more difficult. Excretion of virus from peripheral sites in such individuals is often rare, and, therefore, obtaining tissue for isolation of virus is essential. Detection of viral DNA in the cerebrospinal fluid by PCR is the best diagnostic approach when the test is performed by a reputable laboratory.

THERAPY

The only forms of herpes simplex virus infections that require therapy are those involving the newborn, children with herpes simplex encephalitis, and the immunocompromised child with recurrent herpes simplex infections. Acyclovir is the treatment of choice, and the only formulation currently licensed for use in children is that for intravenous administration (5 to 20 mg/kg given every 8 hours for 14 to 21 days). Some physicians treat gingivosto-matitis with oral acyclovir at 20 mg/kg given every 8 hours.

INFECTIOUS PERIOD

The duration of infectivity is approximately 4 to 5 days once intravenous acyclovir has been initiated. In the absence of therapy, however, infectivity can persist for as long as 3 weeks.

INFECTION CONTROL

Vaccine.   None available.

Exclusion from Child Care or Preschool Attendance.   The child should not attend the child care center or preschool until cutaneous lesions are scabbed.

Recommendations for Other Children.   Once a child is infected, avoid person-to-person contact and contact with vesicles. To accomplish such a goal, existing vesicles can be covered.

Recommendations for Personnel.   Strict handwashing and the use of gloves when changing or manipulating skin that has a vesicular rash will prevent transmission of this virus. Personnel with recurrent herpes labialis (fever blister) should cover their lesions until crusted and be educated to avoid person-to-person contact and touching of and/or contact with vesicular lesions.

Parental Advice.   There is little likelihood that this infection will be transmitted from one child to another.

36

Human Immunodeficiency Virus Infection and Acquired Immunodeficiency Syndrome

Gwendolyn B. Scott

CLINICAL MANIFESTATIONS

Infection with human immunodeficiency virus type-1 (HIV-1) results in a progressive deterioration of the immune system, ultimately leading to opportunistic infections, malignancies, and other conditions representative of the acquired immunodeficiency syndrome (AIDS). By December 2004, 9443 children with AIDS had been reported to the Centers for Disease Control and Prevention (CDC). In recent years, the majority of children have acquired HIV infection through perinatal transmission. It is estimated that approximately 7000 women with HIV infection deliver an infant in the United States yearly. In the absence of antiretroviral therapy, between 20 and 30% of HIV-infected pregnant women will transmit HIV to their infants. Since 1994, however, the use of zidovudine to prevent mother-to-child transmission has significantly decreased the risk of transmission of HIV and the number of children with perinatally acquired AIDS. During infancy and early childhood, many of these children will attend child care or preschool.

HIV infection in children is a chronic multisystem disease characterized by a wide range of complications and conditions. Prior to the availability of highly active antiretroviral therapy, between 10 and 20% of children developed progressive disease with significant immune suppression during the first 2 years of life, with a survival of less than 4 years. The remainder of children had a variable clinical course with a median survival of 8 years. However, earlier identification, diagnosis, and aggressive antiretroviral treatment of HIV infection in children has decreased early complications and prolonged survival. In Miami, 85% of the 310 children followed in our clinic with perinatally acquired HIV infection range in age from 8 to 23 years old.

The clinical course of HIV infection is variable but generally progressive. Particularly for older children, acute complicating infections may be interspersed with periods during which the child functions relatively normally. As the disease progresses, involvement of multiple organ systems and the occurrence of multiple infections or conditions simultaneously are common.

Common early clinical manifestations of HIV infection in children with perinatal infection include failure to thrive or wasting; chronic or recurrent diarrhea without specific cause; generalized lymphadenopathy, hepatosplenomegaly and parotitis; persistent or recurrent oral candidiasis; and a variety of recurrent infections including otitis media, pneumonia, and meningitis, usually of bacterial origin but also including viral, fungal, and parasitic pathogens.

Central nervous system involvement with HIV may present in the infant or young child as developmental delay or loss of milestones. Progressive encephalopathy occurs in about 10% of infected children and is usually associated with significant immune deficiency, failure to thrive, spasticity, poor head growth, and evidence of brain atrophy and/or basal ganglia calcifications on computed tomography scanning of the brain. This condition is associated with a poor prognosis. Older children may manifest learning disabilities or attention deficit disorders. Thus, developmental testing is an important part of routine care so these conditions can be detected early and interventions prescribed. Cardiomyopathy, hepatitis, and nephropathy also occur in some children. Malignancies, particularly non-Hodgkin's lymphomas, occur in about 2% of HIV-infected children.

AIDS is the "late stage" of infection with HIV. The definition, which has been revised several times, includes the presence of opportunistic infection, certain malignancies, recurrent serious bacterial infections, lymphoid interstitial pneumonia in children under 13 years of age, and low levels of CD4-positive lymphocytes (<200 cells/mm^3) in adults and adolescents. Separate disease classification systems have been developed for both children and adults that relate clinical and immunologic status and describe the spectrum of disease.

Lymphoid interstitial pneumonitis occurs in approximately one third of infected children and is usually associated with a good prognosis, although chronic lung disease may occur as a complication in some children. Pneumonia caused by *Pneumocystis jirovecii* is the most frequently described opportunistic infection in AIDS. Other common opportunistic infections include *Candida* esophagitis, disseminated cytomegalovirus infection, and disseminated mycobacterial infection, most often caused by *Mycobacterium avium* complex. Both pulmonary and nonpulmonary tuberculosis is an increasingly common problem, particularly among adults in selected populations. In some areas, tuberculosis and tuberculosis resistant to multiple drugs in people with AIDS has become a significant public health problem.

ETIOLOGIC AGENT

HIV is an RNA cytopathic retrovirus not known to infect other animals naturally: nonhuman primates such as chimpanzees can be infected in the laboratory but do not develop disease. Humans are the only known reservoir of HIV. Two major types of HIV have been identified: HIV-1 and HIV-2. Although both subtypes have been associated with AIDS and related clinical syndromes, HIV-1 has been the predominant cause of disease in the world. HIV-2 infection is endemic in western African countries and is extremely rare in the United States. Considerable genetic variation exists among different isolates of HIV-1 from different individuals. Selected regions of the envelope genes of HIV-1 mutate relatively rapidly, giving rise to numerous strains.

HIV attaches to the cell through the interaction between the viral envelope glycoprotein and its receptor, the CD4 molecule, located on the cell surface. Thus, the cells most commonly infected are CD4-positive lymphocytes and cells of the monocyte-macrophage series. Once a cell has been infected with HIV, the proviral genome is integrated into the host cell DNA and establishes a persistent chronic infection. HIV has a complex gene structure with a number of regulatory genes that appear to control the rate of viral replication, although the interaction of this regulatory mechanism with the infected cell is not yet fully understood.

EPIDEMIOLOGY

Source of the Organism.   Humans are the only known reservoir of HIV.

High-Risk Populations.   In the United States, HIV infection and AIDS primarily occur in young adults. Adults (and adolescents) currently at highest risk of acquiring HIV infection include men who have sex with men (homosexual or bisexual males), people who inject drugs or use crack cocaine (the latter because of its association with multiple sex partners), and men and women who have multiple sex partners (some of whom may be at high risk). Approximately 1 to 2% of all cases of AIDS reported in the United States have occurred in children or adolescents. Children at highest risk for HIV infection are those born to women who are infected; the highest risk for women is injection of drugs, using crack cocaine, having multiple sex partners, or being the sex partner of a man at high risk. Children or adults who have clotting factor disorders (including classic hemophilia) and who received clotting factor therapy before the mid-1980s also are at high risk of HIV infection and AIDS. Major improvements have been made in the safety of clotting factor concentrates since the mid-1980s, and people with hemophilia not infected before 1986 are no longer at high risk of HIV infection through that route. The majority of cases of HIV infection associated with transfusion of infected blood or blood products occurred before 1985. Since 1985, all donated blood has been screened for HIV antibody, and the estimated risk of transmission of HIV by screened blood in the United States is 1 in every 440,000 to 660,000 donated units. This risk usually occurs when the donor has been recently infected and detectable HIV antibodies have not developed.

Mode of Spread.   HIV infection is acquired through (a) sexual contact with an infected person, whether homosexual or heterosexual; (b) direct inoculation of infectious blood or tissue through use of contaminated needles during intravenous drug injection, a mucous membrane exposure, penetrating injury with a needle or sharp object containing infected blood, tissue or organ transplantation, or, rarely, through receipt of a blood transfusion; and (c) perinatal transmission from an infected woman to her fetus in utero or at delivery to her infant, or postnatally during breast feeding. For children with HIV in the United States, perinatal transmission accounts for over 95% of cases. Significant decreases in perinatal HIV infection have been observed in the United States and Europe following the use of zidovudine in pregnant women and their infants to reduce transmission of HIV. In the United States, the risk of perinatal transmission is between 1 and 2% in women receiving zidovudine in combination with other antiretroviral drugs.

Transmission by other means such as through food or water, fomites, or casual contact in a household, workplace, or school setting has not been documented to occur. Several studies of individuals living in households with HIV-infected adults or children have shown no transmission and include 300 children of differing ages followed for more than 1700 person years. Independent of these studies, there are six case reports of household transmission of HIV involving children. In most of these cases the means of transmission is unknown, but percutaneous or intravenous exposure to blood from the infected household contact is possible.

Biting is a common behavior in young children. HIV has been isolated from saliva of some infected persons, but transmission of HIV by bites is rare and has occurred only in association with blood-tinged saliva in the wound. The actual risk of transmission of HIV through biting is thought to be very low. Fluids implicated in the transmission of HIV infection include blood, cervical secretions, semen, and breast milk.

Incubation Period.   In adults, an acute self-limited illness caused by HIV may occur within a few weeks after infection. Onset of chronic illness usually occurs years after infection, with approximately half of infected adults diagnosed with AIDS 10 years after infection. In children with perinatal infection, clinical illness often is apparent during the first or second year of life, although it may occur years later. With other types of infections (e.g., transfusion), clinical illness and a diagnosis of AIDS may not occur for years.

DIAGNOSIS

The diagnosis of symptomatic HIV infection and AIDS is based on the clinical, serologic, and immunologic findings and exclusion of other causes of immunodeficiency. The presence of certain clinical conditions or opportunistic infections may suggest a diagnosis of HIV infection. Serologic tests for HIV infection are highly sensitive and specific if performed by a reliable laboratory. Confirmation is essential. In a child 2 years of age or older, HIV infection is diagnosed by an HIV antibody test that is repeatedly reactive and confirmed by a Western blot assay or an immunofluorescence test. Before 24 months of age, diagnosis is more complex because a positive HIV antibody test may only reflect in utero passive transfer of maternal antibody. The standard test for diagnosis of HIV infection in infants and children under 24 months of age is the polymerase chain reaction (PCR) for detection of HIV DNA sequences. The sensitivity of PCR for diagnosis of HIV is greater than 95% by 6 weeks of age. Consent for testing the infant or child for HIV should be obtained from the parent or legal guardian prior to testing.

THERAPY

Children with HIV infection need close medical supervision with monitoring of their clinical, neurologic, and immunologic status. Most infants and children with HIV infection are seen at 3- to 6-month intervals depending on their clinical status. The child with HIV infection should receive routine childhood care, including vaccinations, and should be evaluated promptly if infection or fever occurs. Therapy of HIV infection includes antiretroviral therapy and prophylaxis against *P. jirovecii* and other infections.

The American Academy of Pediatrics and the CDC have published recommendations for immunization of children with HIV infection against other diseases, and current recommendations should be consulted. Briefly, both symptomatic and asymptomatic children with HIV infection should receive diphtheria-tetanus-acellular pertussis (DTaP) vaccine, inactivated polio vaccine (IPV), *Haemophilus influenzae* type b conjugate, conjugated pneumococcal vaccine, and hepatitis B vaccine following the routine immunization schedule. In general, live viral (e.g., oral polio [OPV]) and bacterial (e.g., bacillus

Calmette-Guérin [BCG]) vaccines should not be given. However, since measles can cause severe or fatal illness in children infected with HIV, measles-mumps-rubella vaccine (MMR) is recommended for those HIV-infected children who are not severely immunocompromised. Varicella vaccine should be considered only for HIV-infected children who are asymptomatic or mildly symptomatic (categories N or A) with CD4 percentage 25% or greater. Inactivated influenza vaccine should be given to children 6 months of age or older annually. Since children with symptomatic HIV infection often have a poor immunologic response to vaccines, these children should be considered candidates for postexposure prophylaxis (e.g., immunoglobulin, varicella-zoster immune globulin) if exposed to diseases for which this is available.

Several antiretroviral drugs have been approved with some restrictions for treatment of HIV infection in children. These include the nucleoside reverse transcriptase inhibitors (zidovudine [azidothymidine, AZT], didanosine [ddI], lamivudine [3TC], emtricitabine [FTC], stavudine [D4T], and abacavir), non-nucleoside reverse transcriptase inhibitors (nevirapine and efavirenz), and four protease inhibitors (ritonavir, amprenavir, nelfinavir, and lopinavir), and an entry inhibitor, entuvirti. Clinical trial data in children show that antiretroviral treatment of symptomatic children slows progression of disease, improves immune status, decreases viral load, and reduces mortality. Present guidelines recommend treatment of all children with HIV infection under 1 year of age independent of clinical or laboratory findings and older children with clinical symptoms of HIV infection or evidence of immune suppression. Infected children who are older than 1 year of age with normal clinical and immune status and a low viral load may be observed with close monitoring, although some experts would also recommend treatment of these asymptomatic children. Initial therapy for HIV-infected children should include two nucleoside reverse transcriptase inhibitors and a protease inhibitor or, alternatively, two nucleoside reverse transcriptase inhibitors and a non-nucleoside reverse transcriptase inhibitor. Compliance with medication regimens is critical for a successful therapeutic outcome. If doses are missed or are suboptimal, then resistance to these drugs may develop, and the regimen will fail. Optimal therapeutic regimens for early infection as well as advanced disease in children are being studied in clinical trials. Antiretroviral agents all have different side effects, and many have interactions with other drugs. Children require close monitoring of both clinical and laboratory parameters. Viral load and CD4 count and percent should be done at least every 3 months, or more frequently if these parameters are changing. Therapy for HIV infection and its complications continues to evolve rapidly, and current recommendations should be sought.

Monthly administration of intravenous immunoglobulin (IVIG) to HIV-infected children is indicated for children with HIV infection who have hypogammaglobulinemia (immunoglobulin G levels below 250 mg%). It has also been recommended as therapy for children with chronic bronchiectasis, for those children with no antibody response to measles immunization living in areas where measles is prevalent, and for treatment of severe HIV-associated thrombocytopenia.

Prompt diagnosis and aggressive treatment of opportunistic infections, maintenance of nutritional status, developmental assessment, and good supportive care are important elements of ongoing medical follow-up. Prophylaxis against *P. jirovecii* pneumonia (PCP) with trimethoprim-sulfamethoxazole is recommended for all children at risk for HIV until their HIV status is determined and for all infected children during the first year of life. Continuation of PCP prophylaxis after 1 year of age in the infected child is determined by the child's clinical and immune status. Prophylaxis against atypical mycobacterial infection (*Mycobacterium avium* complex [MAC]), *Candida* species, herpes simplex, and cytomegalovirus infections are used depending on the clinical situation.

INFECTIOUS PERIOD

Since HIV establishes a chronic infection, an infected person is presumably infectious throughout life. The degree of transmissibility of HIV may vary with the state of infection.

INFECTION CONTROL

Vaccine.   No effective vaccine for prevention of HIV is currently available.

Post-Exposure Prophylaxis for HIV.   The risk for transmission in health care workers exposed to HIV-infected blood following a needlestick injury is 0.3% and is 0.09% following a mucous membrane exposure. There are no large-scale studies available in children who have been exposed to discarded needles in parks, playgrounds, or on the street, but the risk is likely to be small. In the event of such an exposure or an exposure of a child or adult to the blood of an HIV-infected person, the wound or area involved should be washed thoroughly with soap and water and the child or adult referred immediately to his or her physician or the closest emergency room. In some instances, postexposure prophylaxis with antiretroviral therapy is warranted and should be started as soon as possible following an injury.

Exclusion from Child Care or Preschool Attendance.   HIV-infected children should be allowed to attend day care centers and schools and allowed to participate in all activities to the extent that their health permits. Attendance at a day care center should be decided on an individual basis by qualified persons, including the child's physician. Factors to be considered include the type of care the child will receive and whether the infected child would be at significant risk of being exposed to serious infectious diseases. Although the risk of transmission of HIV from one infant or child to another in a child care setting is unmeasurable and highly improbable based on known means of transmission, it has been a major consideration in all discussions about including HIV-infected children in these settings. In general, young children who have open skin lesions should not be in a child care setting with other small children. Because of neurologic impairment and developmental delays with HIV infection, decisions about appropriate care settings should be based on developmental stage rather than chronologic age. Periodic reassessment of the child is urged. The American Academy of Pediatrics publishes current recommendations to provide a guide for evaluation of children in this setting. In addition, other infectious conditions in HIV-infected children should be evaluated to determine whether they pose a risk to other children or adults in the care setting. Preschool care programs should develop policies to inform all parents when a highly infectious illness, such as measles, chickenpox, parvovirus B19 infection (fifth disease), tuberculosis, or cryptosporidiosis or other acute diarrhea, occurs in a child, so families can take appropriate measures to protect their immunodeficient children.

Recommendations for Other Children.   Based on studies of HIV-infected children and adults that have shown no transmission of HIV in a family setting, HIV is highly unlikely to be transmitted from one child to another in a child care center or preschool. No special precautions are warranted; therefore, admission or continued attendance of an HIV-infected child should be based on a careful case-by-case review as recommended above. Screening of children for HIV infection in a child care setting before admission or after a child in the center is found to be infected is not justifiable.

Recommendations for Personnel.   Since a child may not be known to be infected with HIV (or other bloodborne infectious agents such as hepatitis B virus), all child care centers and preschools should adopt reasonable policies and procedures for managing accidents, such as a nosebleed, for all students and for cleaning and disinfecting surfaces contaminated with blood. Gloves should be used if readily available, but direct contact with blood can also be avoided by using several thicknesses of paper towels or folded cloths. Blood-contaminated surfaces should be cleaned and disinfected with freshly prepared chlorine bleach solution (1:10 dilution). Gloves do not need to be used for feeding a child or wiping secretions that do not contain visible blood; they should be used, however (in addition to careful handwashing), for changing diapers that contain bloody stools. Good handwashing is fundamental in prevention of HIV and other infectious diseases. All personnel should have knowledge of appropriate infection control procedures and have access to necessary supplies. The Occupational Safety and Health Administration (OSHA) has published regulations regarding education of employees and routine procedures for handling blood and bloody fluids.

Personnel who are directly involved with the care of an HIV-infected child in a child care setting and who have a need to know should be informed of that fact and should be instructed about the need to respect and maintain the rights of the child and family to privacy and confidentiality of the information; the minimum number of persons necessary should be informed. If medical records are maintained, confidentiality must be assured.

HIV-Infected Personnel.   The American Academy of Pediatrics has stated that HIV-infected adults do not pose a risk of infection to children in child care settings if they do not have open or exudative skin lesions or other medical conditions that would allow contact with potentially infectious (i.e., bloody) fluids. HIV-infected personnel who have other infectious conditions (e.g., active pulmonary or laryngeal tuberculosis, acute diarrhea, herpetic whitlow) that may be transmitted to others in the care setting should be evaluated to determine appropriate management and whether temporary or permanent exclusion from the care setting is warranted. Immunocompromised adults may be highly susceptible to the infectious agents that young children attending child care centers or preschools are likely to have, and they should seek advice from their physician about the advisability of such work and what precautions are recommended.

Parental Advice.   Since the risk of transmission of HIV infection among children in a child care setting is only hypothetical, there is no urgent need to inform parents about the attendance of an infected child at a center. In lieu of special notice, it may be preferable to provide parents with general information about management of infectious diseases, including HIV, before a specific instance arises.

37

Infectious Mononucleosis

Ciro V. Sumaya

CLINICAL MANIFESTATIONS

Most infections by this virus occur mainly in young children and produce no problems (i.e., they are asymptomatic). In some instances, at a frequency that is not very clear, an infection can produce infectious mononucleosis. This illness consists of a typical clinical picture with fever, tiredness, enlarged neck lymph nodes, inflamed throat and tonsils, and enlargement of abdominal organs (liver and/ or spleen). The clinical illness may last 1 to 2 or more weeks.

Sometimes, significant complications can occur during the infectious mononucleosis episode and involve the respiratory tract (pneumonia, severe airway obstruction), nervous system (seizures, meningoencephalitis, nerve palsies), and blood system (decline in platelets and anemia), among others. However, virtually all cases have a transient course with complete resolution and no aftereffects. It also is believed that this virus can cause illnesses characterized by isolated manifestations such as inflamed throats or pneumonia instead of an infectious mononucleosis episode.

ETIOLOGIC AGENT

Epstein-Barr virus (EBV), the cause of infectious mononucleosis, belongs to the herpesvirus group of viruses that produces chickenpox (varicella-zoster virus) and fever blisters or genital herpes (herpes simplex virus).

EPIDEMIOLOGY

Source of the Organism.   It is believed that this virus is present in salival secretions and therefore can be transmitted through body contact that permits salival exchange.

High-Risk Populations.   The virus spreads mainly among children, presumably more rapidly in closed or overcrowded conditions. Why an infection with this virus usually produces no ill effects in young children, while in young adults it is quite likely to produce the infectious mononucleosis syndrome, is unclear. It also seems that if one child in a family develops infectious mononucleosis, there is a greater chance for another child in the family to develop that illness even after a long lapse in time following the initial case. Children with special problems with their immune system or those who have recently received organ or bone marrow transplants are at greater risk for experiencing a serious disease with an infectious mononucleosis episode or other manifestations from their EBV infection.

Mode of Spread.   It is believed that the virus is transmitted through salival exchange. The spread of this virus, however, is not as efficient as that of other herpesviruses, such as herpes simplex or varicella-zoster virus. The transmission of EBV via blood products with the subsequent development of an infectious mononucleosis–like illness is quite uncommon.

Incubation Period.   The incubation period of infectious mononucleosis is usually quite long, 5 to 7 weeks after exposure. The incubation period seems to be a few weeks shorter if the exposure to EBV was through a blood transfusion.

DIAGNOSIS

The diagnosis is made by the presence of the following triad of findings: (a) typical signs and symptoms as mentioned above, (b) a blood count showing a relative lymphocytosis and atypical lymphocyte formation, and (c) a serologic assay indicating the presence of heterophil antibodies or specific EBV antibodies reflecting an acute infection.

THERAPY

Simple measures to reduce or alleviate the signs and symptoms, such as antipyretics to decrease the fever, reduction of activity, and bed rest for the malaise, are commonly recommended for the patient with infectious mononucleosis. Contact sports should be avoided during the time the spleen is felt to be enlarged. Corticosteroids are sometimes administered when the patient has significant complications or an otherwise severe clinical course. The efficacy of the corticosteroids in this condition, however, is still quite obscure. The few patients who may develop pronounced respiratory obstruction because of immense tonsillar inflammation may receive an emergency tonsillectomy or intubation. An antiviral medication, acyclovir, does reduce the amount of EBV in salival excretions of patients with infectious mononucleosis, but does not significantly alter the signs, symptoms, or course of the disease.

INFECTIOUS PERIOD

The length of infectivity is quite unclear, because patients with infectious mononucleosis or other forms of acute EBV infections may excrete the virus intermittently in their saliva for many months, if not years, following their infection. It is presumed, though, that the amount of virus in the saliva during the acute episode of infectious mononucleosis or other form of EBV infection is at its peak and, therefore, more likely to be transmittable to close contacts, in comparison with later in convalescence or after resolution of the illness, when there are progressively decreasing titers of virus present.

INFECTION CONTROL

Vaccine.   An experimental vaccine is being tested but is not available for general use.

Exclusion from Child Care or Preschool Attendance.   The child should probably be removed from the child care setting during the period of time that he or she feels ill and unable to tolerate much general activity. In most cases, this is about 1 to 2 weeks.

Recommendations for Other Children.   There are no specific recommendations for other children in the center other than the adherence to common hygienic practices such as the washing of hands when potentially contaminated with human secretions and the avoidance of mouthing of toys or mouth-to-mouth kissing.

Recommendations for Personnel. There are no specific recommendations other than the adherence to common hygienic practices as noted. The risk of significant problems to a pregnant woman (and her unborn child) from exposure to a child with infectious mononucleosis is considered extremely low.

Parental Advice. The parent (or physician) should notify the center supervisor about the diagnosis. An assurance can be provided that this illness is not easily spread (i.e., the development of a second case or more cases of infectious mononucleosis in the center that are related to contact with the initial case should be a rare event).

Influenza (Flu)

Scott A. Halperin

CLINICAL MANIFESTATIONS

Influenza virus causes a spectrum of clinical symptoms that make up the "flu syndrome." In the first several days of infection, fever, headache, myalgias, and chills are prominent. Burning and tearing of the eyes also occur during this period. Respiratory symptoms, including cough and rhinorrhea, are present at the onset but predominate after the third day when the fever and systemic manifestations subside. Respiratory symptoms persist for 3 or 4 days, although the cough may persist for 1 to 2 weeks.

Influenza infections occur in epidemics during the winter months. The spread is rapid through a community, with widespread absenteeism from work and school. Myalgias, arthralgias, and headache are typically seen in older children and adults. Younger school-aged children and preschool-aged children typically have milder disease, although the fever may be higher. Infants and toddlers have rates of hospitalization similar to the elderly. Secondary complications occur frequently during influenza epidemics, although these are less common in children. Primary viral pneumonia due to influenza virus can occur, as well as secondary bacterial pneumonia due to *Streptococcus pneumoniae*, *Haemophilus influenzae*, or *Staphylococcus aureus*. In young children, croup and bronchitis may occur due to infection with influenza virus. A rare but serious complication of an influenza virus infection in children is Reye's syndrome.

ETIOLOGIC AGENT

Influenza virus is an orthomyxovirus. Three virus types are known: influenza A, influenza B, and influenza C. Influenza virus is an enveloped RNA virus. The unique characteristic of influenza virus is the frequency with which it changes its antigenicity. Antigenic variation involves primarily the two external glycoproteins of the virus, neuraminidase and hemagglutinin. With influenza A, antigenic variation occurs on an almost annual basis. Variation also occurs with influenza B but has not been shown with influenza C virus. This antigenic variation enables the virus to evade the immune system and results in repeated epidemics of influenza virus on a yearly basis.

EPIDEMIOLOGY

Source of the Organism. Influenza virus is found in respiratory secretions of infected individuals.

High-Risk Populations. Because of continual change of the antigenic composition of the virus, individuals may continue to be susceptible to influenza virus infection from year to year. Particularly severe infections occur when major antigenic shifts occur in the influenza virus. Children at high risk include those with chronic lung disease, such as moderate to severe asthma, cystic fibrosis, and bronchopulmonary dysplasia. Severe disease also occurs in children with significant cardiac anomalies, immunosuppressed children, and children with hemoglobinopathies (including sickle cell disease), diabetes, chronic renal failure, and metabolic diseases. Healthy infants younger than 1 year of age have rates of hospitalization for influenza illness comparable to those of the elderly.

Mode of Spread. Influenza is spread from person to person by direct contact with infected secretions or via large- or small-droplet aerosols.

Incubation Period. One to 3 days.

DIAGNOSIS

Influenza virus infection may be diagnosed by culture of the virus in egg or tissue culture. The virus also can be detected directly in nasopharyngeal secretions by using direct or indirect immunofluorescent techniques, enzyme immunoassay, or nucleic acid detection such as polymerase chain reaction. However, during an epidemic, the diagnosis is usually made clinically.

THERAPY

Most children with influenza virus infection do not require specific therapy. In children at risk for severe or complicated disease due to underlying conditions, amantadine and rimantadine therapy have been shown to be effective in reducing the symptoms caused by influenza A virus only, particularly if started very early in the course of the illness. Therapy is usually continued for 3 to 5 days, depending on symptomatic improvement. Zanamivir, an inhaled neuraminidase inhibitor, is effective against both influenza A and B viruses and is approved for use in children 7 years of age and older. To be effective, it must be started within 2 days of symptom onset. Another neuraminidase inhibitor, oseltamivir, is available as an oral suspension and is approved for use in children 1 year of age and older; again treatment must be started within 2 days of symptom onset. Aspirin and aspirin-containing products should be avoided due to their association with the subsequent development of Reye's syndrome in influenza patients. Hospitalization is only required for those with severe illness.

INFECTIOUS PERIOD

The virus may be found in respiratory secretions for 6 days prior to the onset of symptoms until 7 days after the symptoms began for influenza A virus, and from 1 day before to 2 weeks after onset of symptoms for influenza B virus infections.

INFECTION CONTROL

Vaccine.   Influenza vaccine is recommended in children considered to be at high risk. These include children with chronic lung disease, including moderate to severe asthma, bronchopulmonary dysplasia, and cystic fibrosis. It is also recommended for children with significant cardiac disease; children receiving immunosuppressive therapy; children with hemoglobinopathies, diabetes, or human immunodeficiency virus infection; and individuals with rheumatoid arthritis or Kawasaki's disease on long-term aspirin therapy. Immunization is recommended for infants 6 to 23 months of age because of their increased risk of influenza-related hospitalization. Immunization of close contacts of severely immunocompromised children is also recommended because these children may have a suboptimal antibody response to the vaccine. Immunization of close contacts of infants from birth to 6 months of age is also recommended because these infants are at highest risk of influenza-related hospitalization but are too young to receive the vaccine. Influenza vaccine should be encouraged for all day care attendees. A cold-adapted live attenuated vaccine that can be given intranasally and which has been demonstrated to be effective in children is available and may facilitate recommendations for more general use of influenza vaccines in children. Studies involving one of these vaccines are under way to determine whether widespread immunization of healthy children can reduce the risk of infection among the elderly.

Exclusion from Child Care or Preschool Attendance.   Once influenza is introduced into a child care facility, most children will have been exposed before the onset of symptoms. Therefore, exclusion of a child with influenza infection is not necessary, and attendance should be based on the condition of the child. However, it is not uncommon for child care facilities to close during an influenza epidemic because of high absenteeism among staff and high absenteeism among children who are too sick to attend.

Recommendations for Other Children.   Children with symptoms of influenza should be monitored for any complications that would require examination by the family physician.

Recommendations for Personnel.   Influenza virus infection is typically spread from children to their caregivers. The infection spreads rapidly through the facility, and most susceptible individuals will become infected. It is recommended that all day care and preschool providers receive yearly influenza vaccine. Careful handwashing and attention to respiratory secretions may diminish the spread of infection.

Parental Advice.   Parents should be advised that an influenza outbreak is occurring and should be instructed to monitor for any complications or severe infection. Aspirin or aspirin-containing products should be avoided during influenza infections because of the association with Reye's syndrome.

Meningococcus
(Bacteremia, Meningitis, Arthritis)

Eugene D. Shapiro

CLINICAL MANIFESTATIONS

The most common manifestations of illness caused by *Neisseria meningitidis* in children are meningitis, septicemia (with or without septic shock), arthritis, and pneumonia, any of which may occur alone or in combination with one or more of the others. In children with meningitis, fever usually develops, and they may have a stiff neck and often become irritable or lethargic. This condition may progress to obtundation and coma. Children with meningococcal sepsis (with or without meningitis) may develop a characteristic rash that consists of small, flat red spots (petechiae) on the extremities and/or on the trunk. Occasionally, patients develop a fulminant illness with rapidly progressive septic shock, often associated with a hemorrhagic rash (purpura fulminans).

ETIOLOGIC AGENT

Meningococcal infections are caused by a type of bacteria, *N. meningitidis*. These bacteria are divided into more than ten different serogroups (A, B, C, D, 29E, W-135, X, Y, and Z are the most common), based on different characteristics of the outer coating of their cell walls. Most infections in the United States are caused by serogroups B, C, and Y.

EPIDEMIOLOGY

Source of the Organism. The organism is part of the normal bacterial flora of the human mouth. It is usually carried in the nasopharynx (the throat). At any given time, 5 to 10% of asymptomatic people harbor the bacteria in their throat. However, in a day care center in which a case of an invasive meningococcal infection has occurred, up to 50% or more of the children and adults in the group may be colonized with the organism.

High-Risk Populations. Children with deficiencies of antibody or complement or who have anatomic or functional asplenia are at increased risk of infection. Although both children and adults who are exposed may be at risk, younger children are at the greatest risk.

Mode of Spread. The organism is spread by respiratory droplets or by direct oral contact with someone who is colonized with the bacteria. Although many people worry about the organism spreading from an infected child to others, in most instances other children in the group are already colonized before the index child becomes ill. Indeed, the ill child usually acquires the bacteria from other asymptomatic children.

Incubation Period. The incubation period is from 2 days to several weeks. Most people who acquire the organism become temporarily colonized (for weeks to months) with the bacteria and never develop an invasive, symptomatic infection. The majority of the people who do develop an invasive infection do so within 1 week of exposure. However, because the exposure may be to an asymptomatic carrier rather than to an ill person, it is often impossible to identify accurately the time of exposure.

DIAGNOSIS

The diagnosis is usually made by recovering the bacteria from the cerebrospinal fluid or from the bloodstream. This is accomplished by culturing specimens obtained by performing a lumbar puncture (spinal tap) and by drawing a sample of the blood. Throat cultures are *not* useful for establishing a diagnosis.

THERAPY

Children with meningococcal infections are usually hospitalized and treated with an antibiotic (penicillin) that is administered intravenously. Most patients with uncomplicated illnesses are hospitalized for 7 to 10 days.

INFECTIOUS PERIOD

The occurrence of a meningococcal infection is a marker for a high rate of colonization in the entire child care group or preschool class. Consequently, even though the ill child's infectivity diminishes dramatically within 24 hours of the initiation of antimicrobial treatment, the organism may spread within the day care center from other asymptomatically colonized children.

INFECTION CONTROL

Vaccine.   A polysaccharide vaccine against serogroups A, C, Y, and W-135 is available, although it may not be effective in children less than 2 years of age. It takes 1 to 2 weeks for antibodies to develop after immunization. Since the period of greatest risk is in the first 2 weeks after exposure, vaccination is generally not recommended routinely in response to sporadic cases of the illness. However, if there seems to be an ongoing epidemic caused by a serogroup contained in the vaccine, it may be appropriate to institute an immunization program. Protein-polysaccharide conjugate vaccines that are effective in young children are being developed and are being recommended in some countries (e.g., group C conjugate vaccine in Canada and the United Kingdom). A newer conjugate vaccine, Menactra (manufactured by Sanofi Pasteur, Inc.), that contains serogroups A, C, Y, and W-135 has been approved and recommended in the United States for use in all children older than 10 years of age.

Exclusion from Child Care or Preschool Attendance.   The child may return as soon as he or she recovers after treatment.

Recommendations for Other Children.   Chemoprophylaxis with rifampin or ceftriaxone is effective for eliminating colonization with the meningococcus. Rifampin (10 mg/kg/dose [maximum,

600 mg/dose], twice a day for 2 days) or ceftriaxone (125 mg administered intramuscularly in one dose) should be administered to all other children who are regularly cared for in the same room. Rifampin may impart an orangish-red color to urine, tears, and other bodily fluids. Children who develop fever or other symptoms that are consistent with a meningococcal infection should promptly be evaluated by a physician.

Recommendations for Personnel. Rifampin (600-mg dose) twice a day for 2 days, ceftriaxone (250 mg administered intramuscularly in one dose), or ciprofloxacin (500 mg in a single oral dose) should be administered to all personnel who are regularly in the same room (with the exception of pregnant women). Personnel in whom fever or other symptoms develop that are consistent with a meningococcal infection should be promptly evaluated by a physician.

Parental Advice. Prophylactic antimicrobials should be administered promptly to all children and adults in the group. It is usually prudent to try to identify one knowledgeable physician to direct this effort. If each parent goes to his or her own physician, there may be several conflicting recommendations. Since the goal of chemoprophylaxis is to eliminate colonization in the *entire* group, its effectiveness is directly related to the completeness and timeliness with which chemoprophylaxis is implemented.

Parents should realize that most children who are exposed do not become ill. However, at the first sign of an illness that is compatible with a meningococcal infection (fever and/or a petechial rash), the child should be evaluated promptly by a physician.

40

Mumps

Gregory F. Hayden

CLINICAL MANIFESTATIONS

The clinical spectrum of mumps is broad, ranging from subclinical infection to severe illness with involvement of many organ systems. Clinical diagnosis generally depends upon swelling of the salivary glands with prominent parotid enlargement. Other manifestations of mumps may include meningoencephalitis, deafness (usually unilateral), pancreatitis, arthritis, myocarditis, thyroiditis, nephritis, and hepatitis. Orchitis develops in approximately 20 to 30% of affected postpubertal males, but only about 25% of such cases are bilateral, and only a small fraction of these develop progressive testicular atrophy.

ETIOLOGIC AGENT

Mumps is caused by a Rubulavirus in the paramyxovirus family that contains single-stranded RNA in a helical nucleocapsid. Only one serologic type is recognized.

EPIDEMIOLOGY

Reported mumps in the United States has declined substantially since mumps virus vaccine was licensed in 1967. An average of 265 mumps cases had been reported each year since 2001. In the first 4 months of 2006, however, more than 2,500 mumps cases have been reported in 11 states; a thorough investigation of this outbreak is under way.

Source of the Organism.   Humans are the only natural host.

High-Risk Populations.   Mumps infections are uncommon in the first several months of life, but, after this age, unvaccinated children remain at high risk of developing mumps if exposed. The 2006 outbreak has affected primarily young adults, many of whom had previously received mumps vaccine, suggesting possible waning of vaccine-induced immunity. The risk of mumps complications, such as orchitis, meningoencephalitis, and arthritis, is higher in older patients.

Mode of Spread.   The virus is spread by droplets and by direct contact with respiratory secretions of an infected patient.

Incubation Period.   The incubation period is usually 16 to 18 days, but it can range from 12 to 25 days.

DIAGNOSIS

The clinical diagnosis of mumps can be confirmed by using virologic or serologic methods. Mumps virus can be cultured from the throat, urine, and spinal fluid, but viral culture is relatively expensive and not universally available. Reverse transcriptase-polymerase chain reaction (RT-PCR) testing has been introduced recently but is also expensive and not widely available. Several serologic techniques are available, including complement fixation (CF), neutralization (NT), hemagglutination inhibition (HI), and enzyme immunoassay (EIA). A significant rise in titer between acute and convalescent serum specimens is diagnostic of mumps infection. The presence of mumps-specific immunoglobulin M (IgM) antibodies also suggests recent infection. A suspected or confirmed diagnosis of mumps should be reported immediately to the local health department.

THERAPY

No specific therapy is currently available. The selection of treatment, therefore, depends solely on the presence and severity of associated symptoms. Warm or cold compresses and analgesic therapy with acetaminophen, for example, may be used to relieve parotid discomfort. A soft, bland diet may be preferred. Hospitalization is recommended only for those occasional children with very severe or complicated cases requiring intensive supportive care. Children with severe central nervous system involvement, for example, may

206 Section IV. Specific Infections

require hospitalization for bed rest, analgesic/antipyretic therapy, and carefully monitored parenteral fluid therapy.

INFECTIOUS PERIOD

Patients are most contagious from 1 to 2 days before the onset of parotid swelling until 5 days after the onset of swelling. Virus has been isolated from saliva up to 7 days before the onset of parotid swelling until as long as 9 days after onset.

INFECTION CONTROL

Vaccine.   Live, attenuated mumps virus vaccine should be given routinely to children after the first birthday and is usually administered at 12 to 15 months of age as a part of the combined measles-mumps-rubella (MMR) vaccine. The cornerstone of mumps prevention in day care centers and preschools should be the vigilant insistence that all children 15 months or older have received mumps vaccine as a prerequisite for attending the center. A single dose confers long-lasting mumps immunity to most vaccinees, but a second dose at 4 to 6 years of age maximizes the rate of immunity and provides an added safeguard against primary vaccine failures.

Precautions and contraindications to live mumps vaccination include altered immunity, anaphylactic allergy to neomycin or gelatin, severe febrile illness, pregnancy, and recent receipt of an immune globulin preparation or blood products. Persons with anaphylactic allergy to eggs should receive mumps vaccine only with caution, but most children with egg hypersensitivity can be safely immunized with MMR vaccine. MMR vaccine is recommended for children infected with the human immunodeficiency virus if they are not severely immunocompromised.

Exclusion from Child Care or Preschool Attendance.   Since the period of communicability can extend as long as 9 days after the onset of parotid swelling, infected children should be excluded for this interval. By this time, the parotid swelling should have subsided, and any other manifestations of mumps should have resolved. Since patients are often contagious before the onset of parotid swelling, however, and since inapparent infections can be communicable, attempts to control spread by means of isolation are commonly ineffective.

Recommendations for Other Children. The first step is to verify that other children attending the center have already been immunized against mumps in accordance with established center policy. Children with documented previous immunization against mumps are highly unlikely to develop illness and may continue to attend the center. In the unlikely occurrence of an outbreak involving young children, a second dose of mumps vaccine could be considered for children 1 to 4 years old (at a minimum interval of 28 days between doses), recognizing that vaccine may not be effective in preventing incubating mumps infection.

The management of unvaccinated children is somewhat more complex. It is not known whether the administration of mumps vaccine after exposure can prevent or modify illness. Adverse reactions to this vaccine are uncommon, however, and vaccination after exposure is not known to increase the severity of incubating mumps. If an exposed child is not already incubating infection, mumps vaccination should protect the child against subsequent exposures to mumps. Vaccination can, therefore, be recommended for unimmunized children at least 12 months of age, especially if they have been exposed for no more than a few days. Parents must understand, however, that the vaccine may not block the progression of incubating mumps, so that they will not wrongly blame the vaccine for mumps illness that develops after vaccination.

For children younger than 1 year of age, vaccination is a less attractive option because the rate of seroconversion is lower, and protection is less likely. Standard immunoglobulin is ineffective in protecting against mumps infection. These infants could be excluded from the center during the period when they might be expected to become ill and contagious themselves. Since patients may be contagious up to 7 days before the onset of parotid swelling and since the incubation period may vary from 12 to 25 days, this policy would require exclusion of infants from the child care center or preschool for 3 weeks or longer. Since mumps is usually not severe in young infants, simple observation seems reasonable if coupled with careful documentation of immunization among those

12 months of age or older. If additional cases of mumps were to occur among younger infants, however, a strict exclusionary policy could be enforced.

Recommendations for Personnel. Ideally, all staff members should provide a documented history of adequate mumps immunization, a physician-documented diagnosis of infection, or serologic evidence of immunity at the time of employment. Adequate immunization has been recently defined as 1 dose of mumps vaccine for adults not at high risk of exposure, and 2 doses for those at high risk of exposure (such as health care workers, international travelers, and students at post–high school educational institutions). Since relatively few cases of mumps are currently reported in young children, most child care center and preschool staff are at low risk for mumps exposure. If mumps were to become reported more commonly in young children, however, the risk of mumps exposures among staff workers would increase, and a second dose of mumps vaccine could be considered. Birth before 1957 is generally considered presumptive evidence of immunity to mumps because most such persons will have contracted mumps illness and developed natural immunity. If mumps were to become more common in young children, however, unvaccinated staff members born before 1957 who do not have either a history of physician-diagnosed mumps or laboratory evidence of mumps immunity could consider receiving one dose of mumps vaccine.

Strict adherence to such a policy reduces or eliminates the disruption that can arise among personnel when mumps is diagnosed in a child attending the center. If appropriate preparations have not been made before such a case occurs, the first step is to determine whether any center personnel are likely to be susceptible to mumps. The mumps skin test was unreliable in predicting clinical immunity to mumps and is no longer readily available. A positive mumps neutralization titer or enzyme-linked immunosorbent assay (ELISA) index strongly suggests mumps immunity, but these tests are not always readily available. The determination of probable immunity usually rests, therefore, upon simple historical information. A history of having received 2 doses of mumps vaccine previously is highly, but not perfectly, predictive of mumps immunity. A history of physician-diagnosed mumps illness is also highly predictive of mumps immunity. In contrast, a negative history of mumps illness is poorly predictive of mumps susceptibility. Most adults with such negative histories are immune to mumps on the basis of previous, unrecognized infection. Most persons born before 1957 are immune, but if such persons lack a history of physician-diagnosed mumps or laboratory evidence of mumps immunity, they may consider receiving a single dose of mumps vaccine for added protection. Younger adults with a negative history of mumps immunization or illness are at somewhat greater risk of infection and can consider immunization after the exposure, recognizing that the vaccine may not be effective in preventing incubating mumps infection.

Parental Advice. Parents should be advised that a suspected (or confirmed) case of mumps has occurred in a child at the center. They should be advised that the risk to their child is minimal so long as the child has already received mumps vaccine. Parents of unimmunized children should be advised to seek medical advice immediately concerning the prompt vaccination of children older than 1 year of age. Parents should also be urged to verify their own immunity status as well as the immunization status of any older children in the family, especially adolescents, who do not attend the center, and to seek vaccination as appropriate.

Mycoplasma pneumoniae
(Pneumonia)

Ronald B. Turner

CLINICAL MANIFESTATIONS

Mycoplasma pneumoniae infection may result in symptoms at any level of the respiratory tract. Pneumonia is the most commonly recognized manifestation of infection and is characterized by prominent cough and fever. Other respiratory syndromes associated with *Mycoplasma* infection are pharyngitis and bronchiolitis. Most preschool children infected with *Mycoplasma* are asymptomatic.

M. pneumoniae has rarely been associated with a variety of nonrespiratory illnesses. Arthritis, carditis, and a variety of neurologic syndromes have been reported in patients infected with *M. pneumoniae*. These manifestations of infection have generally been reported in patients older than those who would be seen in a day care setting.

ETIOLOGIC AGENT

Mycoplasmas are free-living organisms that can be cultured on agar or in broth medium. Four of these organisms are associated with clinical illness. *M. pneumoniae* causes respiratory illness. *M. hominis*, *M. genitalium*, and *Ureaplasma urealyticum* are associated with genitourinary infections.

EPIDEMIOLOGY

Source of the Organism.   Infected humans are the only known source of infection.

High-Risk Populations.   No populations have been identified that are at high risk for acquisition of infection. Infection of children with sickle cell disease has been associated with severe lower respiratory disease.

Mode of Spread.   The mechanism of transmission is not known with certainty but is thought to be person-to-person spread by large-particle aerosols. Small-particle aerosols may rarely play a role in transmission of infection.

Incubation Period.   The incubation period for *Mycoplasma* infection is 2 to 3 weeks.

DIAGNOSIS

Culture of *M. pneumoniae* is relatively easily accomplished by experienced personnel. The organism grows slowly, however, so culture is generally not useful in the clinical setting. Serology has been the cornerstone of the etiologic diagnosis of *M. pneumoniae* infections. A fourfold rise in titer or a high titer obtained during a typical illness is generally consistent with an acute *Mycoplasma* infection. Serologic techniques for the detection of immunoglobulin M antibody directed against *M. pneumoniae* and methods for detection of *Mycoplasma* antigens or nucleic acid have adequate sensitivity and specificity for the rapid diagnosis of acute infections. Diagnostic testing by polymerase chain reaction is available.

THERAPY

Erythromycin, 50 mg/kg/day given orally on an every-6-hour dosing schedule for 10 to 14 days, is the usual treatment for *Mycoplasma* infections in children. Hospitalization is usually not necessary. Azithromycin is also effective against *Mycoplasma*.

INFECTIOUS PERIOD

The period of infectivity is not known; however, infected individuals should be considered capable of transmitting infection for the duration of the cough.

INFECTION CONTROL

Vaccine.   None available.

Exclusion from Child Care or Preschool Attendance.   Exclusion from child care or preschool settings is not necessary for children infected with *Mycoplasma.*

Recommendations for Other Children.   No special precautions are indicated.

Recommendations for Personnel.   No special precautions are indicated.

Parental Advice.   *Mycoplasma* infections spread very slowly and have not been associated with outbreaks in the day care or preschool setting. No special precautions are indicated.

42

 Necator americanus
(Hookworm)

Jonathan P. Moorman

CLINICAL MANIFESTATIONS

The initial manifestation of an infection with *Necator americanus* may consist of itching and burning ("ground itch"), followed by the development of a papular or vesicular rash at the site of larval penetration into the skin. Although many infected individuals remain asymptomatic, heavy infections can be associated with the development of gastrointestinal symptoms, including abdominal pain, anorexia, diarrhea, and weight loss. The most debilitating effect of hookworm infections is chronic intestinal blood loss resulting in the development of iron-deficiency anemia. The severity of the anemia is variable, depending on the worm burden and dietary iron intake. The average daily loss of blood for this worm is 0.03 ml/day, a less significant loss than is found with *Ancylostoma duodenale* infections. It may be associated with pallor, lassitude, dyspnea, palpitations, cardiomegaly, and impaired growth. Infected individuals may also have hypoalbuminemia, hypoproteinemia, and eosinophilia. The hematologic, cardiac, and nutritional effects of hookworm infections contribute significantly to the morbidity of pediatric and adult populations worldwide.

ETIOLOGIC AGENT

N. americanus is one of the two most common hookworms found in humans. Along with *A. duodenale*, it affects one quarter of the world's population. Humans acquire the infection percutaneously by coming into contact with infective larvae present in contaminated soil. The larvae penetrate the skin, migrate through the circulation to the lungs, pass through the alveolar walls, and ascend the trachea. They are then swallowed and move to the small intestine where they attach to the duodenal and jejunal mucosa and mature into adults. After mating, the female worms lay eggs, discharging thousands per day in the feces. Under favorable environmental conditions, the eggs will hatch and larvae will develop into infective forms. This process generally requires 5 to 10 days in the soil, during which time the eggs and larvae are not infective for humans.

EPIDEMIOLOGY

Source of the Organism.   Hookworms continue to be endemic in a number of tropical and subtropical areas. *N. americanus* is the prevailing species in parts of the southern United States, Central and South America, the Caribbean, central and southern Africa, and southern Asia. Hookworm has remained endemic in areas where fecal pollution and environmental conditions favoring the development of hookworm eggs are present. The infective larvae are found in soil contaminated with human feces, and transmission is generally the result of direct contact with the soil, often through bare feet. Although transmission of *A. duodenale*–infective larvae occurs through food and possibly breast milk, this does not appear to occur with *N. americanus*.

High-Risk Populations.   Individuals who have direct contact with fecally contaminated soil in hookworm-endemic areas will be at risk of acquiring the infection. Because children are more likely to go barefoot and to play in dirt, they are also likely to acquire hookworm infections. However, since the larvae are not infective unless they undergo development in soil, direct person-to-person spread of hookworm does not appear to occur. Therefore, institutional or child care settings should not increase a child's risk of infection.

Mode of Spread.   Transmission occurs percutaneously through contact with soil containing infective hookworm larvae. Larvae require 5 to 10 minutes of contact for penetration.

Incubation Period.   The time interval between the acquisition of *N. americanus* and the passage of eggs in the feces ranges from approximately 40 to 60 days. Considerable variability has also been observed in the time between exposure and development of symptoms; some individuals develop gastrointestinal symptoms 20 to 45 days following an acute infection.

DIAGNOSIS

The diagnosis is established by identifying the characteristic hookworm eggs in feces; *N. americanus* eggs cannot be distinguished from those of *A. duodenale*. Most moderate to severe hookworm infections will be detected by direct microscopic examination of a fecal smear. However, the detection of light infections may require the use of concentration methods such as the zinc sulfate flotation or formalin-ether techniques. Although larvae or adult worms are rarely seen in stool specimens, the larvae can be grown from specimens by using Harada-Mori fecal cultures. This technique is rarely used diagnostically.

THERAPY

In countries where hookworm infections are endemic and reinfection is common, light infections are often not treated. In this country, hookworm infections are generally treated with either mebendazole or pyrantel pamoate. Mebendazole is given in a dose of 100 mg twice a day for 3 days or 500 mg once. Pyrantel pamoate is given as a single daily dose of 11 mg/kg (maximum, 1 g), repeated for 3 days. Albendazole can be given in a single oral dose of 400 mg. Although pyrantel pamoate and albendazole are approved drugs, the U.S. Food and Drug Administration considers them investigational for this condition. Both regimens are effective against *N. americanus* and are associated with few significant adverse reactions. However, since none of these therapies has been used widely in children younger than 2 years old, the drugs should be used with caution, determining the potential risks and benefits of therapy on an individual basis in this age group. One to 2 weeks following treatment with any of the regimens, a repeat stool examination should be performed, and if the infection is still present, retreatment undertaken.

In addition to the use of antihelmintic agents, iron supplementation should be provided to individuals with significant anemia.

INFECTIOUS PERIOD

If untreated, hookworm infections, in particular those caused by *N. americanus*, may persist for many years. Since egg production tends to decrease over time, individuals may become somewhat less infectious.

INFECTION CONTROL

Vaccine.   None available, although several candidates are currently being studied.

Exclusion from Child Care or Preschool Attendance.   Children with hookworm infections do not need to be isolated. Since human-to-human transmission does not occur and the eggs passed in feces are not infectious, an infected child does not need to be kept out of any child care setting.

Recommendations for Other Children.   Other children will acquire hookworm only if they come into contact with soil containing infective larvae. Unlike the situation with many other enteric pathogens, they should not become infected if they inadvertently ingest fecal material contaminated with hookworm eggs. Therefore, no additional precautions need to be undertaken for children in a center when one child is found to have hookworm infection.

Recommendations for Personnel.   Personnel should be instructed to maintain techniques that decrease fecal-oral transmission of pathogens, including good handwashing and appropriate disposal of fecal material. Obviously, no child should be allowed to defecate in the playground areas where fecal contamination of the soil may be a problem, and children should not be allowed to go barefoot or play in the soil.

Parental Advice.   Parents should be told that the risk of person-to-person transmission is minimal. If the attendee appears to have acquired the infection locally, the need for sanitary disposal of feces and the potential for spread through contaminated soil should be reviewed with all of the parents.

Papillomaviruses
(Warts)

David A. Whiting

CLINICAL MANIFESTATIONS

Warts are unusual in infancy and early childhood and have a peak incidence at 12 to 16 years of age. Warts are intraepidermal tumors that affect skin and mucous membranes and are caused by a DNA virus known as the human papillomavirus (HPV).

Common warts (verruca vulgaris): These occur as firm papules with a rough, horny surface that range in size from 1 to 12 mm in diameter and are usually discrete but may be confluent. They often contain black specks from thrombosed capillaries. They can occur anywhere on the body but are seen most commonly on the backs of the hands and fingers and on the knees. Sixty-five percent disappear spontaneously within 2 years.

Plane warts (verruca plana): These are multiple, small, tan or flesh-colored, flattened, round, or polygonal lesions 1 to 5 mm in diameter and are found mostly on the face, backs of the hands, and shins.

Plantar warts (verruca plantaris): These are inverted, flattened, circumscribed horny papules of the soles often containing black specks from thrombosed capillaries. A wart interrupts the natural skin lines and is separated from the surrounding skin by a plane of cleavage. Plantar warts may be single, multiple, or mosaic. They are rare in the preschool-aged child.

Venereal warts (condylomata acuminata): These manifest as multiple pointed papules, single or confluent, on or around the genitalia and the anus. In children, the possibility of child abuse should always be considered in cases of venereal warts.

ETIOLOGIC AGENT

HPVs, a subgroup of the Papovaviridae family, are small, double-stranded DNA viruses that are host-specific. More than 100 types of HPV have now been characterized by Southern blot testing of the viral genome. The most common viral types are associated with different warts.

Common warts (verruca vulgaris): HPV 2 and 4, 29, 57.

Plane warts (verruca plana): HPV 3, 10.

Plantar warts (verruca plantaris): HPV 1, 2, 4, 10.

Venereal warts (condylomata acuminata): HPV 6, 11, 42, 54 (HPV 16, 18, 31, and 45 cause venereal warts less commonly but are oncogenic and can cause dysplasia in adolescents and adults).

EPIDEMIOLOGY

Source of the Organism.   Other humans.

High-Risk Populations.   Schoolchildren 12 to 16 years of age or immunosuppressed individuals. Abused children may have genital warts.

Mode of Spread.   Warts are spread by direct contact with the infected individual, by indirect contact through contamination of objects and immediate environment, and by autoinoculation.

Incubation Period.   1 to 20 months, with an average of 4 months.

DIAGNOSIS

The clinical appearance is usually diagnostic, and the presence of warts may be confirmed by demonstrating black dots in them after paring down the horny surfaces. A biopsy is sometimes diagnostic. HPV DNA testing can be confirmatory.

THERAPY

Therapy is local and is done on an outpatient basis. Hospital admission is not required unless it is for very extensive condylomata acuminata.

There is no specific antiviral therapy, although intralesional alpha-2b interferon has been used successfully in some cases, and imiquimod cream is indicated for genital warts.

Common warts: Light electrodesiccation and curettage, cryosurgery, keratolytics, monochloroacetic acid or bichloracetic acid, laser surgery.

Plane warts: Cryosurgery, monochloroacetic acid or bichloracetic acid, light electrodesiccation and curettage, topical tretinoin. Imiquimod cream may prove useful following its reported success in treating molluscum contagiosum.

Plantar warts: Keratolytics, light electrodesiccation and curettage, formalin soaks, laser surgery. Cryosurgery is painful when treating the soles of the feet.

Venereal warts: Podophyllin 25% in compound tincture of benzoin or podophyllotoxin (Condylox gel), imiquimod cream (Aldara), monochloroacetic acid or bichloracetic acid, cryosurgery, light electrodesiccation and curettage, laser surgery.

Note that a wait-and-see attitude is advisable in children, since many warts disappear spontaneously and wart treatment is often destructive and painful and liable to cause scars. The least destructive therapy possible is always advisable.

INFECTIOUS PERIOD

How long the infectious period will last is uncertain, but it may last as long as the lesion is actually present, which can be months or years.

INFECTION CONTROL

Vaccine.   Two vaccines have been FDA approved for the prevention of HPV infection and are recommended for administration prior to the initiation of sexual activity. Both contain HPV strains 16 and 18, which cause 70% of cervical cancer cases, and one also contains HPV strains 6 and 11, which commonly cause genital warts.

Exclusion from Child Care or Preschool Attendance.   Isolation is unnecessary, although it is advisable to cover the warts, if practical.

Recommendations for Other Children.   Wait and see if warts develop, and treat if necessary.

Recommendations for Personnel.   Wait and see if warts develop, and treat if necessary.

Parental Advice.   Wait and see if warts develop, and treat if necessary.

44

Parainfluenza Virus

Scott A. Halperin

CLINICAL MANIFESTATIONS

Parainfluenza virus causes both upper and lower respiratory tract disease in children. Upper respiratory infection with fever is the most common manifestation of parainfluenza virus infection and is indistinguishable from the common cold caused by other viruses. The disease is characterized by coryza, bronchitis, and pharyngitis and may be associated with a low-grade fever.

Parainfluenza virus is the most common etiologic agent of croup, which is characterized by hoarseness, a barking cough, and inspiratory stridor. Parainfluenza viruses also are important causes of bronchiolitis, bronchitis, and pneumonia. Outbreaks of croup caused by parainfluenza virus often occur each fall, although sporadic infection occurs throughout the year. Reinfections with parainfluenza virus occur but are usually mild.

ETIOLOGIC AGENT

Parainfluenza virus is a member of the paramyxoviruses. Parainfluenza viruses are enveloped RNA viruses that, although similar to influenza virus, have remained antigenically stable. There are four antigenic types that cause disease in humans. Parainfluenza virus types 1 and 2 are the most common causes of croup, while parainfluenza virus type 3 is an important etiologic agent of pneumonia and bronchiolitis. Types 1, 2, and 3 also are associated with symptoms of the common cold. Parainfluenza virus type 4 causes very mild disease of the upper respiratory tract.

EPIDEMIOLOGY

Source of the Organism.   Parainfluenza virus is spread from person to person or found in infected respiratory secretions. Although parainfluenza-like viruses exist in animals, these do not cause infection or disease in humans.

High-Risk Populations.   Infants and young children are susceptible to parainfluenza viruses, and almost all children will have been infected with all four types by the age of 6 years. The severity of the illness depends on the parainfluenza virus type, the age of the child, and whether it is a primary infection or a reinfection. Severe prolonged infection can occur in the immunocompromised host.

Mode of Spread.   Parainfluenza viruses are spread from person to person by direct contact or by large droplets and contaminated nasopharyngeal secretions.

Incubation Period.   Two to 4 days.

DIAGNOSIS

Specific virologic diagnosis of parainfluenza virus infection is not routinely necessary because treatment is nonspecific and symptomatic. Because of the epidemic nature of certain parainfluenza virus infections, a diagnosis can occasionally be deduced by using knowledge of the predominant viral infection in a community at that time. When indicated, virologic diagnosis of parainfluenza virus infection can be established through isolation of the virus in tissue culture. The diagnosis can also be made (a) by detection of the virus in infected secretions by using direct or indirect immunofluorescent techniques, (b) by antigen detection methods, or (c) by nucleic acid detection such as polymerase chain reaction.

THERAPY

No specific antiviral therapy is yet available for parainfluenza virus infection. Most infections due to parainfluenza virus are self-limited; however, parainfluenza virus infections of the lower respiratory tract may be severe and require hospitalization for supportive care. Oxygen, epinephrine, and oral, parenteral, and aerosolized steroid therapy are effective in the management of some patients with croup.

INFECTIOUS PERIOD

Parainfluenza viruses may be shed for 4 to 21 days, depending on the type.

INFECTION CONTROL

Vaccine.   None available.

Exclusion from Child Care or Preschool Attendence.   Exclusion from child care or preschool settings is not necessary for children infected with parainfluenza virus.

Recommendations for Other Children.   No specific precautions are indicated.

Recommendations for Personnel.   No specific precautions are indicated.

Parental Advice.   No specific precautions are indicated.

45

Parvovirus B19
(Fifth Disease, Erythema Infectiosum)

William C. Koch

CLINICAL MANIFESTATIONS

The most common manifestation of infection with the human parvovirus B19 is a benign rash illness of childhood called erythema infectiosum (EI) or "Fifth Disease." EI occurs most often in school-aged children, with a peak season from late winter to early spring. The illness begins with a prodromal phase of mild fever and nonspecific symptoms of headache, malaise, and myalgia. This phase lasts only a few days and is followed by the eruption of the characteristic rash. This begins as an intensely red symmetric facial rash, giving the child a "slapped-cheek" appearance. It then spreads to the trunk and the extremities as an erythematous, maculopapular eruption. As the rash progresses, there is central clearing that gives it a reticular or lacy character, especially on the arms and legs. The palms and soles are spared. When the rash appears, the child has usually begun to feel better, and fever, if present, resolves. The rash may persist for weeks and may recur in response to various stimuli such as exposure to sunlight, a warm bath, or exercise.

B19 also causes more serious illnesses in other groups of individuals. These include a syndrome of acute, self-limited arthritis in adults; transient aplastic crisis in individuals with chronic hemolytic anemia such as sickle cell anemia or hereditary spherocytosis; fetal hydrops and stillbirth in pregnant women; and chronic anemia in adults and children with impaired immunity. Asymptomatic infections occur commonly, and atypical rashes (rubella-like, petechial, etc.) have been reported. There is no evidence that parvovirus B19 causes congenital anomalies.

ETIOLOGIC AGENT

Parvovirus B19 is a small, single-stranded DNA virus; it is one of the smallest DNA-containing viruses known to infect mammalian cells. It has no envelope and is relatively heat-stable and resistant to inactivation by detergents. Parvovirus B19 is a member of the family Parvoviridae, which includes a number of animal pathogens, but it is infectious only among humans. There is only one serotype of parvovirus B19.

EPIDEMIOLOGY

Source of the Organism.   The virus is contracted from infected individuals during their period of viremia. Virus can be detected in respiratory secretions at this time, suggesting that these secretions are involved in transmission. For patients with EI, this occurs during the prodromal phase, prior to the onset of the rash. In patients with parvovirus B19–induced aplastic crisis or chronic anemia, viremia occurs at presentation and is of much greater intensity.

High-Risk Populations.   There are no conditions that predispose to acquisition of parvovirus B19 infection. Although the infection occurs most commonly in school-aged children, it can be spread to their younger siblings through household contact and is thus subsequently introduced into the child care or preschool setting. There are certain groups who are at risk for more serious consequences if they acquire a parvovirus B19 infection, and these include children with conditions of chronic hemolysis, immunocompromised patients (including human immunodeficiency virus [HIV] infection), and pregnant women.

Mode of Spread.   The virus is spread by close contact, presumably through respiratory secretions. The secondary attack rate for susceptible household contacts is about 30 to 50%. In school outbreaks, the secondary attack rate has varied from 10 to 60%.

Potential mechanisms of transmission include direct personal contact, large-particle and small-particle droplets, and fomites (shared objects and surfaces such as toys, doorknobs, etc.). Transmission by blood or blood products is also possible.

Incubation Period.   The incubation period for EI is reported to range from 4 to 14 days on average, with the longest reported incubation time being 28 days. However, results of experimental parvovirus B19 infection in adults suggest an incubation period of 17 to 18 days based on time to onset of the rash. This correlates well with the reported case-to-case interval of 6 to 14 days observed in most studies. The incubation period for the parvovirus B19–related aplastic crisis is generally shorter as it coincides with the onset of viremia, usually 6 to 8 days after exposure.

DIAGNOSIS

EI is usually diagnosed on clinical grounds. It can be confirmed by serologic tests for parvovirus B19 antibodies. The most reliable single test for acute infection is detection of anti-B19 immunoglobulin M (IgM). This is detectable by 8 to 10 days after infection and persists for 2 to 3 months. Infection can also be diagnosed by seroconversion from negative to positive on a test for anti-B19 immunoglobulin G (IgG) antibody. IgG is detectable a few days after IgM and persists for life. These serologic tests are available at commercial laboratories and some state health departments. However, their sensitivity and specificity are variable, especially for IgM detection, making interpretation of results difficult. In immunocompromised patients, specific antibody production may be impaired, so diagnosis usually requires detection of viral DNA by nucleic acid hybridization or polymerase chain reaction (PCR), tests which are not widely available.

THERAPY

Children with EI require no therapy, as the great majority will recover without incident. Children with aplastic crisis will usually require hospitalization for supportive care with oxygen and transfusions until their hematocrit and hemoglobin return to baseline. There is no antiviral agent available. Although the use of commer-

cial preparations of immune globulin have been reported to ameliorate parvovirus B19 infections in immunocompromised children,
their use as either treatment or postexposure prophylaxis in pregnant caretakers cannot be recommended until controlled studies are
performed.

INFECTIOUS PERIOD

Children with EI are infectious during the prodromal phase of their
illness when the virus is detectable in their respiratory secretions, a
period of 1 to 6 days. This phase may go unnoticed but usually
occurs about 7 to 10 days prior to the onset of the rash. The
appearance of the rash coincides with production of virus-specific
antibodies; once the rash develops, the child is no longer infectious.

INFECTION CONTROL

Vaccine.   None available.

Exclusion from Child Care or Preschool Attendance.   Children
with EI do not need to be excluded from day care, as they are
unlikely to be infectious after the rash appears and the clinical
diagnosis is made. Children with aplastic crisis are infectious at
presentation with fever and anemia, and they remain infectious for
a longer period of time. Such children will most likely be hospitalized until their hematologic status is stable. They should be isolated
for at least 1 week after presentation and should not return to the
child care or preschool setting until after this time.

Recommendations for Other Children.   Once an outbreak of EI
has been identified in a child care center or preschool, parents of
children at risk for more serious complications as a result of
parvovirus B19 infection (chronic hemolytic conditions, immunocompromised, etc.) should be notified. They may wish to consult
their pediatricians for individual advice. A general policy of exclusion is not recommended.

Recommendations for Personnel.   There are no studies documenting the effectiveness of handwashing or decontamination of
toys and environmental surfaces in preventing the transmission of

parvovirus B19; however, handwashing and careful control of respiratory secretions are recommended.

When an outbreak of EI is identified in a center, there is some risk that the adult personnel will become infected. This is primarily of concern for those who are pregnant. Approximately 50% of adults will already be seropositive and, therefore, immune to infection. If a pregnant woman becomes infected, the risk of an adverse outcome (e.g., fetal loss) caused by parvovirus B19 is low, with risk estimates ranging from 1.6 to 6% in large, prospective studies. Infection occurring in the first half of pregnancy appears to be associated with the highest risk. Personnel who are pregnant should be aware of ways to minimize exposure by proper handwashing, avoidance of shared utensils, etc. If available, serologic testing for the presence of anti-B19 IgG could be of benefit by identifying those women who are already immune. Individuals who desire more information on the risks and management of parvovirus B19 exposure should contact their health care provider. Again, a routine policy of exclusion of pregnant caretakers is not recommended.

Parental Advice.   Once an outbreak of EI has been identified in a center, parents of children in attendance should be informed of the risk for transmission of the virus both in the center and from susceptible contacts at home. They should be made aware of the generally benign nature of the illness and those underlying conditions that are considered higher risk. Those families who desire more information about parvovirus B19 infections should be referred to their health care provider or local health officials.

46

 # Pediculosis (Lice)

David A. Whiting

CLINICAL MANIFESTATIONS

The characteristic feature of all types of pediculosis is pruritus. Intense itching, usually worse at night, leads to excoriations, lichenification, pigmentation, secondary infection, and lymphadenopathy. The actual louse bites are relatively painless and cause small, red macules. These may develop into papules over hours or days or, in a sensitized individual, may cause immediate whealing. The nit or egg case of the developing louse is attached firmly to human hair or threads of clothing and is usually somewhat translucent in appearance. It is often easier to find the nit than the actual louse.

Head lice: Pruritus is most severe around the back and sides of the scalp. Nits can be found attached to scalp hair in those areas. Excoriation with secondary infection and lymphadenopathy is common, and foul matted hair can result. Common bacterial invaders causing secondary infection include *Staphylococcus aureus* and group A *Streptococcus pyogenes*.

Body lice: Body lice can only survive in conditions of poor hygiene and are therefore found in homeless or displaced persons who are unable to maintain any reasonable standard of personal cleanliness. The lice live in clothing and lay eggs on the inner seams of clothes and occasionally on body hairs. Pinpoint red macules, papules, wheals, excoriations, secondary infection, and, perhaps, pigmentation can occur all over the body. Note that body lice are vectors of epidemic or louseborne typhus (caused by *Rickettsia prowazekii*), trench fever (caused by *Rochalimaea* [*Rickettsia quintana*]), and Euro-

229

pean or louseborne relapsing fever (caused by *Borrelia recurrentis*). Body lice are human-to-human vectors of murine typhus or are vectors of endemic or fleaborne typhus caused by *Rickettsia typhi* (*mooseri*).

Pubic lice: Pubic lice affect not only the pubic hair but also the adjacent hair on the thighs, abdomen, chest, breasts, and axillae and sometimes the hair on the eyebrows, eyelashes, or scalp. Intense irritation with excoriation and eczematization occurs. Occasionally, blue-gray macules, the so-called maculae ceruleae, are found on the lower abdomen and upper thighs.

ETIOLOGIC AGENT

Sucking lice of the order *Anoplura* are dorsoventrally flattened, wingless insects, and two species of these are obligate parasites of humans. The first is *Pediculus humanus*, a louse 3 to 4 mm long that exists in humans in two distinct populations, namely, *Pediculus humanus capitis*, affecting the scalp, and *Pediculus humanus corporis*, affecting the body. The other species is *Phthirus pubis* or the crab louse, which is 2 to 3 mm in length and is adapted for clinging onto body hairs.

EPIDEMIOLOGY

Source of the Organism.   Human body.

High-Risk Populations.   *Head lice*: Age and sex: Highest prevalence of head lice is usually between the ages of 3 and 10 years with equal sex incidence. More females are affected in the teens and in adult life. Socioeconomic and ethnic factors: Head lice can affect all levels of society and all ethnic groups except for low levels of infestation in North American blacks. Lack of grooming: Inadequate washing and grooming as seen in individuals with mental disabilities or in those with elaborate hairstyles can lead to higher populations of head lice.

Body lice: Socioeconomic factors: Body lice are confined to economically deprived persons of no fixed abode and no means of achieving personal cleanliness. The term "vagabond's disease" is self-explanatory here. Lack of personal hygiene: Chronically ill individuals or persons with mental disabilities who are unable to look after themselves also may be infested by body lice, and children living in that environment may become infested.

Pubic lice: Children are not usually affected by this sexually transmitted disease, but the presence of crab lice or nits in eyelashes or scalp hair in children does indicate the possibility of sexual abuse.

Mode of Spread.   Direct spread is frequent, but lice can survive for at least a week off the human body, so indirect spread can occur.

Head lice: The commonest method of spread is head-to-head contact, especially in crowded sleeping quarters. Head lice can also be spread by infested headgear, towels, hairbrushes, combs, pillows, bedding, and earphones.

Body lice: Body lice are spread by person-to-person contact or contact with infested clothing or bedding.

Pubic lice: Crab lice are spread by person-to-person contact and sometimes by infested towels and bedding.

Incubation Period.   The incubation period from egg laying to emerging adult is 17 to 25 days for *Pediculus humanus capitis* and *corporis* and 22 to 27 days for *Phthirus pubis*.

DIAGNOSIS

The diagnosis is established by the identification of nits on hairs or clothing, which show pale blue fluorescence on Wood's light, or the identification of actual lice on skin, hair, or clothing. Supporting the diagnosis is a clinical picture of intense pruritus, excoriations, secondary infection, and lymphadenopathy.

THERAPY

Outpatient therapy is adequate.

Head lice: The treatment of choice, after shampooing and rinsing the hair, is to work 1% permethrin creme rinse (Nix) into the hair and scalp, leave for 10 minutes, and then rinse it out with clear water. An alternative but less effective therapy is to apply 1 to 2 ounces of 1% lindane shampoo to the dry hair and work it in thoroughly.

Then add small quantities of water until a lather forms, and leave it in place for 4 minutes. Rinse thoroughly and dry briskly. An effective ovicidal treatment available in various countries is 0.5% malathion (Ovide) lotion, applied to the scalp once, for 8 to 12 hours. One method of nit removal is a creme rinse containing 8% formic acid, followed by a metal nit comb (Nit Removal System Step II). A Lice Meister nit comb is also effective. However, increasing numbers of patients who are infested with lice that are resistant to permethrin are being reported. There are anecdotal reports of successful therapy for head lice with a single oral dose of 200 mcg/kg of ivermectin (an antihelmintic). These treatments can be repeated weekly if necessary.

Body lice: Current treatment is to sterilize clothing and bedding and to apply 1% lindane lotion from head to toe for 8 to 10 hours or for 6 to 8 hours in small children. A better alternative is to apply 5% permethrin topical cream (Elimite).

Pubic lice: One method of treatment is 1% lindane lotion from neck to toes for 8 to 12 hours. Alternatively, 5% lindane shampoo can be used on the affected hair-bearing areas in the same manner as it is on the scalp, or, preferably, 1% permethrin creme rinse (Nix) or 0.5% malathion can be applied.

Floors, play areas, and furniture should be vacuumed thoroughly for affected hairs. Mattresses and furniture can be sprayed with synergized pyrethrins or synthetic pyrethroids (Li-Ban, R&C Spray). All clothing, bedding, and headgear should be disinfected by machine washing and machine drying or dry cleaning. Clothing can also be bagged and sealed in tight plastic bags for 2 weeks. Combs and brushes should be soaked in 2% Lysol for 1 to 2 hours or boiled in water for 10 minutes. Combs, brushes, grooming aids, towels, sponges, and facecloths should not be shared. Any secondary infection should be treated with appropriate compresses and antibiotics.

INFECTIOUS PERIOD

The child is infectious as long as live lice or viable ova (nits) are present on the child.

INFECTION CONTROL

Vaccine.   None available.

Exclusion from Child Care or Preschool Attendance.   Until live lice and viable ova are eradicated. This usually means isolating the child until effective treatment has been provided. Retreatment is advisable after 1 week to eradicate new lice hatching out of any surviving viable ova.

Recommendations for Other Children.   Examine unaffected children for results of pruritus, such as excoriations, infections, and lymphadenopathy, examine with Wood's lamp for nits, and examine for lice. If any symptoms or signs of pediculosis are found or develop, treatment is indicated.

Recommendations for Personnel.   Check personnel for pruritus, excoriations, infections, lymphadenopathy, nits, and lice. If any symptoms or signs develop, treatment is indicated.

Parental Advice.   All domestic contacts should be checked for symptoms or signs and treated as necessary.

47

Pertussis
(Whooping Cough)

Judy M. Vincent

CLINICAL MANIFESTATIONS

Pertussis evolves in three clinical stages: catarrhal, paroxysmal, and convalescent. The catarrhal stage is manifested by mucoid rhinorrhea, nasal congestion, sneezing, and cough. This stage lasts 1 day to several days and is indistinguishable from the common cold. The paroxysmal stage follows and is manifested by violent, protracted bouts of coughing in severe paroxysms lasting up to several minutes. Gasping musical inspirations, "the whoop," often occur during these paroxysms in older infants and preschool children, but they may be absent in infants less than 6 months of age and in older children and adults. This stage lasts from only a few days to 3 to 4 weeks but averages about 2 weeks in duration. The convalescent stage begins when cough paroxysms cease while chronic cough continues. It usually lasts 3 to 4 weeks, with decrease in frequency and severity of cough. Rarely, this stage may persist for months.

ETIOLOGIC AGENT

Pertussis, or the "whooping cough syndrome," is caused by *Bordetella pertussis* (90 to 95% of cases) or *Bordetella parapertussis* (5%). The clinical illness caused by the two organisms is the same except that *B. parapertussis* infections are said to be less severe. Since immunization against pertussis does not protect against *B. parapertussis* infection, the relative incidence of *B. parapertussis* infection in areas with high pertussis immunization rates has been reported to be as high as

20%. Small outbreaks of whooping cough–like illness due to *Bordetella bronchiseptica* have been reported in families or laboratory workers in contact with small animals. All three organisms are small gram-negative coccobacilli that are morphologically similar.

EPIDEMIOLOGY

Pertussis is one of the most highly communicable diseases of humans. Attack rates approach 100% in close susceptible contacts. The distribution of the disease is worldwide. It is a leading cause of sickness and death in children in developing countries where immunization against pertussis is not practiced.

Source of the Organism.   The only natural reservoir of *B. pertussis* and *B. parapertussis* organisms is the human being, and a healthy carrier state in humans has not been demonstrated. Only a few experimental animals have been infected.

High-Risk Populations.   In the United States, the epidemiology of pertussis has changed dramatically over the past two decades, with the incidence of pertussis gradually increasing since 1981. Prior to 2000, the majority of pertussis cases were in infants less than 1 year of age, but since 2000 the majority of cases have been found in adolescents aged 10 to 19 years. Between 1994 and 2004 a 1054% increase was seen in the reported incidence of pertussis in the 10- to 19-year age group.

Adolescents and adults are the major reservoir of pertussis and a significant source of infection for infants and children. Adolescents and adults should be considered susceptible to pertussis, regardless of childhood vaccination status, because vaccine-induced immunity wanes with time, and natural pertussis infection does not confer long-lasting immunity. Adolescents and adults with pertussis may have classic symptoms of whooping cough or may have only a mild cough.

Infants less than 1 year of age are at greatest risk for severe, life-threatening illness. Lack of placentally transferred passive immunity to pertussis and the delay in active immunity until infants receive the standard vaccine series leave them vulnerable to pertussis throughout most of the first year of life.

Mode of Spread. Mode of spread is by the airborne route directly by droplets and droplet nuclei from aerosols generated by the intense cough of infected individuals. Less often, infection may be acquired indirectly by handling objects freshly contaminated with nasopharyngeal or oropharyngeal secretions.

Incubation Period.   The incubation period is usually 7 to 10 days but may range from 5 to 20 days.

DIAGNOSIS

Culture of *B. pertussis* from secretions obtained from the posterior nasopharynx (NP) by a through-the-nose swab remains the "gold standard" for laboratory diagnosis of pertussis in infants and children. *B. pertussis* is rarely cultured from adults. Oropharyngeal swab culture and cough plates are less efficient and are no longer used.

Unfortunately, culture requires a minimum of 3 to 5 days for adequate growth for identification, and positive cultures are obtained in only 35 to 80% of patients with obvious clinical pertussis, varying significantly with the experience and skill of the laboratory personnel and with timing of the culture. Organisms are most likely to be recovered from patients in the catarrhal stage of illness when almost pure cultures may be obtained, particularly in very young infants. The diagnosis, however, is seldom suspected until the onset of the paroxysmal stage. Cultures are most likely to be positive during the first paroxysmal week; however, the likelihood of identifying the organism by culture decreases thereafter, and it is seldom possible to recover the organism from patients beyond 3 weeks after onset of the paroxysmal stage of illness. Positive cultures are also less likely with prior antibiotic therapy (with erythromycin, clarithromycin, azithromycin, or trimethoprim-sulfamethoxazole) or in vaccinated persons.

DNA amplification by polymerase chain reaction (PCR) is being used more frequently to detect *B. pertussis*. PCR can be used to diagnose pertussis when the case also meets the clinical case definition (2 weeks of cough with paroxysms, inspiratory whoop, or posttussive emesis). PCR has a higher sensitivity and shorter turnaround time than culture. When symptoms of classic pertussis are present (2 weeks of paroxysmal cough), PCR is 2 to 3 times more likely than culture to detect a positive *B. pertussis* sample. However, analytical sensitivity, specificity, accuracy, and quality control of PCR-based *B. pertussis* tests vary widely among laboratories. Use of PCR tests with low specificity can result in unnecessary investigation and treatment of persons with false-positive PCR test results and inappropriate chemoprophylaxis of their contacts.

Early presumptive diagnosis may be made using the direct fluorescent antibody (DFA) test. DFA tests provide results in hours, but are less sensitive than culture. With the use of monoclonal agents, the specificity of DFA should be >90%; however, the interpretation of the test is subjective, and interpretation by an inexperienced microbiologist can result in lower specificity.

Serology has been a useful tool in clinical studies, but this test is not standardized. Serologic results are difficult to interpret, and in the absence of standardization, serology cannot be used for case confirmation and/or national reporting.

The characteristic lymphocytosis seen with pertussis may be a helpful diagnostic aid, but it is nonspecific. Lymphocyte counts ranging from 20,000 to over 100,000 mm^3 are seen in the late catarrhal stage and throughout most of the paroxysmal stage. Lymphocytosis may not be present in children less than 6 months of age and in adults or partially immunized individuals.

THERAPY

General Medical Management.   Experienced and efficient nursing care is probably the most important factor in survival of infants with severe pertussis. Seventy percent of children who die of pertussis are less than 1 year of age and are most commonly 2 to 4 months of age. For this reason it is wise to hospitalize children in this age group until it can be determined that the child does not have life-threatening paroxysms, apnea, cyanosis, or severe feeding problems. Children with these problems may require frequent suctioning of secretions and oxygen administration during severe paroxysms. Parenteral fluid and electrolyte supplementation and, in protracted cases, parenteral alimentation may be required.

Mist therapy is not helpful. Continuous supplemental well-humidified oxygen may be needed for some patients who have sustained hypoxemia. These patients usually have pulmonary complications such as atelectasis or pneumonia. Cough suppressants, expectorants, and sedatives have not been shown to be of benefit in the treatment of pertussis.

Antimicrobial Agents.   Pertussis organisms are eradicated from patients with the disease if they are treated with antimicrobial agents active against *B. pertussis* organisms, provided that the drug diffuses in significant concentrations into respiratory tract secretions. No antimicrobial drug has been shown to alter the subsequent clinical course of the illness when given in the paroxysmal stage of the disease. However, drugs that meet these criteria attenuate the illness when given in the catarrhal or pre-paroxysmal stage of the disease and abort or prevent the disease in individuals during incubation (asymptomatic susceptibles who are culture, PCR, or fluorescent antibody–positive for *B. pertussis*). Their administration to patients at any stage of pertussis regularly produces bacteriologic cure and may render them noninfectious. These reasons constitute the rationale for the use of antimicrobials in pertussis. Erythromycin is the drug of choice. The optimal dose is 40 to 50 mg/kg/day (maximum, 1 g per day) in four divided doses for 14 days. Treatment for less than 14 days results in a 10% incidence of bacteriologic relapse, and these children may again become contagious. Recent reports indicate that erythromycin may be equally effective when given in three and even two divided doses daily if tolerated. Trimethoprim-sulfamethoxazole is a possible alternative for patients who do not tolerate erythromycin, but the efficacy of this treatment regimen is unproven. Clarithromycin and azithromycin have also been shown to be effective for treatment and chemoprophylaxis of pertussis, offering the advantage of shorter duration of treatment, less frequent dosing, and better tolerance.

Children who develop fever or an elevated erythrocyte sedimentation rate usually have secondary suppurative infections, most often acute otitis media, sinusitis, or pneumonia. The bacterial pathogens implicated are those that usually cause these infections in infants and children, and thus require more targeted antimicrobial therapy.

Corticosteroids.   Corticosteroids given orally or intramuscularly have both been shown to be effective in reducing the incidence and severity of cough paroxysms in controlled studies of children with pertussis. Additional studies are needed, but it appears that corticosteroids may be beneficial in the treatment of pertussis even after onset of paroxysms and that treatment may be indicated in young infants with life-threatening paroxysms.

Albuterol. Several controlled studies evaluating the use of albuterol in the treatment of pertussis have been reported, and most have shown a beneficial effect. Its use may be indicated for treatment of pertussis in small infants with severe life-threatening paroxysms.

INFECTIOUS PERIOD

Individuals with pertussis should be considered infectious from just before the onset of the catarrhal stage of the disease until 3 weeks after the development of the paroxysmal cough.

INFECTION CONTROL

Vaccine. Effective control of pertussis depends on achieving universal immunization of infants and children and initiation of booster immunization for adolescents and adults. Infants and children should be immunized with a series of vaccinations containing diphtheria toxoid, tetanus toxoid, and acellular pertussis vaccine (DTaP). Adolescents and adults should receive booster immunization using a single dose of an age-appropriate tetanus toxoid, reduced diphtheria toxoid, and acellular pertussis vaccine (Tdap). Adolescents aged 10 to 18 years of age may receive a single dose of Tdap as BOOSTRIX (manufactured by GlaxoSmithKline Biologicals), or adolescents aged 11 to 18 years may receive a single dose of Tdap as ADACEL (manufactured by Sanofi Pasteur, Inc.) if they have completed the recommended childhood vaccination series. ADACEL is also licensed for adults up to age 64 years. Adults should receive a single dose of Tdap for booster immunization against tetanus, diphtheria, and pertussis if they received the last dose of tetanus toxoid–containing vaccine ≥10 years earlier. To protect against pertussis, Tdap may be given at an interval shorter than 10 years since the last dose of tetanus toxoid–containing vaccine. The safety of an interval as short as 2 years between administration of Td and Tdap is supported by a Canadian study of children and adolescents. Adults who have or who anticipate having close contact with an infant 12 months of age or younger (e.g. parents, child care providers, health care providers) should receive a single dose of Tdap. Tdap should be given at least 1 month before beginning close contact with the infant. Women should receive a dose of Tdap in the immediate post-partum period if they have not already received Tdap. Any woman who might become pregnant is encouraged to receive a single dose of Tdap. Health care personnel who work in hospitals or ambulatory care settings and have direct patient contact should receive a single dose of Tdap. Close contacts of a newly infected patient should be vaccinated if they have not received a dose within the previous 2 years. Those who are unimmunized or children who are less than age 7 years who have received fewer than four doses of DTaP should be immunized in accordance with current recommended age-appropriate schedules.

Chemoprophylaxis.   All persons who have been exposed to a patient with pertussis should be considered infected and should receive chemoprophylaxis with an appropriate antibiotic, as outlined under Therapy. Chemoprophylaxis that is begun before or during the catarrhal phase may abort or ameliorate illness.

Exclusion from Child Care or Preschool Attendance.   Children with clinical pertussis should be considered contagious from the earliest signs and symptoms of the catarrhal stage of illness to 3 weeks after onset of the paroxysmal stage. Nearly all children with pertussis who are treated with erythromycin are culture-negative for *B. pertussis* organisms after 5 days, so that if compliance can be assured, these children may be considered noncontagious and return to the child care setting. However, treatment should be continued for at least 14 days if erythromycin is used.

Recommendations for Other Children.   All children in a child care center or preschool where pertussis has been confirmed in one or more children should be considered infected, and they should be isolated from other children until it can be determined if they are contagious. After nasopharyngeal culture, PCR, or DFA studies are obtained, it is recommended that these children be treated with antibiotics as outlined under Therapy.

Recommendations for Personnel.   When the diagnosis of pertussis has been confirmed in a day care center, it should be recommended that all day care center personnel receive antibiotic prophylaxis with erythromycin, azithromycin, clarithromycin, or trimethoprim-sulfamethoxazole as outlined under Therapy, and be immunized with the Tdap vaccine.

Parental Advice.   Parents should be told that pertussis or "whooping cough" has been diagnosed in children in the center and that measures have been taken to control the infection. These include isolation of infected or possibly infected individuals, "booster" pertussis vaccine administration to children who have not completed their immunization series, booster immunization with Tdap for adult personnel, and antibiotic prophylaxis for all children and adults in the center.

48

 # Pneumococcus
(Otitis Media, Sinusitis,
Bacteremia, Pneumonia, Meningitis)

Keith R. Powell

CLINICAL MANIFESTATIONS

The most common diseases caused by *Streptococcus pneumoniae* are otitis media, sinusitis, and more invasive infections, including bacteremia, pneumonia, and meningitis. The incidence of invasive pneumococcal infections has decreased dramatically since 2000 when immunization of all infants with pneumococcal conjugate vaccine was recommended. The incidence of pneumococcal otitis media has remained about the same, although pneumococcal serotypes included in the vaccine seem to be playing a decreasing role. *S. pneumoniae* is isolated from 30 to 40% of cases of acute otitis media and acute maxillary sinusitis in which a bacterial pathogen is identified. Pneumococcal otitis media frequently accompanies a viral respiratory infection. There are no clinical features that distinguish acute pneumococcal otitis media or sinusitis from infections with other pathogens. *S. pneumoniae* also can cause purulent conjunctivitis in young infants. *S. pneumoniae* pneumonia is characterized by fever, tachypnea, localized findings on chest examination, and consolidative pneumonia of one or more lobes seen on chest roentgenogram. Symptoms usually improve dramatically after 1 or 2 days of appropriate antibacterial therapy.

The rate of occult bacteremia in children between 3 and 36 months of age with temperatures above 39°C for which no source can be identified has fallen to less than 1% in the *Haemophilus influenzae* type B and pneumococcal vaccine era. Nonetheless *S. pneumoniae* continues to be the organism most often isolated from the blood of bacteremic infants. Occult bacteremia is most often associated with upper respiratory infections, pharyngitis, or fever alone. Pneumococcal meningitis cannot be distinguished clinically from other types of bacterial meningitis.

ETIOLOGIC AGENT

S. pneumoniae are lancet-shaped, gram-positive cocci that occur in pairs. When grown on blood agar plates, there is a greenish discoloration around colonies because of partial (alpha) hemolysis. Pneumococci are serotyped based on chemically distinct capsular polysaccharides. There are currently over 90 recognized serotypes.

EPIDEMIOLOGY

Source of the Organism.   *S. pneumoniae* are ubiquitous. Asymptomatic carriage of this organism is extremely common and carriage rates as high as 60% have been documented in young children. For adults living with children, the carriage rate approaches 20 to 30%, while the rate for adults without children in the household is only 6%. Pneumococci are rapidly developing resistance to our usual antibacterial therapies. People recently treated with antibacterial agents and children attending day care are more likely to be colonized with resistant pneumococci.

High-Risk Populations.   About 70% of pneumococcal infections in children occur in infants younger than 2 years old, and as many as 25% of children with systemic pneumococcal infections have underlying conditions. Children are considered at high or moderate risk for invasive pneumococcal infection if they have sickle cell disease, congenital or acquired asplenia, splenic dysfunction, human immunodeficiency virus infection, congenital immune deficiency, chronic cardiac disease, chronic pulmonary disease, cerebrospinal fluid leak, chronic renal insufficiency, immunosuppressive chemotherapy, diabetes mellitus, or a cochlear implant.

Mode of Spread.   The mode of spread of *S. pneumoniae* is from person to person via respiratory droplets. Spread can occur in association with viral upper respiratory tract infections.

Incubation Period.   There is no distinct incubation period for pneumococcal diseases. However, infection most often occurs within 1 month after an individual acquires a new serotype.

DIAGNOSIS

The diagnosis of infection caused by *S. pneumoniae* is usually made by isolation of the organism from body sites that are normally sterile (e.g., blood, spinal fluid). A diagnosis of pneumococcal pneumonia can be made by typical clinical and roentgenographic findings and the presence of gram-positive, lancet-shaped diplococci in an adequate gram-stained sputum specimen. Since sputum is difficult to obtain in young children, an alternative is to assay concentrated urine for the presence of pneumococcal capsular polysaccharides by countercurrent immunoelectrophoresis or latex particle agglutination.

THERAPY

Pneumococci with reduced susceptibility to penicillin, cephalosporins, macrolides, and trimethoprim-sulfamethoxazole are being isolated with increasing frequency from children in day care settings. However, with increasing coverage with the pneumococcal conjugate vaccine, there is some evidence to suggest that a decrease in colonization with vaccine serotypes is resulting in fewer isolates that are penicillin resistant. It is important to know what the susceptibility trends are at the community level. Penicillin G remains the antibacterial agent of choice for most noninvasive infections caused by penicillin-susceptible *S. pneumoniae*. Otitis media, sinusitis, and pneumonia are often treated empirically with amoxicillin. With the increasing incidence of penicillin-resistant pneumococci isolated from day care attendees, higher-dose amoxicillin (80 to 90 mg/kg/day) should be considered for day care children requiring therapy targeted against the pneumococcus. Conjunctivitis can be treated with ophthalmic preparations of polymyxin B-bacitracin, sulfacetamide, or erythromycin. For children with life-threatening infection, namely meningitis, bacteremia, and pneumonia requiring hospitalization, the empiric use of ceftriaxone or cefotaxime plus vancomycin has been recommended until susceptibility information is available. Children with bacterial meningitis require hospitalization for 7 to 10 days of parenteral antibacterial therapy, and children with more severe pneumococcal pneumonia require hospitalization until they are ready for oral therapy. Children found to have occult pneumococcal bacteremia are usually treated for 10 days. The route of administration and whether the child is hospitalized will depend on the clinical setting.

INFECTIOUS PERIOD

There is no evidence that children with *S. pneumoniae* infections are more likely to transmit the organism than are asymptomatic carriers.

INFECTION CONTROL

Vaccine. The heptavalent pneumococcal conjugate vaccine (PCV) is recommended by the Advisory Committee on Immunization Practices and the American Academy of Pediatrics for universal administration to infants 2, 4, and 6 months of age, with a booster dose at 12 to 15 months of age. Infants starting pneumococcal immunization between 7 to 11 months of age should receive 2 doses 6 to 8 weeks apart and a booster dose at 12 to 15 months of age. If the first dose is not given until 12 to 23 months of age, the child should receive 2 doses, 6 to 8 weeks apart. Children receiving the first dose after 24 months of age require only 1 dose unless they are in one of the high-risk groups mentioned above. High-risk infants should receive 2 doses given 2 months apart. The 23-valent pneumococcal polysaccharide vaccine (PPV) is recommended in addition to PCV for children over 2 years of age who are at high risk for pneumococcal infection (e.g., heart disease, lung disease, sickle cell disease, diabetes, immunocompromised).

A PPV has been available since 1983; however, it is not effective in children under 2 years of age. Current recommendations are that children with sickle cell disease and children who have anatomic or functional asplenia, are immunocompromised, have human immunodeficiency virus infection or other chronic illnesses (chronic cardiac disease, particularly cyanotic congenital heart disease; chronic pulmonary disease, excluding asthma unless on high-dose corticosteroid therapy; cerebrospinal fluid leaks; cochlear implants; and diabetes mellitus) should receive 1 dose of the PPV at age 2 years or older and 6 to 8 weeks after their last dose of the 7-valent pneumococcal vaccine.

Exclusion from Child Care or Preschool Attendance.   Children should only be kept out of child care or preschool if they are too ill to participate in usual activities.

Recommendations for Other Children.   Universal vaccination is recommended.

Recommendations for Personnel.   There are no recommendations for personnel in the day care center once one child is known to be infected.

Parental Advice.   Nearly all children have *S. pneumoniae* in their upper respiratory tract at one time or another, and such "colonization" is seldom associated with disease. The fact that one child in the day care center has an illness caused by *S. pneumoniae* probably does not increase the risk of another child having an illness with these bacteria. Children recently treated with antibacterial agents are more likely to have infections with resistant pneumococci than children who did not receive antibacterial therapy. Antibacterial agents should be used only when there are clear indications of bacterial infection.

Over 80% of children with acute otitis media recover in 1 to 7 days without antibacterial therapy. Antibacterial therapy should be reserved for children who clearly have purulent fluid in the middle ear and children whose symptoms do not improve after 3 days of pain control with acetaminophen. Antibacterial agents should not be used for colds, upper respiratory infections, bronchitis, or bronchiolitis.

49

Respiratory Syncytial Virus

Caroline Breese Hall

CLINICAL MANIFESTATIONS

Respiratory syncytial virus (RSV) is the major cause of lower respiratory tract infection in infants and young children. It is the most frequent cause of bronchiolitis and also the most frequent cause of pneumonia during the first 2 years of life. The lower respiratory tract disease caused by RSV in the first year of life may vary in severity from mild to life-threatening or even fatal. Although essentially all first RSV infections are symptomatic, the vast majority have an uncomplicated course. The morbidity and mortality are greatest in the very young infant and in children with underlying diseases, especially those affecting the cardiac, pulmonary, and immunologic systems. Apnea may be a manifestation of RSV infection, especially in premature infants and those in the first several months of life. RSV is a major cause of tracheobronchitis in pre-school-age children and occasionally may be manifest as croup. Close to half of primary infections are manifest as lower respiratory tract disease, and the other half are manifest as upper respiratory tract infections and otitis media.

RSV causes frequent and repetitive infections throughout life. In children approximately 3 years of age or older, these infections are most often expressed as upper respiratory tract infections, otitis media, and tracheobronchitis. RSV is commonly associated with recurrent wheezing and occasionally may present as a febrile, influenza-like syndrome. Adults may manifest recurrent RSV infection as bronchitis, wheezing, febrile upper respiratory tract infection, a cold, or with little in the way of symptoms. These mild infections are more apt to occur in those with recent or frequent exposure to children with RSV infections, such as staff in child care centers. Such mild infections may nevertheless be a source of spread of RSV.

ETIOLOGIC AGENT

RSV is an enveloped RNA virus of medium size that is currently classified in the family Paramyxoviridae and in the genus *Pneumovirus*. RSV strains are divided into two major groups, A and B. These groups are based mostly on the antigenic variations in the two major surface glycoproteins, the F, or fusion protein, and the G, or attachment protein. The F protein is relatively well conserved and thus antigenically similar among strains A and B. The major antigenic differences occur in the largest surface glycoprotein, the G protein. The immunologic, clinical, and epidemiologic importance of strain variation is currently unclear but may contribute to the frequency of repetitive RSV infections within a short time, even within the same season.

EPIDEMIOLOGY

Source of the Organism.   RSV is highly contagious and is spread from person to person. In the normal host, the presence of the virus in the secretions indicates an acute infection. Repetitive infections occasionally may be asymptomatic, but carriage or latent infection does not occur.

High-Risk Populations.   The major risk factor for acquisition and severity of RSV infection is young age. RSV tends to occur in annual winter outbreaks; many children acquire RSV infection during the first outbreak they experience, and essentially all children experience RSV infection by 3 years of age. In day care settings studies have shown that during the first year of life the infection rate is close to 100%, and about half will have lower respiratory tract disease. Even in the second and third year of life in child care settings, two-thirds to three-fourths of the children will become infected with RSV. The rate of reported infection is lower for children cared for at home than for those who are cared for in child care settings, but it is still high. Approximately two-thirds of the infants cared for at home in the first year of life have been shown to acquire RSV infection, and an even higher percentage have been shown to acquire RSV in the second year. During the third and fourth year of life, one-third to one-half of children will become infected each year.

Children at risk for the most severe and complicated disease from RSV are those with premature birth, chronic lung disease, and cardiac disease, especially congenital heart disease with pulmonary hypertension, compromised immunity, and multiple congenital anomalies or neurologic diseases that affect pulmonary function or may predispose to gastroesophageal reflux and aspiration. Older children with hyperreactive airway disease may have exacerbations of wheezing and more prolonged illness.

Mode of Spread.   RSV is spread by direct contact with infectious secretions. This appears to be primarily by large-particle aerosols from infected individuals within close proximity and from contact with infectious secretions contaminating the environment. In this latter mode of spread, infectious secretions on surfaces, toys, clothes, and other objects are transmitted by touching, with subsequent inoculation of the virus occurring when the eyes or nose is touched. The virus may remain infectious on surfaces and skin from half an hour to more than a day, depending on the temperature, humidity, and type of surface.

Incubation Period.   The incubation period ranges from 3 to 7 days but most frequently appears to be 4 to 5 days.

DIAGNOSIS

The season, age, and clinical presentation, especially bronchiolitis, allow a presumptive diagnosis in many infants. Specific diagnosis may be made by viral isolation from respiratory secretions, which usually requires 3 to 7 days, or by a rapid diagnostic test for antigen in respiratory secretions. A variety of commercial antigen detection tests are currently available, most of which employ monoclonal antibodies in an immunofluorescent or enzyme-linked immunosorbent assay technique. These tests have variable sensitivity and specificity and are generally considered as screening tests. Detection by reverse transcriptase polymerase chain reaction (RT-PCR) in respiratory secretions is highly sensitive and specific and is becoming more widely available. Serologic diagnosis is generally impractical and insensitive.

THERAPY

Most children attending day care who acquire RSV infection require no more than the usual supportive care for an upper respiratory tract infection. Some may benefit from antipyretic therapy, although fever associated with RSV infection is usually not high and does not correlate with the severity of the illness.

An appreciable proportion of these children also may manifest wheezing, which may be intermittent and variable in severity, from mild enough to be detectable only on auscultation, to severe with overt respiratory distress. Bronchodilators, mostly nebulized, are frequently used, but for most children with acute RSV infection, especially young infants with a first episode of wheezing, they provide little or no benefit and may be associated with adverse effects. For some children with moderately severe bronchiolitis, some studies have suggested that a modest clinical benefit may be observed with nebulized bronchodilators.

For more severely ill children requiring hospitalization, supportive care remains the mainstay of therapy. Ribavirin may be considered for use in children with severe illness or with high-risk conditions.

INFECTIOUS PERIOD

The period of infectivity correlates with the shedding of the virus in the nasopharyngeal secretions. In young infants this is most frequently 1 to 2 weeks but may occasionally be 3 weeks or longer. In older children and adults, shedding of the virus is less, usually 3 to 7 days.

INFECTION CONTROL

Vaccine.   None.

Immunoglobulin Prophylaxis.   Two products have been licensed for prophylaxis of a select group of premature high-risk infants and those with chronic lung diseases: intravenous immunoglobulin containing high titers of neutralizing antibody to RSV, and a monoclonal antibody directed to an epitope on the RSV F protein (palivizumab). Both are approved for administration once per month during the RSV season. In most cases the preferred product for prophylaxis is the monoclonal antibody because of the ease of its intramuscular administration, fewer side effects, and its greater availability.

Exclusion from Child Care or Preschool Attendance.   Because of the ubiquitous and prevalent nature of RSV during a winter community outbreak, and because the clinical presentation may be variable and not distinguishable from respiratory illnesses caused by many other pathogens, preventing an infected child from attending a child care or preschool setting is impractical in most instances. Furthermore, children may be highly infectious just prior to the onset of symptoms. For those children known to have RSV infection, particularly with lower respiratory tract infection, the best guideline for return to the child care setting is when the child is clinically well enough to be able to attend and participate in the usual activities.

Recommendations for Other Children.   Studies have shown that once one child in a child care or preschool setting is infected, spread of infection is often rapid and inevitable. The risk of infection is so high for young children in or out of the day care setting during a community outbreak that recommendations for other children in a center once a child has become infected usually are of little value. Routine handwashing is probably the most effective means of protection against spread of RSV infection, and should be consistently practiced by staff in the day care center. Although enforcing good handwashing in children is difficult, emphasis on routine hand cleaning in day care centers has been shown to result in fewer respiratory and gastrointestinal illnesses. Recent studies, however, have suggested that the routine use of alcohol gel hand sanitizers by staff and children is a feasible and preferable means for effective hand cleansing and has resulted in a reduced rate of acute infections among staff and children.

Communal toys should be routinely cleaned, and when possible, toys should be assigned to individual child use.

Recommendations for Personnel.   Personnel in a child care center or preschool frequently may become infected with RSV, which most often is manifest as an upper respiratory tract infection. Nevertheless, they may serve as disseminators of the infection to others in the center. The most effective infection control method, as noted above, is good and constant handwashing since the primary mode of spread is by direct contact with infectious secretions, which may remain contagious on skin and environmental surfaces for some time. Since compliance with routine handwashing is notably poor, gel hand sanitizers may have some benefit in diminishing the chance of spread of infection to personnel by self-inoculation, as noted in Recommendations for Other Children.

Parental Advice.   Parents should be informed about the prevalence and contagiousness of RSV among young children in any setting during a community outbreak of RSV infection. They should understand that all children acquire RSV infection in the first few years of life, and if the child is over 1 year of age or has been in the day care center through a previous RSV epidemic, the child is highly likely to have already experienced RSV infection. Thus, if their child acquires a respiratory infection, they should treat it as any other respiratory illness and seek the advice of their private physician.

Rhinoviruses
(Common Cold)

Ronald B. Turner

CLINICAL MANIFESTATIONS

The rhinoviruses are an important cause of the common cold. The symptoms of rhinovirus colds are limited to the upper respiratory tract in most people; fever or myalgia is uncommon. Gastrointestinal symptoms are not associated with rhinovirus infections. The first symptom noted by many individuals is a mild sore throat. This is soon followed by development of nasal stuffiness and rhinorrhea. About one-third of rhinovirus illnesses are associated with cough. Symptoms reach a peak after 1 to 2 days of illness and usually resolve within 7 to 10 days.

Although rhinovirus infection is usually minor and self-limited, a small proportion of infected individuals will have complications. Rhinovirus colds may be complicated by otitis media due to either the rhinovirus itself or a secondary bacterial infection. Sinusitis may also complicate the viral infection. Lower respiratory symptoms, especially exacerbations of asthma, are reported in about 1% of these infections.

ETIOLOGIC AGENT

The rhinoviruses are members of the family Picornaviridae, which also includes the enteroviruses. This family is composed of small (approximately 25 nm) nonenveloped RNA viruses. The rhinoviruses are distinguished from the enteroviruses by their inactivation by exposure to acid. There are more than 100 different serotypes of rhinovirus. Serotype-specific antibody generally protects against infection, although the degree of protection is dependent upon the size of the inoculum received.

EPIDEMIOLOGY

Source of the Organism. Infection with the rhinoviruses is acquired exclusively from other infected individuals. There is no animal host for this virus. The virus can survive on inanimate objects for several hours, and contaminated objects can presumably serve as a source of infection.

High-Risk Populations. There is no population that is known to be at increased risk of infection with the rhinoviruses. Patients with asthma may be at risk of more severe illness if infection with rhinovirus occurs.

Mode of Spread. Spread of rhinovirus infection has been demonstrated to occur by direct contact, via fomites, and in aerosols. The relative importance of these different routes of spread in the natural setting is not known.

Incubation Period. The incubation period for rhinovirus infection is 1 to 2 days.

DIAGNOSIS

Rhinovirus illnesses are generally mild, and specific etiologic diagnosis is not generally attempted. Laboratory diagnosis is accomplished by isolation of the organism in cell culture. Optimal conditions for cell culture require that the specimen be incubated at 33°C on a roller drum. There are no reliable antigen detection methods for rhinovirus, and serologic diagnosis is generally not attempted because of the large number of distinct serotypes. Polymerase chain reaction is commonly used for detection of rhinovirus in the research setting.

THERAPY

There are no anti-infective therapies of proven benefit for treatment of rhinovirus infections. Cold symptoms can be palliated with over-the-counter medications. Topical adrenergic agents are the most efficacious decongestants. Antihistamines have a modest effect on the runny nose and cough associated with colds; however, drowsiness is a frequent side effect.

INFECTIOUS PERIOD

Infected individuals may shed virus in nasal secretions for as long as 3 weeks. Transmission is most likely when nasal symptoms are present.

INFECTION CONTROL

Vaccine.   None available.

Exclusion from Child Care or Preschool Attendance.   Exclusion of rhinovirus-infected children from child care settings is not indicated.

Recommendations for Other Children.   Transmission of infection may be reduced by frequent handwashing.

Recommendations for Personnel.   Transmission of infection may be reduced by frequent handwashing.

Parental Advice.   No special measures are indicated.

Roseola
(Exanthema Subitum)

Mary Anne Jackson

CLINICAL MANIFESTATIONS

Roseola (also called exanthema subitum) is the most common acute febrile exanthem of children ages 6 months to 2 years and is typically caused by human herpesvirus 6 (HHV-6) or, in some cases, HHV-7 infection. In typical cases, high, sustained fever is present and lasts for 3 to 5 days. Irritability, malaise, and runny nose may be present during this time, but usually, despite the high fever, most children are alert and playful. A red throat with small lesions on the palate or tonsils may be seen in 65% of patients, and lymphadenopathy involving the occipital, cervical, and posterior auricular chains may be the only other pertinent findings. Children with roseola may have eyelid swelling that gives them a "sleepy" or "droopy" appearance. Many clinicians believe this is a classic pre-rash finding, although it occurs in only 30% of infants with roseola.

The exanthem or rash phase of roseola generally occurs coincident with the disappearance of fever. (The Latin translation of exanthema subitum is sudden rash.) Pale rose-pink macules measuring 2 to 5 mm are surrounded by a white halo and scattered over the neck and trunk, sparing the face and extremities. The rash lasts 24 to 48 hours, and a total clinical course of 5 to 7 days is typical.

High fever without localizing signs occurs frequently in primary infection. One population-based study suggests that the acquisition of HHV-6 in infancy often results in fever, fussiness, diarrhea, rash, or roseola presentation. Medical evaluation in such children is common, with nearly 4 in 10 children generating a physician visit. Febrile seizures resulting in hospitalization occur in both HHV-6 and HHV-7 infection. Fatal liver failure has been described in an infant with primary HHV-6 infection.

Primary infection in adults can present with a mononucleosis-type illness. Various neurologic manifestations, including encephalitis, are well described in compromised hosts as well as immunocompetent adults and are typically associated with reactivated disease.

Fever, hepatitis, pneumonia, and bone marrow suppression have also been reported in compromised hosts in whom reactivation has occurred. An association with graft rejection has been noted in liver and kidney transplant patients. There is some support for the possibility of an intrauterine or perinatal infection based on reports of finding viral genome in maternal, fetal, and neonatal samples. HHV-6 DNA was detected in 1% of 5638 cord bloods tested, and all neonates were asymptomatic. Vertical transmission is suspected to be blood borne and occurs during periods of maternal reactivated infection.

ETIOLOGIC AGENT

HHV-6 and -7 are neurotropic viruses first described in 1986 and 1990, respectively. The viruses are lymphotropic, with T cells being the targets for both. These agents are ubiquitous and acquired early in life. HHV-6 infection is most common; primary infection occurs in the first year of life in 40% of infants, in 77% by age 24 months, and seroprevalence rates approach 100% by age 3 years. Two variants of HHV-6 are recognized (A and B), with primary infection with HHV-6B causing most cases of roseola. Variant 6A has only rarely been associated with clinical diseases. Primary HHV-7 infection appears to occur slightly later in life. Twenty percent of healthy children are seropositive by 1 year, 40% by 2 years, 50% by 3 years, and greater than 90% of adults demonstrate evidence of past infections.

At times, roseola-like illness has been associated with other viruses including enteroviruses (most commonly ECHO-16 virus), adenoviruses, and parvovirus.

EPIDEMIOLOGY

Source of the Organism.   The human is the only known host for roseola. There is no distinct seasonality.

High-Risk Populations.   Reactivated disease has been reported in immunocompromised hosts.

Mode of Spread.   Contact with infected respiratory secretions of healthy persons is the probable mode of spread. Older siblings may serve as a source for intrafamily spread.

Incubation Period.   Nine to 10 days.

DIAGNOSIS

Although this test is not readily available, HHV-6 and -7 can be isolated from blood and detected by polymerase chain reaction (PCR). Confirmation of acute infection by documenting an increase in neutralizing antibody to the virus is complicated by cross-reactivity. Antibody avidity immunofluorescence testing has shown to be a reliable discriminator of HHV-6 and -7. Discrimination between primary and reactivated infection is not possible; high persistent HHV-6 viral load detected by PCR has been noted in primary infection.

Diagnosis of roseola is generally made on clinical grounds. The major requirement in establishing the diagnosis of roseola is to document the fever, defervescence, and the rash pattern of the disease.

THERAPY

Treatment is supportive. Febrile seizures and other neurologic manifestations of roseola may require further evaluation and other diagnostic studies. In the United Kingdom, 26 (17%) of 205 two- to thirty-five-month-old children who were prospectively followed and hospitalized for suspected encephalitis or severe illness with fever and seizures had HHV-6 or -7 infection. Hospitalization averaged 7 days with almost half requiring intensive care. While ganciclovir or foscarnet may be considered in severe disease in the compromised host, there are no prospective studies to confirm efficacy.

INFECTIOUS PERIOD

The period of communicability is unknown.

INFECTION CONTROL

Vaccine.   None available.

Exclusion from Child Care or Preschool Attendance.   Generally speaking, children with febrile exanthems should not return to a child care or preschool setting until their rash is gone and they are well.

Recommendations for Other Children.   No contact prophylaxis is necessary.

Recommendations for Personnel.   No special recommendations are necessary for child care personnel.

Parental Advice.   Cases usually occur sporadically throughout the year. Occasionally outbreaks have been reported, but parents can be reassured as to the benign nature of this infection. There is no known risk to pregnant women, and roseola in children less than 3 months or children over 4 years of age is uncommon.

52

 # Rotavirus

Theresa A. Schlager

CLINICAL MANIFESTATIONS

Rotavirus infection is the most common cause of gastroenteritis occurring in the winter among infants and young children in the United States. The clinical features of rotavirus infection vary from asymptomatic fecal shedding of the virus to severe vomiting and diarrhea associated with circulatory collapse. Symptomatic illness usually is manifested by vomiting and low-grade fever followed by watery, nonbloody diarrhea. Vomiting and dehydration occur more frequently with rotavirus infection than with other causes of gastroenteritis. Diarrhea typically lasts between 3 and 8 days but may be prolonged in immunocompromised children. Respiratory symptoms are associated with rotavirus, but the virus has not been isolated from respiratory secretions. The overall course of rotavirus infection ordinarily is self-limited and without sequelae if appropriate therapy for dehydration is provided.

ETIOLOGIC AGENT

Rotaviruses are RNA viruses: at least seven distinct antigenic groups (A to G) have been described, and group A is the major cause of infantile diarrhea. Five strains account for over 90% of clinical illness in developed countries; however, strain distribution may be more diverse in developing countries. Thus, an effective vaccine must provide protection against several strains that a child may be exposed to. Rotavirus appears to cause disease by invading and altering (morphologically and functionally) small bowel mucosal cells, resulting in malabsorption and diarrhea.

EPIDEMIOLOGY

Source of the Organism.   Rotavirus is one of the most common causes of diarrhea in the child care center for children younger than 4 years of age and represents a source of infection for parents and child care providers. Among the many viruses causing diarrhea, rotavirus is one of the most common causes of severe illness. Although symptomatic disease in adults is unusual, asymptomatic shedding of the virus by adults can be a source of infection. Animals are known to have rotavirus diarrheal disease, but animal-to-human transmission has not been documented under natural conditions.

High-Risk Populations.   The peak age for symptomatic rotavirus infection is 6 to 24 months, and virtually all children are infected by 3 years of age. The disease is highly contagious, and contact with infected patients in the 6- to 24-month age group constitutes the greatest risk factor for disease acquisition. The immunocompromised child is at risk for developing chronic diarrhea. Reinfections are usually milder than the primary infection.

Mode of Spread.   Fecal-oral spread is the most common mode of spread, but contaminated fomites may also transmit rotavirus.

Incubation Period.   One to 3 days.

DIAGNOSIS

Although a specific diagnosis is usually not necessary in sporadic cases, it may be useful in outbreaks, in isolating hospitalized patients, and in epidemiologic studies. Commercial enzyme immunoassay and latex agglutination assays for group A rotavirus provide rapid inexpensive detection with a sensitivity and specificity that exceeds 90%.

Fresh stool specimens from the first 4 days of illness have the highest yield for rotavirus detection and correlate with the highest degree of viral shedding. The presence of detectable rotavirus in feces usually correlates with acute diarrheal symptoms. In some patients, rotavirus may be shed for as long as 3 weeks, thereby permitting a diagnosis well after the initial onset of diarrhea.

THERAPY

No specific antiviral therapy is available. Adequate fluid replacement is the mainstay of treatment. Most patients can be managed appropriately with oral rehydration, but infants with marked dehydration may require hospitalization for aggressive fluid and electrolyte repletion. In one study, lactobacillus GG, a probiotic, significantly reduced the duration of acute rotaviral gastroenteritis in immunocompetent children when compared to placebo. The routine use of oral immunoglobulin for rotavirus gastroenteritis has not proved to be beneficial when compared to rehydration therapy alone. However, in immunodeficient children with chronic rotavirus infection, orally administered rotavirus-specific immunoglobulin preparations may ablate shedding or ameliorate disease.

INFECTIOUS PERIOD

The infectious period is usually less than 1 week, paralleling diarrhea that usually ceases in 4 to 5 days. However, severe rotavirus disease in young and immunocompromised patients may be followed by extended excretion of rotavirus.

PREVENTION

Breast Feeding. Breast milk antibodies coat infant mucosal surfaces and may play a role in protecting infants from infection by pathogens such as rotavirus that have a mucosal portal of entry.

Vaccine. The first vaccine was licensed in the United States in 1999 and withdrawn 9 months later due to reports of an association between the vaccine and intussusception. Several new orally administered rotavirus vaccines have demonstrated clinical efficacy in preventing gastroenteritis and resulted in lower rates of infant hospitalization. Studies to date have demonstrated no difference in the rates of intussusception between vaccine and placebo groups. In 2006, the Advisory Committee on Immunization Practices (ACIP) to the Centers for Disease Control and Prevention (CDC) recommended that all infants receive 3 doses of the oral vaccine RotaTeq (marketed by Merck & Co., Inc.) at 2, 4, and 6 months of age. Children should receive the first dose of the vaccine by 12 weeks of age and should receive all doses of the vaccine by 32 weeks of age. There are insufficient data on safety and efficacy outside of these age ranges. This new vaccine is the only vaccine approved in the United States for prevention of rotavirus gastroenteritis.

INFECTION CONTROL

Exclusion from Child Care or Preschool Attendance. The infected child should be kept out of the child care or preschool setting as long as diarrhea or vomiting is present.

Recommendations for Other Children. Routine testing for rotavirus of case contacts within a child care center or preschool is not recommended. Washing of children's hands on arrival at the center, after a diaper change or use of the toilet, and before meals and snacks should be consistently practiced. Use of liquid soap in a dispenser along with disposable paper towels is recommended. Rotaviruses are inactivated by 70% ethanol, which is the preferred solution for cleaning contaminated surfaces.

Recommendations for Personnel. Symptomatic staff members should not attend the center until fever, diarrhea, or vomiting ceases. Without failure, staff members should practice careful hand-washing (10 seconds with soap and warm running water) upon arrival at the center, after changing a child's diaper, after using or providing assistance to a child using the toilet, and before food handling. Disinfecting diaper-changing surfaces along with proper diaper disposal is recommended.

Parental Advice. A child care center or preschool should notify parents of children who have been in direct contact with a child who has diarrhea. Parents should contact their physician for advice if their child develops diarrhea.

53

Rubella
(German Measles)

Gregory F. Hayden

CLINICAL MANIFESTATIONS

Rubella (German measles) is commonly inapparent and unrecognized. When clinical illness occurs, it is generally benign and is manifested by rash and lymphadenopathy with mild constitutional symptoms. The pink maculopapular rash appears first on the face and then spreads downward and peripherally. The usual duration of rash is 2 to 5 days, leading to the lay term "3-day measles." The illness is often more severe among adolescents and adults whose illness may begin with a prodrome of fever, malaise, headache, and respiratory symptoms. Arthralgia and arthritis may occur, especially in adult women. Rare complications include thrombocytopenic purpura and encephalitis.

In contrast to the usually mild nature of postnatal rubella, gestational rubella can be devastating to the developing fetus. Virtually every organ system can be affected, but especially the eyes, heart, and central nervous system. The clinical expression of congenital rubella depends on the timing of infection, with the risk of major anomalies being greatest during the first trimester.

ETIOLOGIC AGENT

Rubella is a spherical, enveloped, RNA-containing virus that is classified as a rubivirus in the togavirus family. Only one serologic type is recognized.

EPIDEMIOLOGY

Reported rubella has declined substantially since rubella vaccine was licensed in 1969. Fewer than 25 cases of rubella have been reported in the United States each year since 2001, and rubella is no longer considered endemic. It remains important, however, to maintain high immunization rates among children and to respond rapidly to any outbreak.

Source of the Organism. The human is the only known natural host and source of infection.

High-Risk Populations. Rubella is uncommon in the first several months of life, but after this age, unvaccinated children remain at high risk of developing rubella if exposed.

Mode of Spread. Transmission is via respiratory droplets or direct contact with an infected patient.

Incubation Period. The incubation period is usually 16 to 18 days but can range from 14 to 23 days.

DIAGNOSIS

The clinical diagnosis of postnatal rubella can be confirmed by using virologic or serologic methods. Rubella virus can be isolated from the nose, throat, and other sites, but viral culture is relatively expensive and not universally available. Reverse transcriptase polymerase chain reaction (RT-PCR) testing has been recently introduced, but is expensive and not widely available. Several serologic techniques are available, including latex agglutination, fluorescence immunoassay, passive hemagglutination, hemolysis-in-gel, enzyme immunoassay (EIA), and a number of older methods. A significant rise in titer between acute and convalescent serum specimens is diagnostic of rubella infection. The presence of rubella-specific immunoglobulin M (IgM) antibodies also suggests recent postnatal infection. A suspected or confirmed diagnosis of rubella should be reported immediately to the local health department.

THERAPY

No specific therapy is currently available.

INFECTIOUS PERIOD

The period of maximum communicability occurs from up to 5 days before rash onset until 5 to 7 days after rash onset. More rarely, virus has been detected in the nasopharynx as long as 7 days before and 14 days after rash onset.

INFECTION CONTROL

Vaccine.   Live, attenuated rubella virus vaccine should be given routinely to children after the first birthday, and is usually administered at 12 to 15 months of age as a part of the combined measles-mumps-rubella (MMR) vaccine. The cornerstone of rubella prevention in child care centers and preschools should be the vigilant insistence that all children 15 months of age or older have received rubella vaccine as a prerequisite for attending the center. A single dose confers long-lasting rubella immunity to more than 90% of vaccinees, but a second dose at 4 to 6 years of age maximizes the rate of immunity and provides an added safeguard against primary vaccine failures.

Precautions and contraindications to live rubella vaccination include altered immunity, pregnancy, severe febrile illness, and recent administration of an immune globulin preparation or blood products. Children with minor illnesses, with or without fever, may be vaccinated. MMR vaccine is recommended for children infected with the human immunodeficiency virus (HIV) if they are not severely immunocompromised.

Exclusion from Child Care or Preschool Attendance.   Children with postnatal rubella should be excluded from child care or preschool for 7 days after rash onset. Since patients are often contagious before rash onset, however, and since inapparent infections can be communicable, attempts to control spread by means of isolation are commonly ineffective.

Children with congenital rubella should be considered contagious until they are 1 year old, unless nasopharyngeal and urine cultures after 3 months of age are repeatedly negative for rubella.

Recommendations for Other Children.   The first step is to verify that other children attending the center have already been immunized against rubella in accordance with established center policy. Children with documented previous immunization against rubella are highly unlikely to develop illness and may continue to attend the center. The management of unvaccinated children is more complex. Live rubella vaccine is not known to prevent illness when given after exposure, but theoretically it can prevent illness if administered within 3 days of exposure, and it will at least protect against subsequent exposures if the child is not already incubating wild rubella infection. Immunization of a child who is incubating natural rubella is not known to be harmful. For unvaccinated children who have reached their first birthday, vaccination can therefore be recommended. Parents must understand, however, that the vaccine may not block the progression of incubating rubella, so that they will not wrongly blame the vaccine for rubella illness that develops after vaccination.

For infants younger than 1 year of age, vaccination is a less attractive option because the likelihood of seroconversion is believed to be lower. Although limited data suggest that it can potentially prevent or modify infection in exposed susceptibles, immunoglobulin is not generally recommended in this instance because of its expense, its questionable efficacy, and the usually mild clinical course of rubella in young children.

Recommendations for Personnel. Ideally, all staff members should provide a documented history of immunization or serologic evidence of immunity at the time of employment. Strict adherence to such a policy will reduce or eliminate the needless disruption that can arise among personnel when rubella is diagnosed in a child attending the center. If appropriate preparations have not been made before such a case occurs, the first step is to determine whether any staff members are susceptible to rubella. This determination is particularly crucial for any personnel who may possibly be pregnant. Documented history of previous rubella immunization on or after the first birthday strongly suggests immunity to rubella. The detection of antibody by a properly performed test before or at the time of exposure provides strong evidence that the individual is immune and not at risk for developing rubella. If antibody is not detectable immediately after an exposure of rubella, additional blood testing will be necessary to determine whether infection has occurred. A pregnant woman exposed to rubella should consult her obstetrician immediately to discuss and evaluate the possible implications of this exposure. In most instances, the woman will already be immune to rubella and can be reassured that the exposure poses little or no risk to her developing fetus.

Parental Advice.   Parents should be advised that a suspected (or confirmed) case of rubella has occurred in a child at the center. They should be advised that the risk to their child is minimal so long as he or she has already received rubella vaccine. Parents of unimmunized children should be advised to seek medical advice immediately concerning the prompt vaccination of children over 1 year of age and concerning the potential risk their child may pose to susceptible pregnant contacts. Parents should also be urged to verify their own immunity status as well as the immunization status of any older children, especially adolescents, who do not attend the center and to seek vaccination as appropriate. A mother who is pregnant should discuss this possible exposure with her obstetrician.

Rubeola (Measles)

Caroline Breese Hall

CLINICAL MANIFESTATIONS

The onset of rubeola is usually marked by fever followed by the "three C's"—coryza, conjunctivitis, and cough. These signs peak after about 3 to 4 days, which is when the rash first appears. The typical morbilliform eruption starts on the head, around the hairline, and progresses to the feet over 3 days, changing from discrete maculopapular lesions to a confluent rash. About 2 days prior to the onset of the rash the characteristic Koplik spots may appear on the buccal mucosa. Once the rash appears, the respiratory signs and fever tend to abate. The rash fades over the subsequent several days, leaving a brown stain and then a generalized desquamation that has the appearance of bran. The course of classic measles generally resolves over a 10-day period, but the cough may persist. Bronchitis, otitis, croup, and pneumonia may complicate the course of rubeola.

The severity of the disease and mortality rates are increased in immunocompromised children, such as those with malignancy and human immunodeficiency virus (HIV). The rash in these children, however, may be uncharacteristic or even absent, resulting in the diagnosis being unsuspected.

Clinical variants of classical measles include modified measles, atypical measles, and vaccine measles. Modified measles is a mild form of measles with a shortened course occurring in patients who possess some measles antibody, such as those who have received gamma globulin, occasionally in infants with passive maternal antibody, and possibly in those with waning immunity from vaccination. Atypical measles is a severe and clinically unusual form of measles occurring in patients who have previously received inactivated measles vaccine, which ceased to be marketed after 1968. After exposure to the wild virus these patients developed a high fever, sometimes nodular pulmonary infiltrates, and an unusual exanthem that could be petechial, vesicular, nodular, or urticarial, as well as macular-papular. Fortunately, with time and widespread use of live vaccine, this atypical disease is no longer seen. Vaccine measles is the mild illness that appears in some children following administration of the live attenuated vaccine. A mild rash and fever may appear approximately a week after immunization.

Acute encephalitis may be associated with measles in approximately 0.1% of cases. Subacute sclerosing panencephalitis is a late complication of measles occurring in approximately 1 in 100,000 cases.

ETIOLOGIC AGENT

Measles virus is classified as a paramyxovirus. It is an RNA-enveloped virus possessing six major proteins: NP, the nucleocapsid that contains the viral genomic RNA and the structural proteins associated with the nucleocapsid and RNA polymerase activity; associated with the envelope are the surface glycoproteins H, the hemagglutinin, F, the fusion protein, and M, an internal membrane protein. Measles is a relatively large (120 to 250 nm in diameter) and spherical virus related to canine distemper virus and rinderpest virus.

EPIDEMIOLOGY

Source of the Organism.   Measles is spread from person to person, and humans are the only source of the virus, although monkeys may be infected with measles.

High-Risk Populations.   Measles is highly contagious, and anyone who does not possess specific measles antibody is at high risk of acquiring infection. Infants, pregnant women, adults, and those with underlying diseases, especially immunocompromising conditions, including HIV, tend to be at increased risk for severe and complicated disease.

Mode of Spread.   Measles is spread by contact with secretions of infected persons. Infectious secretions may be spread by large-particle droplets, requiring close contact, or by small-particle aerosols that may allow rapid and distant transmission of the virus. Direct contact with infectious secretions also may occur via contact with contaminated surfaces or objects. Inoculation appears to occur through the nasopharynx and possibly the conjunctiva.

Incubation Period.   The incubation period is usually 8 to 12 days.

DIAGNOSIS

Diagnosis is often made clinically in the classic case. Confirmation of the diagnosis of measles may be made by isolation of the virus in appropriate tissue culture or by assays identifying the antigen which are usually much more readily available than viral isolation. Diagnosis by polymerase chain reaction is also now available and is highly sensitive and specific. Serologic diagnosis may be made by hemagglutination-inhibition (HI), complement fixation (CF), neutralizing, and ELISA assays of acute and convalescent sera, which may be obtained as early as 1 to 2 weeks after the onset of the rash. Detection of measles-specific immunoglobulin M (IgM) antibody on a single acute specimen is often the fastest and simplest test for diagnosis and is usually readily available. The measles-specific IgM may not be present in the first 3 days after the onset of the rash, and the assay is of variable sensitivity during that period.

THERAPY

Measles is usually a self-limited disease, and therapy is mainly supportive. The antiviral drug ribavirin has been shown in vitro to have activity against measles virus. In controlled studies in children in other countries, oral ribavirin therapy has appeared to shorten the course of the disease. In the United States, aerosolized and intravenous ribavirin has been used for severe measles pneumonia, but the experience is anecdotal, and the drug is not approved for this use.

Vitamin A treatment of children with measles in developing countries has resulted in diminished measles severity and mortality, and thus is recommended by the World Health Organization to be administered to all children with measles in areas where vitamin A deficiency exists and where the mortality from measles is 1% or more. In the United States vitamin A deficiency generally is not a problem, but low vitamin A levels have been documented in the sera of some children with severe measles. The American Academy of Pediatrics, therefore, recommends that vitamin A supplementation be considered for children 6 months to 2 years of age with measles severe enough to require hospitalization and for those children 6 months of age or older who have certain risk factors, such as those with immunodeficiency, nutritional problems, including impaired intestinal absorption, and for children from areas in other countries in which measles mortality is high.

Antibiotics should be used only for proven bacterial complications of measles, such as otitis media.

INFECTIOUS PERIOD

Measles is considered to be contagious from the onset of symptoms, usually 3 to 5 days before the onset of the rash to 3 to 4 days after its appearance. In immunocompromised children the duration of viral shedding and thus the infectivity are prolonged. Measles is most infectious during the catarrhal stage when diagnosis is most difficult. Once the rash appears, the communicability of the disease rapidly declines.

INFECTION CONTROL

Vaccine. The live, further-attenuated (Moraten strain) measles vaccine combined with mumps and rubella (MMR) is recommended routinely for all children at 12 to 15 months of age. A second dose of measles vaccine or MMR should be administered by the time of school entry. In outbreak situations the initial measles immunization may be given as a monovalent vaccine to children as young as 6 months of age. Children receiving their initial vaccination before the first birthday should be revaccinated at 12 to 15 months of age, and a third dose should be administered at 4 to 6 years of age.

Exclusion from Child Care or Preschool Attendance. A child with a known or suspected case of measles should be excluded from the child care or preschool setting until 5 days after the onset of the rash.

Recommendations for Other Children. If a case of measles is suspected in a child care center, the local health department should be notified immediately. In a child care center or preschool in which measles has occurred, a program of revaccination with MMR is recommended. Unvaccinated children who are 6 months of age or older also should receive the live measles vaccine. If the vaccine is given within 72 hours of exposure, it may give protection against infection. Immunoglobulin can be administered to unvaccinated children within 6 days of exposure (0.25 ml/kg). If the immunoglobulin is given, live measles vaccine must be delayed for 5 months or longer if doses larger than 0.25 ml/kg were administered.

Recommendations for Personnel. Since susceptible adults are at risk for severe measles infection, it is essential that personnel exposed in a child care or preschool setting know their immunization status, preferably at the time of employment. Although recommendations specific for this setting do not exist, the recommendations for those in medical facilities and for young adults in the college setting are that at the time of employment or enrollment they must have proof of immunity or proof of having had two doses of vaccine. Similar recommendations would seem advisable for personnel in the child care setting who were born after 1956. Once measles has been introduced into the child care or preschool setting, all adults who do not have clear proof of having had measles or of having received two doses of the vaccine should be immunized, especially if born after 1956.

Parental Advice. Parents of children attending a child care center or preschool in which measles has occurred should be immediately notified, and the recommendations for their children, as stated above, should be given to them in written form, and they should be urged to consult their physician immediately. The importance and urgency of this should be stressed, and the contagiousness of measles emphasized. The parents also should understand that children who are susceptible and those who do not comply with the above recommendations will have to be excluded from child care or preschool until the risk of the spread of measles is over, which may mean 4 weeks from the time of the onset of the last case.

Salmonella

Linda A. Waggoner-Fountain

CLINICAL MANIFESTATIONS

Diseases caused by *Salmonella* can be classified into four categories: typhoid fever, enteric fever, focal infection, and diarrheal disease.

Typhoid fever is a multisystem illness that may or may not be associated with diarrhea. Enteric fever is the syndrome of diarrhea and high fever often associated with bacteremia. Following bacteremia, which may or may not be symptomatic, *Salmonella* organisms can localize in virtually any organ of the body and cause focal infection. The most common are meningitis, skeletal infections, urinary tract infections, and gallbladder disease.

Gastrointestinal syndromes take several forms. The most common is a mild to moderately severe diarrhea with mushy or soupy consistency of the stools without abdominal pain, tenesmus, or systemic symptoms. There is no fever or low-grade fever. The illness resolves spontaneously within a few days. When heavily contaminated food is ingested, a food poisoning syndrome ensues that is characterized principally by repeated vomiting for a few hours. On occasion, *Salmonella* causes colitis with a dysentery syndrome identical to that seen with *Shigella*. Finally, a failure-to-thrive syndrome occurs in some young infants who have indolent *Salmonella* enteritis without frank diarrhea.

ETIOLOGIC AGENT

Salmonella organisms are gram-negative enteric bacilli. Typhoid fever syndrome is caused by *Salmonella typhi*, *S. paratyphi A*, *S. paratyphi B*, or *S. choleraesuis*. The other illnesses are caused by any one of several hundred named species of *Salmonella* that sometimes are referred to collectively as *S. enteritidis*. *S. typhimurium* is the most common species causing gastroenteritis.

EPIDEMIOLOGY

Source of the Organism. In typhoid fever the human is the principal reservoir of infection, whereas in other *Salmonella* infections domestic animals, especially chickens, are the reservoir. Pet turtles were a common source of infection until laws were enacted to control the problem. Iguanas, snakes, and other reptiles remain a potential reservoir of infection.

High-Risk Populations. Immunocompromised persons are susceptible to infection after ingesting small numbers of salmonellae that would not cause disease in healthy individuals.

Mode of Spread. Person-to-person spread can occur, but this mode is very unusual except in the case of immunocompromised individuals. The usual source of infection is contaminated food. Eggs and products containing raw eggs are especially high-risk foods. Because healthy individuals are resistant to small numbers of salmonellae, improper cooking and storage of contaminated foods under conditions that promote growth of the organism are important epidemiologic factors. There have been numerous epidemics of *Salmonella* infection from common source-contaminated foods. Person-to-person spread has not been a major problem in child care centers.

Incubation Period. The incubation period is from 6 to 72 hours for gastroenteritis and from 7 to 14 days for typhoid fever.

DIAGNOSIS

Diagnosis of gastroenteritis is by culture of feces. In typhoid fever the organism can be cultured from blood, bone marrow, urine, or feces. Serologic tests for agglutinins to O and H antigens of *S. typhi* are suggestive of the diagnosis if the titer is greater than 1:160 and a fourfold or greater change in titer occurs between acute and convalescent serum specimens.

THERAPY

Fluid and electrolyte therapy are given as needed. Antibiotic therapy is given for typhoid fever for 2 weeks. Antibiotics that are effective when the organism is susceptible in vitro are ampicillin (intravenously), amoxicillin, trimethoprim-sulfamethoxazole (intravenously or orally), cefixime, cefotaxime, ceftriaxone, azithromycin, and ciprofloxacin (for adults). Bacteremia and focal infections caused by nontyphoid fever strains of *Salmonella* are treated with the same antibiotics. The usual case of *Salmonella* gastroenteritis is not treated with antibiotics; exceptions are those patients with an increased risk to progress to invasive disease. Those patients include immunocompromised persons, those with chronic inflammatory bowel disease, patients with hemoglobinopathies, those with dysentery, and young infants with a failure-to-thrive syndrome or less than 3 months of age.

INFECTIOUS PERIOD

Asymptomatic individuals with *Salmonella* colonization often excrete the organisms for many months; this is particularly true of children less than 5 years of age. *Salmonella* infection in child care centers and preschools has not been a problem, probably because the infectious dose of organisms is high.

INFECTION CONTROL

Vaccine.   The live, attenuated oral vaccine is administered as a capsule on days 1, 3, 5, and 7, and is suitable for children >6 years of age. The Vi capsular polysaccharide vaccine is available for parenteral use in children >2 years of age. Both vaccines are given to family members of a typhoid carrier, selected travelers to endemic areas, persons with continued household contact with a documented typhoid fever carrier, selected laboratory workers, and military personnel.

Exclusion from Child Care or Preschool Attendance.   Children should be excluded from child care or preschool attendance until the diarrhea ceases.

Recommendations for Other Children.   There is no action indicated for other children in the child care or preschool setting once one child is known to be infected. Other children with diarrhea should be seen by their physician.

Recommendations for Personnel. There is no action indicated for personnel in the child care or preschool setting once a child is known to be infected other than scrupulous handwashing. Staff members diagnosed with *S. typhi* should not work if symptomatic and should not be involved with food preparation until three consecutive stool cultures are negative for *S. typhi*. If more than one case occurs, public health providers should assist in screening food handlers and potentially infected personnel.

Parental Advice. Parents should be advised that spread of *Salmonella* is extremely unlikely in the child care or preschool setting. If diarrheal symptoms arise, the child should be examined and the stool cultured by his or her health care provider.

56

Scabies

David A. Whiting

CLINICAL MANIFESTATIONS

Scabies causes a severe itch that is usually worse at night. Burrows and vesicles are indicative of mite infestation. Burrows are 5 to 15 mm long and often are curved or S-shaped. They usually occur on wrist flexures, on the ulnar border of the hand, and in fingerwebs. They also involve the elbows, anterior axillary folds, nipples, genitalia, natal cleft, and buttocks. Nodular lesions that contain mites sometimes occur, especially on the buttocks and genitalia. Secondary lesions with small urticarial papules and excoriations and crusts may occur on the abdomen, thighs, and buttocks.

In infants, bullous lesions can occur on the palms and soles. Secondary infection is common, due to group A *Streptococcus pyogenes* or *Staphylococcus aureus*. Nodules can be very persistent. Lesions are rare on the scalp and usually only occur in infants.

ETIOLOGIC AGENT

Scabies is caused by *Sarcoptes scabiei* var. *hominis*. This is a white, hemispherical mite with four pairs of short legs. The average size of the female is 0.3 to 0.4 mm.

EPIDEMIOLOGY

Source of the Organism. The human body is the only known source of this mite.

High-Risk Populations.   Populations at high risk of infection are those in congested housing with overcrowded sleeping quarters. Scabies can be widespread in immunosuppressed individuals or in mentally disabled patients who do not scratch.

Mode of Spread.   Spread is from human to human. The mite can only survive up to a few days off the human body, so spread by bedding and clothing is rare.

Incubation Period.   The incubation period from egg to adult is 14 to 17 days.

DIAGNOSIS

Definitive diagnosis depends on the microscopic demonstration of a scabies mite from a burrow on the skin. Supporting evidence is provided by an intense pruritic dermatosis affecting the wrists, finger-webs, elbows, axillary folds, nipples, buttocks, and genitalia, or palms and soles in infants, and by a history of contact with other cases.

THERAPY

Outpatient therapy is adequate.

The traditional treatment is 1% lindane lotion applied from the neck to the toes for 6 to 8 hours. It can be applied to older children and adults for 8 to 12 hours and to small children for a maximum of 6 hours. Due to possible toxicity to the central nervous system, it should not be used in infants, nor in very sick children, nor in children with inflamed and secondarily infected skin. The treatment should not be repeated in less than 7 days, the 1% strength of lindane should not be exceeded, and as little as possible should be used. A safer and more effective treatment for all ages is 5% permethrin topical cream (Elimite), applied once from head to foot, for 8 to 14 hours. Another safe treatment for small children is 3 to 10% sulfur in Eucerin applied to the whole body from the neck to the toes for 3 successive nights. Normal laundering of clothes and bedding in a domestic washing machine and dryer is all that is required after treatment.

Ivermectin (an antihelmintic), in a single oral dose of 200 mcg/kg, has been found to be effective in treating scabies in various parts of the world.

INFECTIOUS PERIOD

The condition is infectious as long as living mites are present on the patient.

INFECTION CONTROL

Vaccine.   None available.

Exclusion from Child Care or Preschool Attendance.   The child should be isolated until effective treatment has been provided.

Recommendations for Other Children.   Once one child is infected, it is recommended that all children in the center be treated as though infected.

Recommendations for Personnel.   Treatment is recommended for all personnel in the center.

Parental Advice.   Parents and family contacts of an affected child should be treated.

Shigella

Linda A. Waggoner-Fountain

CLINICAL MANIFESTATIONS

The principal illness caused by *Shigella* species is diarrhea. Rare manifestations are bacteremia, hemolytic-uremic syndrome, pneumonia, skeletal infections, meningitis, urinary tract infection, and vaginitis.

There are three clinical syndromes of diarrheal disease caused by *Shigella*. The first is the classic bacillary dysentery syndrome manifested by low-grade or moderate fever, cramping abdominal pain, tenesmus, and frequent small-volume stools containing mucus, fecal leukocytes, and sometimes blood. Untreated with antibiotics, it persists for a week or longer.

The second syndrome is the small bowel diarrheal illness. It is characterized by the abrupt onset of high fever, sometimes associated with a seizure; vomiting one or two times; and large-volume, explosive, watery stools. There is spontaneous cure in 24 to 72 hours.

The third syndrome is the small bowel illness just described progressing to dysentery. During the watery diarrhea phase, one can predict this sequence if leukocytes are seen in microscopic examination of the stool.

ETIOLOGIC AGENT

Shigella is a gram-negative enteric bacillus whose only natural host is the human. There are four species. *S. flexneri* is most common in developing countries, while *S. sonnei* predominates in developed countries. *S. dysenteriae* is uncommon but produces virulent disease often complicated by hemolytic-uremic syndrome. *S. boydii* is rare. There are several serotypes of each of the species except *S. sonnei*.

EPIDEMIOLOGY

Source of the Organism.   Humans. There are no animal reservoirs of *Shigella* infection.

High-Risk Populations.   Crowded, unsanitary conditions and lack of refrigeration for food are risk factors. Child day care populations are a particularly high-risk group. Incidence of disease is also high in institutions for individuals with mental retardation or other disabilities. Sexual transmission can occur, especially with oral-anal contact.

Mode of Spread.   Spread is from person to person by the fecal-oral route either directly or indirectly through contaminated food or fluids. *Shigella* organisms are easily spread by direct fecal-oral contact because the number of organisms needed to produce disease is small. Rodents, flies, and cockroaches have been implicated in the mechanical transfer of organisms. The chronic carrier state is unusual except in malnourished individuals.

Incubation Period.   The interval from ingestion of organisms to onset of symptoms is usually 12 to 48 hours but can be as long as 7 days.

DIAGNOSIS

The diagnosis is based on culture of the organism from feces. There is no rapid antigen detection test available, and there are no useful serologic tests. A stool smear stained with methylene blue may show polymorphonuclear leukocytes or an elevated fecal lactoferrin, which are findings consistent with *Shigella* infection.

THERAPY

Antibiotic therapy of the dysenteric form of illness is effective in shortening the period of morbidity and of infectivity. Antibiotic resistance is common in *Shigella* organisms, so in vitro susceptibility testing is important. Trimethoprim-sulfamethoxazole is most commonly used; other drugs effective when the strain is susceptible in vitro are ampicillin, azithromycin, cefixime, tetracycline, nalidixic acid, and fluoroquinolones. The latter are not approved for use in children. The duration of antibiotic therapy is 5 days. Fluid and electrolyte therapy is accomplished with oral rehydration solutions or intravenous fluids. Antidiarrheal compounds should not be used because they may prolong the clinical and bacteriologic course of disease.

INFECTIOUS PERIOD

Shigella cannot be recovered in stool cultures 1 to 4 days (average, 2 days) after the start of antibiotic therapy. Untreated patients carry the organism for 7 to 30 days and rarely longer than that.

INFECTION CONTROL

Vaccine. There have been many candidate vaccines tested, but no vaccine is available for use.

Exclusion from Child Care or Preschool Attendance. The child should not attend child care or preschool until completion of 5 days of antibiotics or until two successive stool cultures are negative or until the diarrhea and systemic symptoms have resolved.

Recommendations for Other Children and Personnel. No action is required for a single case. If there are multiple cases, stool cultures should be obtained on all symptomatic children and personnel to identify and treat infected individuals. Handwashing practices should be reviewed and improved when necessary.

Parental Advice. Other family members are at risk of becoming infected from children. If diarrhea develops, parents should inform their physician that their child has shigellosis.

58

Staphylococcus
(Impetigo, Boils, Abscess, Cellulitis, Lymphadenitis, Osteomyelitis, Endocarditis)

Stephanie H. Stovall
Richard F. Jacobs

CLINICAL MANIFESTATIONS

Staphylococcal infections (in particular *Staphylococcus aureus*) are commonly associated with diseases of the skin (bullous impetigo, furuncles, or boils), bones and joints (osteomyelitis, septic arthritis), pneumonia, and endocarditis. Staphylococci cause a wide variety of localized suppurative (pus-producing) diseases but also may cause sepsis or toxin-mediated diseases (food poisoning, toxic shock syndrome, and staphylococcal scalded skin syndrome). Skin and soft tissue infection is the most prevalent staphylococcal infection of children in child care centers and preschools. These infections vary in severity from impetigo to furuncles (subcutaneous abscesses), folliculitis (infection of the hair follicles), cellulitis, or wound infections. Staphylococci are also a frequent cause of pyogenic lymphadenitis seen most commonly in the cervical area in children. Respiratory tract infections, including otitis media, sinusitis, and mastoiditis, have variable involvement by staphylococci, but these organisms can cause severe extensive pneumonia.

Staphylococci are the most common cause of osteoarticular infections in children and should be suspected in children with a limp and fever, refusal to walk, and swollen extremities or joints, and in younger children with fever and irritability but no other obvious source of infection. Staphylococcal food poisoning is characterized by the abrupt onset of severe cramps, vomiting, and diarrhea. The short incubation (30 minutes to 7 hours), short duration of illness, epidemiology, and lack of fever help distinguish it from the other causes of food poisoning. Staphylococcal scalded skin syndrome (SSSS) is recognized by exfoliation with cleavage of the stratum granulosum layer of the epidermis. Staphylococcal toxic shock syndrome is an acute febrile illness with hypotension, myalgias, vomiting, diarrhea, pharyngitis, rash (diffuse macular erythro-derma/sunburn appearance with subsequent desquamation), and mucous membrane inflammation.

ETIOLOGIC AGENT

Staphylococcus aureus is a gram-positive coccus that appears in grape-like clusters that grow on most bacteriologic media and produce an enzyme, coagulase, which is important in tissue breakdown and pus formation. The organisms multiply aerobically and anaerobically, are resistant to heating (up to 122°F), drying, and high salt concentrations, and can survive indefinitely on surfaces, in clothing, and on fomites. *S. aureus* is one of three staphylococcal species.

Prior to the late 1990s semi-synthetic penicillin resistance patterns of *S. aureus* isolates were primarily seen in patients with significant health care exposure. Most of these isolates exhibited multiple-class antibiotic resistance. Over the last 5 to 10 years, community-acquired methicillin-resistant *Staphylococcus aureus* (CA-MRSA) has become an increasing concern. In many communities, CA-MRSA has become the leading pathogen in skin and soft tissue infection. Many urban areas now report methicillin resistance rates of CA-MRSA greater than 50% (many even above 70%). In addition to drug resistance, many strains of CA-MRSA encode virulence factors such as the Panton-Valentine leukocidin genes (pvl). These genes allow for production of certain cytotoxins that cause severe tissue necrosis and leukocyte destruction, which likely contributes to overall increases in skin and soft tissue infection rates. CA-MRSA, like health care–associated MRSA, is resis-tant to semisynthetic penicillins (like methicillin) and is also usually resistant to erythromycin. These isolates are usually susceptible to clindamycin and trimethoprim-sulfamethoxazole (TMP-SMX). Some CA-MRSA isolates may encode a small resistance cassette (macrolide-lincosamide-streptogramin B) that confers inducible clindamycin resistance. The current mainstay of outpatient management of patients with CA-MRSA infections includes clindamycin or TMP-SMX. Varying reports of inducible clindamycin resistance from around 4 to 6% (even higher for MSSA isolates) makes this problematic and necessitates culture and susceptibility testing of lesions to avoid antibiotic-discordant therapy.

EPIDEMIOLOGY

Source of the Organism.   Staphylococci are ubiquitous and are found on most environmental surfaces. *Staphylococcus aureus* frequently colonizes the skin and mucous membranes of children and adults. Common sites of colonization include: the anterior nares, throat, axilla, hands (transient), and inflamed skin (desquamating and chronic skin disorders).

High-Risk Populations.   Newborns, immunodeficient children, and children with recent surgical placement of indwelling devices (intravascular catheters, ventriculoperitoneal shunts) are high-risk populations. Crowding, poor hygiene, or inadequate infection control measures are predisposing factors.

Mode of Spread.   Multiple routes: contact with infected persons, contact with asymptomatic carriers, airborne spread, and contact through contaminated objects.

Incubation Period.   Usually 1 to 10 days for skin and soft tissue infections. Other staphylococcal infections may have an incubation period from days to weeks.

DIAGNOSIS

Purulent drainage, bullous lesions, or osteoarticular infection in a child suggests staphylococcal infection. Gram-stained smears of material from suppurative lesions can provide a presumptive diagnosis. Culture of infected material remains the confirmatory test. Due to recent increases in CA-MRSA isolates, susceptibility testing should be done on all isolates.

THERAPY

The severity, extent of involvement, organ system involvement, age of the child, and antibiotic susceptibilities dictate the necessity for hospitalization and parenteral antibiotic therapy. For superficial infections, aggressive local care and topical antibiotics may be sufficient. Abscesses should be surgically drained. The mainstay of antistaphylococcal therapy remains antibiotics. Most mild to moderate staphylococcal infections can be treated with 7 to 10 days of oral antibiotics. The site of infection in serious staphylococcal disease (pneumonia, endocarditis) dictates the duration of intravenous therapy. The identification of invasive MRSA or disseminated infection may require intravenous vancomycin therapy.

INFECTIOUS PERIOD

Patients with draining staphylococcal lesions should be isolated for 48 hours after starting effective therapy and until the active drainage has diminished. Due to the increasing prevalence of CA-MRSA colonization, isolation for carriage alone is not practical. Thorough hand hygiene should be emphasized.

INFECTION CONTROL

Vaccine.   None available.

Exclusion from Child Care or Preschool Attendance.   The child with staphylococcal infection should not attend child care or preschool for at least 48 hours after the initiation of appropriate antibiotics and until drainage of infected material has stopped or diminished to the point that barrier protection is effective.

Recommendations for Other Children.   The best recommendation is prevention of spread. This includes proper disinfection procedures, good handwashing, avoidance of open infected wounds, improved hygiene, and reduced crowding. Children with any sign of early staphylococcal infection should be referred to their pediatrician. In situations of multiple cases (outbreak), all infected children should be referred to their pediatrician, and consideration of temporary closure of the facility should be discussed until the infections are controlled. This should also involve local experts and public health officials. In an MRSA outbreak, cohorting and good handwashing are critical.

Recommendations for Personnel.   The involved personnel should implement contact isolation, improved handwashing, and early recognition and treatment of infected children. No routine cultures or antibiotic therapy (oral or topical) is indicated for contacts unless an epidemic occurs.

Parental Advice.   Parents should institute close observation for early signs of staphylococcal infection with prompt recognition and treatment. Symptomatic children or relatively asymptomatic children with clinical evidence of staphylococcal disease should be taken to their local pediatrician for diagnosis and therapy.

59

Streptococcus
(Cellulitis, Impetigo, Pharyngitis)

Stephanie H. Stovall
Richard F. Jacobs

CLINICAL MANIFESTATIONS

The most common illnesses associated with group A beta hemolytic streptococci (GABHS) are pharyngitis and impetigo. Pharyngitis varies greatly in severity from subclinical (30 to 50%) to severe, with high fever, nausea, vomiting, and collapse (less than 10%). The onset is acute, with sore throat, fever, headache, or abdominal pain. The pharynx and tonsils usually appear red and swollen with exudate (50 to 90%) and palatal petechiae. Exudate usually appears around day 2, is whitish-yellow, and appears early as discrete patches with progression to confluence. Swollen, tender cervical lymph nodes are found in 40 to 60% of cases. Clinical manifestations usually subside spontaneously in 3 to 5 days unless suppurative complications (peritonsillar abscess) occur. An infantile form (children less than 3 years of age) may occur with GABHS and is more prolonged with persistent purulent nasal discharge, fever, and lymphadenopathy. Nonsuppurative complications may occur in approximately 10 days (nephritis) to 18 days (acute rheumatic fever). Scarlet fever represents a manifestation of GABHS, with a red papular rash on the trunk, spreading peripherally within several hours to days. The typical "sandpaper" rash fades on pressure, usually desquamates, has petechiae in joint folds (Pastia's lines), and is associated with a strawberry tongue and red swollen lips. Scarlet fever occurs commonly with pharyngitis, but may also occur with GABHS skin infection. This presentation should trigger the consideration of Kawasaki's syndrome in the clinical differential diagnosis.

A scarlatiniform rash also may accompany impetigo, the most common cutaneous manifestation of GABHS. Impetiginous lesions most commonly occur over excoriated areas, such as insect bites, where GABHS is introduced into normal skin. The skin lesions usually start as superficial vesicles or erythematous pustules and progress to thick yellowish crusted lesions that last from days to several weeks. Fever or constitutional symptoms rarely accompany impetigo. Secondary infection with staphylococci is common and may lead to purulent pustules or cellulitis. This type of superficial pyoderma may complicate abnormal skin (eczema) or follow trauma or burns. Glomerulonephritis is the most common nonsuppurative complication and has a latent period of around 3 weeks.

Other infections associated with GABHS include more serious skin infections (cellulitis, erysipelas), otitis media, sinusitis, pneumonia, perianal cellulitis, vaginitis, and invasive disease (streptococcal toxic shock syndrome, necrotizing fasciitis; usually following varicella-zoster virus [VZV] infection).

ETIOLOGIC AGENT

GABHS are gram-positive cocci that form chains that produce clear hemolysis (beta) on blood agar plates. Presumptive differentiation from other streptococci can be provided by GABHS susceptibility (inhibition) to a bacitracin disc on blood agar. More than 80 different types of GABHS are known. They are separated on the basis of different serologically distinct surface proteins, M proteins. Some GABHS strains are known to be rheumatogenic and cause outbreaks of acute rheumatic fever; others have been associated with invasive disease.

EPIDEMIOLOGY

Source of the Organism.   Upper respiratory tract and skin lesions are the most common source of GABHS. Cases of invasive GABHS disease in close contacts of patients with invasive disease have been reported. Contaminated food or milk has caused some outbreaks, and anal carriage has been linked to several hospital outbreaks. Recent evidence indicates that children in day care centers are colonized with GABHS at an earlier age. Reports of several outbreaks of GABHS in day care centers have recently been published.

High-Risk Populations.   Crowding, poor hygiene, and improper handling of infected children are associated with the greatest risk of transmission and predisposition to GABHS disease. Children with diagnosed acute rheumatic fever are a high-risk population for acquisition and recurrences. Children with VZV infection are pre-disposed to invasive GABHS disease.

Mode of Spread.   Close contact with an infected individual by direct projection of large respiratory droplets (not aerosols) or physical transfer of respiratory secretions or infected skin lesions.

Incubation Period.   Streptococcal pharyngitis: 12 hours to 4 days. Streptococcal impetigo: few days to several weeks (usually around 10 days). Invasive GABHS disease: few days to a week (case reports).

DIAGNOSIS

The clinical appearance and epidemiology should provide the caretaker with a high degree of suspicion. Culture of the tonsillo-pharyngeal bed or infected skin lesions with the isolation of GABHS is confirmatory. Due to the time frame for this procedure, a number of rapid detection kits for identifying GABHS pharyngitis in min-utes to hours have been developed. Caution should be used in interpreting negative tests for purposes of treatment in areas where rheumatic fever is prevalent. Cultures should be obtained on these cases to confirm a negative rapid test.

THERAPY

The therapy for GABHS pharyngitis is antibiotics; penicillin is the drug of choice. It is usually given as a single intramuscular injection of long-acting penicillin or oral penicillin three or four times a day for 10 full days. Amoxicillin suspension given in daily or twice daily doses is often preferred to penicillin suspension because of taste. Erythromycin given four times a day for 10 days or azithromycin given daily for 5 days are alternative regimens for penicillin-allergic children. Reports of GABHS resistant to erythromycin warrant consideration in treatment failures. Most treatment failures likely result from non-compliance as opposed to bacteriologic failure. Neither sulfonamides nor tetracyclines should be used for the treatment of GABHS infections because of resistance and failure to eradicate the organisms from the respiratory tract. For GABHS impetigo, local care with abrasive cleansing of lesions is effective. Oral penicillin or an antistaphylococcal antibiotic may be beneficial in children with numerous lesions. Hospitalization is only required for suppurative (peritonsillar abscess, cellulitis, erysipelas) or non-suppurative complications. The current recommendation for treatment of invasive GABHS disease is the combination of penicillin plus clindamycin.

INFECTIOUS PERIOD

The period of maximal infectivity is in the acute phase of the illness with most secondary cases occurring within 2 weeks of acquisition.

INFECTION CONTROL

Vaccine.   None available. However, immunization with VZV vaccine can reduce the risk of varicella-associated invasive GABHS disease.

Exclusion from Child Care or Preschool Attendance.   At least until afebrile and 24 hours after appropriate therapy is started.

Recommendations for Other Children.   The best current control measure is prompt recognition and treatment of GABHS infections. The best current control measure for invasive GABHS disease is immunization with VZV vaccine.

Contacts with recent or current clinical evidence of GABHS infection should be cultured and treated if culture-positive to reduce transmission and nonsuppurative complications. Siblings do have a higher acquisition rate (up to 50%).

No data are available to allow for a recommendation about the usefulness of throat cultures or antigen detection tests in identifying contacts at increased risk for invasive GABHS disease. Because the risk of streptococcal infection in contacts is low, chemoprophylaxis is not routinely recommended in families, schools, or child care facilities. However, some experts have encouraged consideration of chemoprophylaxis for persons with other risk factors for severe GABHS disease (human immunodeficiency virus, age >65 years, diabetes mellitus) who are or have been in close contact with patients with severe invasive GABHS disease. In these cases, rifampin plus intramuscular benzathine penicillin or a 10-day course of a second-generation cephalosporin or clindamycin has been shown to be more effective than penicillin in eradicating GABS from the pharynx of chronic carriers.

Recommendations for Personnel. In nonepidemic situations, only symptomatic personnel should be cultured and treated if positive. Screening asymptomatic children or personnel, especially in nonepidemic situations, is not warranted. In epidemics or in family situations in which a child has acute rheumatic fever, selective cultures of contacts may be warranted.

Parental Advice. If the child becomes symptomatic, he or she should be taken to the local pediatrician for culture and treatment if positive. If the child has a previous diagnosis of acute rheumatic fever and a history of close contact with a proven GABHS patient, he or she should be taken to the local pediatrician for culture and initiation of prophylactic antibiotics to prevent recurrences of rheumatic fever. Children should be immunized with VZV vaccine.

Syphilis
(*Treponema pallidum*)

Michael F. Rein

CLINICAL MANIFESTATIONS

Syphilis is an extremely protean and complex disease. It may be encountered in two forms in the day care center or preschool: congenital and acquired. Early congenital syphilis usually manifests during the first 3 months of life and includes generalized rash, which may be bullous and often involves the palms and soles; hepatomegaly or hepatosplenomegaly; generalized lymphadenopathy; or meningitis. Of particular public health importance are "snuffles," a chronic nasal discharge, and mucous patches, which are painless ulcers inside the mouth. Both contain large numbers of organisms and are highly contagious. Warty lesions, called *condyloma lata*, may develop around the anus or vagina. Late congenital syphilis is not contagious and presents with a variety of skeletal lesions, including frontal bossing, sabre shins, saddle nose, or notching of the secondary incisors. One may also see interstitial keratitis; inflammation of the corneas, which appears between the ages of 5 and 16; and mild to moderate nerve deafness.

Acquired syphilis results from contact, usually sexual, with an infected lesion. Infected patients develop a painless chancre at the point of inoculation, the exact site of which depends on the practice that resulted in infection. Secondary syphilis occurs weeks to months later and consists initially of a nonspecific febrile illness followed by a generalized, relatively indolent rash and generalized lymphadenopathy. There may be patchy hair loss and mucous patches. The dry skin lesions are not contagious, but the mucous patches contain large numbers of organisms and can spread infection. Secondary syphilis may also present as hepatitis or nephritis. Primary and secondary syphilis resolve without specific treatment, but the patient remains infected. Intercurrent antibiotic therapy for other infections may modify or completely mask the clinical manifestations of syphilis.

ETIOLOGIC AGENT

Treponema pallidum is a spirochete that does not survive in the environment. It can penetrate mucous membranes and even intact-appearing skin, and it remains highly sensitive to many antibiotics.

EPIDEMIOLOGY

Source of the Organism. The fetus can be infected by spirochetes passing through the placenta from the maternal circulation. Newborns may also acquire the organism from mothers during delivery. In older children, acquisition is almost exclusively sexual.

High-Risk Populations. Syphilis in pregnant women, and hence congenital syphilis, is usually associated with youth, poverty, and psychosocial problems. Older children with syphilis tend to come from similar backgrounds, and/or have been sexually abused by infected persons.

Mode of Spread. Acquisition of the organism after birth requires direct contact with infectious material. Thus older children with acquired syphilis must be evaluated for sexual abuse. However, the organism may be transmitted in blood and by some of the lesions of secondary syphilis, such as mucous patches of the mouth.

Incubation Period. The incubation period of acquired syphilis is usually 10 to 21 days but may extend to 90 days.

DIAGNOSIS

Syphilis is subclinical or latent during much of its course, and thus diagnosis usually depends on testing for antibodies using nontreponemal blood tests (e.g., rapid plasma reagin [RPR]), with positives confirmed by treponemal tests (e.g., fluorescent treponemal antibody absorption [FTA-ABS], microhemagglutination test for *T. pallidum* [MHA-Tp], and *T. pallidum* particle agglutination [TP-PA]). Diagnosis in the newborn is more complicated, because maternal antibody acquired transplacentally may obscure the infant's immune response for several months. Organisms in chancres, condylomata lata, mucous patches, and the infected nasal secretions of newborns may be visualized with darkfield microscopy.

THERAPY

Penicillin remains effective treatment for congenital or acquired syphilis. Infants with congenital syphilis require either procaine penicillin, 50,000 units/kg intramuscularly once daily for 10 days, or aqueous crystalline penicillin G (APG), in a regimen approximating 50,000 units/kg intravenously three times daily for 10 days. Hospitalization is required for intravenous therapy of congenital syphilis and is usually indicated for intramuscular therapy. Hospitalization may also be indicated for management of sexually abused children. Older children should be treated with APG, 50,000 units intravenously every 4 to 6 hours for 10 days. Children with acquired syphilis may be treated with benzathine penicillin G, 50,000 units/kg intramuscularly, up to a total single dose of 2.4 million units. The treatment of persons allergic to penicillin is complex and should be undertaken in consultation with an expert.

Congenital syphilis should be considered a "sentinel health event" that indicates a breakdown of health care for the family. Acquired syphilis must be evaluated as sexual abuse.

INFECTIOUS PERIOD

The infected person is no longer contagious within 24 hours of receiving effective treatment. Without therapy, the period of contagiousness may last for months.

INFECTION CONTROL

Vaccine.   None available.

Exclusion from Child Care or Preschool Attendance. The child may return to day care the day after being given effective treatment.

Recommendations for Other Children. The risk of nonsexual transmission to other children is low, but real. If the child acquired infection elsewhere and has been treated, no further measures for control of infection are necessary. The child, however, may be at risk of emotional and behavioral problems.

Recommendations for Personnel. Careful handwashing is essential. The risk of transmission to personnel is low but real.

Parental Advice. If the infection was not acquired at the child care center or preschool, other parents should not be informed, because the infection is stigmatizing, and the risk of transmission is extremely low. Detection of the infection may have forensic implications for the child care center or preschool.

61

Tinea Capitis, Corporis, Cruris, and Pedis
(Ringworm, Athlete's Foot, Jock Itch)

David A. Whiting

CLINICAL MANIFESTATIONS

Tinea capitis: This condition causes partial hair loss. Patches vary from well-circumscribed, round lesions to vague and irregular areas of hair thinning that are difficult to detect. Redness and scaling may be present and can range from mild to severe. In the United States, affected hairs are generally broken off flush with the scalp and appear as black dots when due to infection by *Trichophyton tonsurans*, but occasionally are grayish-white and are broken off 1 to 3 mm above the skin surface when due to *Microsporum canis* infection. Inflammatory types of scalp ringworm sometimes cause fluctuant, boggy, purulent masses associated with hair loss, a so-called kerion infection. The incidence of tinea capitis is equal in males and females. Tinea capitis peaks at age 5 and usually disappears at puberty, although black-dot ringworm and favus can affect adults.

Tinea corporis: This condition usually starts as small, reddish, itchy, scaly macules that gradually expand outward, clearing in the middle, forming annular lesions with scaly margins and clear centers. Sometimes, new lesions form in the middle of an expanding lesion and spread outward to cause concentric rings. The lesions are usually single but, if multiple, are often unilateral or at least asymmetrical.

Tinea cruris: This condition is rare before puberty. It causes itchy, reddish, and scaly lesions in the groin and on the adjacent thighs, and may extend around the anus onto the buttocks, with advancing scaly borders and central clearing. Some types of tinea cruris, especially those due to *Trichophyton rubrum*, may produce large, circinate lesions around the genitalia.

Tinea pedis: This condition is also rare before puberty. There are three types; namely, the interdigital, the vesicular, and the moccasin. The interdigital type usually starts in the lateral toe webs and spreads medially, and the vesicular type generally affects the instep. The lesions are usually unilateral and asymmetrical, except for the moccasin type of tinea pedis in which both feet are affected by a diffuse, scaling rash. Tinea pedis is aggravated by heat and sweating.

ETIOLOGIC AGENT

Tinea infections are caused by one or more of the dermatophytes, which are imperfect fungi (phylum Deuteromycetes) belonging to genera *Trichophyton*, *Microsporum*, and *Epidermophyton*. Infection is confined to keratin, the dead horn of skin, hair, and nails. At present, 39 species of dermatophytes are recognized in humans: 21 in the genus *Trichophyton*, 16 in the genus *Microsporum*, and 2 in the genus *Epidermophyton*. Almost all human infections are caused by 16 species, only 5 of which are common in the United States; namely, *T. rubrum*, *T. tonsurans*, *T. mentagrophytes*, *E. floccosum*, and *M. canis*. Infrequent causes of disease are *T. schoenleinii*, *T. violaceum*, *T. verrucosum*, *T. megninii*, *T. terrestre*, *M. audouinii*, *M. distortum*, *M. gypseum*, *M. ferrugineum*, *M. nanum*, or *M. fulvum*.

EPIDEMIOLOGY

Source of the Organism. Anthropophilic (human): *T. tonsurans*, *M. audouinii*, *T. rubrum*, and *E. floccosum*. Zoophilic (animals): *M. canis*, *T. mentagrophytes*, and *T. verrucosum*. Geophilic (soil): *M. gypseum*. Patterns of infection in tinea capitis: small-spore ectothrix: *M. audouinii*, *M. canis*, and *M. ferrugineum*; large-spore ectothrix: *T.*

mentagrophytes (interdigitale), *T. verrucosum*, and *T. megninii*; endothrix: *T. tonsurans*, *T. violaceum*, *T. soudanense*, *T. gourvilii*, and *T. yaoundei*. Favic pattern in hair (no spores): *T. schoenleinii*.

High-Risk Populations.   Children especially, aged 2 to 20 years. Overcrowding with head-to-head contact predisposes to tinea capitis. Contact with cattle and horses can result in animal ringworm.

Mode of Spread.   Tinea is spread by direct contact with humans, animals, or soil or by indirect contact with contaminated combs, brushes, headgear, towels, pillows, bedding, or clothing.

Incubation Period.   It takes 3 to 5 days for microscopic infection and 2 to 3 weeks for clinical manifestations to develop. The condition can spread for 3 to 4 months, and then after a refractory period, spontaneous regression may occur.

DIAGNOSIS

The diagnosis is made on the clinical appearance; positive Wood's light in some cases of tinea capitis; microscopic demonstration of fungal hyphae in potassium hydroxide preparations of skin, hair, and nails; and fungal culture.

THERAPY

All treatment is managed on an outpatient basis.

Tinea capitis: The preferred treatment is griseofulvin taken orally in a dose of 20 mg/kg body weight daily for 6 to 12 weeks. Second-choice therapy is ketoconazole, 3.3 to 6.6 mg/kg body weight for 6 to 12 weeks. Oral itraconazole, fluconazole, and terbinafine are other effective therapies. Itraconazole is given as pulse therapy at a dose of 5 mg/kg/day for 1 week with 2 weeks off between two or three consecutive pulses. Fluconazole is given at a dose of 8 mg/kg once a week for 8 to 12 weeks. Terbinafine can be given in a dose of 10 mg/kg/day for 4 weeks. To prevent cross infection, clip the affected hairs and shampoo with selenium sulfide 2.5% twice weekly, or apply a topical antifungal preparation, as for tinea corporis, daily.

Tinea corporis: Topical clotrimazole (Lotrimin), econazole (Spectazole), ketoconazole (Nizoral), miconazole nitrate (Monistat-Derm), oxiconazole (Oxistat), sulconazole (Exelderm), naftifine (Naftin), butenafine (Mentax), terbinafine (Lamisil), or ciclopirox olamine (Loprox) can be used once or twice daily. A salicylic acid and benzoic acid combination (Antinea) can be used. In severe cases, oral griseofulvin, terbinafine, or itraconazole (see above) can be used for 2 to 4 weeks.

Tinea pedis: In the inflammatory stage, soaks with Burow's solution or potassium permanganate solution can be used. The fungal infection can be treated topically as for tinea corporis, and undecylenate powder (Desenex) can be sprinkled in the socks. Oral griseofulvin, itraconazole (Sporanox), or terbinafine may be necessary (see above).

Tinea cruris: Topical antifungal therapy as for tinea corporis. In addition, oral griseofulvin or terbinafine may be necessary in extensive cases.

INFECTIOUS PERIOD

The patient is infectious as long as organisms can be found invading the tissue on potassium hydroxide examination or culture. Tinea capitis may persist from 3 months to several years. Tinea corporis may persist or recur for many years, as may tinea cruris or tinea pedis.

INFECTION CONTROL

Vaccine. None available.

Exclusion from Child Care or Preschool Attendance. No isolation needed after effective treatment is started.

Recommendations for Other Children. Watch for development of infection and treat if necessary.

Recommendations for Personnel. Watch for development of infection and treat if necessary.

Parental Advice. Parents should be notified that there has been a case or cases of tinea in the center. They should watch for the development of infection and seek medical attention for diagnosis and therapy as necessary.

62

Toxocara

Jonathan P. Moorman

CLINICAL MANIFESTATIONS

The clinical manifestations of toxocariasis depend on the size of the infecting dose of larvae. Individuals who ingest small numbers of larvae may remain asymptomatic, while those ingesting large numbers may develop visceral larva migrans. Characteristic findings in visceral larva migrans include fever, hepatomegaly, eosinophilia, and hypergammaglobulinemia. A cough, wheezing, and pulmonary infiltrates may also be present, and, rarely, myocarditis or encephalitis may develop. *Toxocara* larvae may invade the eye, producing retinal granulomas or endophthalmitis and occasionally resulting in blindness. Ocular larva migrans is not characterized by hepatomegaly and eosinophilia, and visceral and ocular larva migrans are rarely observed concurrently.

ETIOLOGIC AGENT

Toxocariasis is caused by *Toxocara canis* and *Toxocara cati*, common roundworms of dogs and cats; the majority of cases in this country are due to *T. canis*. Less often, visceral larva migrans can be caused by infection with other helminths. Dogs and cats are commonly infected by *Toxocara* spp., with most having acquired the infection early in life. Infected animals harbor adult worms that pass eggs in the feces. After several weeks of embryonation in soil, infective larvae develop within the eggs. Humans acquire toxocariasis by ingesting embryonated eggs that hatch in the small intestine, releasing larvae. After penetrating the intestinal wall, the larvae begin to migrate throughout host tissues. The larvae cannot complete their normal development in humans, and therefore they do not mature into adult worms capable of passing eggs in human feces. After a variable period of migration, the larvae within a human host will eventually die.

EPIDEMIOLOGY

Source of the Organism. *Toxocara* infections occur in both temperate and tropical areas, being most prevalent where dogs are common and hygiene is poor. Eggs passed in dog and cat feces become infective in approximately 3 weeks and may persist in the environment for months. Parks and playgrounds are often heavily contaminated, providing a ready source of infective eggs. Ingestion of even small amounts of dirt may result in the transmission of relatively large numbers of eggs.

High-Risk Populations. Children less than 6 years of age are at higher risk of acquiring toxocariasis because they are more likely to eat dirt and to contaminate their hands and food with soil.

Mode of Spread. Humans acquire *Toxocara* infections by ingesting soil containing infective eggs. Transmission is generally the result of geophagia in young children and of exposure to hands or possibly food contaminated with infective eggs in older children. Since humans do not pass *Toxocara* eggs in their feces, person-to-person transmission of the infection does not occur.

Incubation Period. The time interval between acquisition of infection and the development of visceral larva migrans appears to be quite variable, ranging from days to months. Although not well established, the incubation period prior to the development of ocular larva migrans appears to be longer, ranging from months to years.

DIAGNOSIS

Visceral larva migrans should be considered in any child with a history of geophagia or exposure to dogs who presents with hypereosinophilia and hypergammaglobulinemia. Elevated titers of isohemagglutinins to the A and B blood group antigens are also often present in toxocariasis. The diagnosis can be confirmed by demonstration of larvae in a liver biopsy; however, the larvae may be difficult to find, and a negative liver biopsy does not rule out the diagnosis. An enzyme-linked immunosorbent assay, available at the Centers for Disease Control and Prevention, can be used to establish a serologic diagnosis.

THERAPY

To date, no controlled studies have proved the effectiveness of any therapeutic regimen against toxocariasis. However, treatment with diethylcarbamazine (6 mg/kg/day in 3 doses for 7 to 10 days) has been reported to decrease symptoms in some patients. Mebendazole (100 to 200 mg twice a day for 3 to 5 days) has also been used to treat toxocariasis and appears to be associated with fewer adverse effects. Albendazole also can be used (400 mg orally twice a day for 3 to 5 days). These drugs are considered investigational for this condition by the U.S. Food and Drug Administration, and it is unclear whether treatment may actually worsen the disease. Corticosteroids have also been used in individuals with significant involvement of the heart or central nervous system. Optimal therapy for ocular larva migrans has not been well established; past approaches have included the use of antihelmintic agents and corticosteroids.

INFECTIOUS PERIOD

Humans with toxocariasis are not infectious.

INFECTION CONTROL

Vaccine.   None available.

Exclusion from Child Care or Preschool Attendance.   A child with toxocariasis cannot transmit the infection to other individuals and therefore does not need to be kept out of any child care or preschool setting.

Recommendations for Other Children.   Other children in the center will acquire toxocariasis only if they ingest soil containing infective eggs. Given the high prevalence of infective eggs in most communities, children should not be allowed to eat dirt, and good hygiene should be enforced.

Recommendations for Personnel. Personnel should minimize their exposure to infective *Toxocara* eggs by maintaining good hygienic practices. They should also attempt to diminish children's exposure by not letting them eat dirt and by covering play areas such as sandboxes in order to prevent animals from defecating in them.

Parental Advice. Parents should be reassured that a child with toxocariasis will not transmit the infection to their own children. The mode of spread should be explained to them, emphasizing the need to keep their children from eating dirt and to properly dispose of cat and dog feces. Pet owners should be encouraged to seek expert advice from a veterinarian regarding treatment of puppies and kittens with appropriate antihelmintics to avoid exposing their children to *Toxocara*. In addition, dogs and especially puppies should be periodically examined for the presence of helminths.

Trichuris trichiura
(Whipworm)

Jonathan P. Moorman

CLINICAL MANIFESTATIONS

The clinical manifestations associated with *Trichuris trichiura* infections depend on the intensity and duration of the infection and on the age of the host. Light infections are generally asymptomatic. Heavy infections, most often seen in young children, may be associated with malnutrition, mild anemia, diffuse colitis, chronic diarrhea, and rectal prolapse. Stunted growth of children can occur with even moderate infections.

ETIOLOGIC AGENT

T. trichiura is an intestinal nematode also known as the human whipworm. Humans acquire trichuriasis by ingesting infective-stage ova derived from human feces. The eggs hatch in the small intestine, and the larvae mature into adult worms and attach to the superficial mucosa of the cecum and ascending colon, where they can survive for 5 years. Female worms produce eggs that are passed in the feces; if exposed to favorable conditions of soil, moisture, and temperature, the eggs embryonate, developing into infective-stage ova within 11 to 30 days. Eggs that have not embryonated are not infective.

EPIDEMIOLOGY

Source of the Organism. Although *T. trichiura* infections are found worldwide, they are most prevalent in the tropics, particularly in overcrowded communities with poor sanitation. Infective-stage eggs are found in soil contaminated with human feces, and infection may result from direct ingestion of soil or indirectly through contaminated hands, utensils, or food.

High-Risk Populations. In areas where *T. trichiura* is endemic, children are often infected by the time they are 2 years old, and reinfection is common. Infection of young children is often a consequence of geophagia, whereas older children and adults are more likely to be infected through indirect contamination by flies and insects.

Mode of Spread. Transmission occurs through ingestion of infective eggs. Since *T. trichiura* eggs are not infective until after they have embryonated in the soil, person-to-person transmission of the infection does not occur.

Incubation Period. The interval between the acquisition of *T. trichiura* and the passage of eggs in the feces is approximately 30 to 90 days. The time from infection to the development of symptoms has not been well established.

DIAGNOSIS

The diagnosis can be made fairly easily by microscopic stool examination with detection of the characteristic eggs. In symptomatic individuals it may be important to quantitate the intensity of the worm burden, since significant symptoms are rarely associated with light *T. trichiura* infections and may indicate the presence of other pathogenic processes. Adult worms may be seen on proctoscopy or during rectal prolapse in heavy infections. Eosinophilia is rare.

THERAPY

In countries where trichuriasis is endemic and where reinfection is common, light infections are often untreated. However, in this country, *T. trichiura* infections are generally treated with mebendazole given in an oral dose of 100 mg twice daily for 3 days or 500 mg once. Although mebendazole appears to be fairly effective with low toxicity, data regarding its use in children younger than 2 years are limited. Albendazole is an alternative therapy and is given at a dose of 400 mg once. Heavy infestation may require extension of treatment to 3 days, but this medication is considered investigational for this condition.

INFECTIOUS PERIOD

If untreated, trichuriasis may persist for many years.

INFECTION CONTROL

Vaccine.   None available.

Exclusion from Child Care or Preschool Attendance.   Children with trichuriasis do not need to be isolated or kept out of any child care setting. Human-to-human transmission does not appear to occur, and *T. trichiura* eggs are not immediately infectious when passed in feces.

Recommendations for Other Children.   Other children in the center will become infected with *T. trichiura* only if they ingest eggs that have embryonated after several weeks in the soil. If fecal contamination of the environment is a problem in the center, children must be kept from ingesting infected dirt either directly or indirectly through contaminated hands or food.

Recommendations for Personnel.   Inadvertent contamination of food, utensils, and hands with soil containing infective eggs should be avoided. Personnel should maintain good handwashing practices and ensure the appropriate disposal of fecal material.

Parental Advice.   The mode of spread should be explained to parents, reassuring them that person-to-person transmission does not occur. In *T. trichiura* endemic areas, the need to discourage geophagia among young children and to encourage good hygiene among older children should be emphasized to parents.

64

Tuberculosis

Jane D. Siegel

CLINICAL MANIFESTATIONS

Approximately 40 to 50% of infections in infants less than 1 year of age, and 80 to 90% of infections in older children will cause no recognizable symptoms or merely a low-grade fever. This is referred to now as "latent tuberculosis" or previously as "tuberculous infection." Symptomatic disease may develop within a few weeks of the initial infection or many years later when the body's normal immune system becomes suppressed either by another disease process or by chemotherapeutic agents used to treat the disease (e.g., human immunodeficiency virus [HIV] infection, leukemia, tumors, bone marrow, or organ transplant). The presence of active disease in one or more organs is referred to as "active tuberculosis." Overall, only 5 to 15% of patients with latent tuberculosis will become ill with active tuberculosis. Pulmonary disease is the most common manifestation of tuberculous infection. Children with primary pulmonary tuberculosis have fever, cough, poor appetite, weight loss, and occasionally wheezing. Enlarged hilar and sometimes paratracheal lymph nodes and small focal or lobar infiltrates are present on chest x-ray. Some children may have persistent fever, weight loss, and night sweats without a cough, but pulmonary infiltrates are present on chest x-ray. Infants and young children usually do not have the more classic cavitary lesions that are observed in adolescents and adults. Infection of the cervical lymph nodes (scrofula) is another early form of disease caused by *Mycobacterium tuberculosis*.

Less frequently, the mycobacteria may spread from the original site of infection in the lungs through the lymphatic system and bloodstream to other organs and cause "extrapulmonary" tuberculosis. The clinical picture that results is determined by host susceptibility and by the quantity of mycobacteria that are released. The most serious complications of tuberculosis are miliary tuberculosis and meningitis, both of which occur at 3 to 6 months following the initial infection. The onset of miliary disease may be insidious or abrupt with a rapid progression of respiratory symptoms and multiple organ involvement. The chest x-ray pattern of uniform distribution throughout both lung fields is diagnostic. Meningitis develops in approximately 1 of every 300 primary infections. Children 4 months to 6 years of age are at greatest risk for this complication. There is a high case fatality rate, and many serious neurologic sequelae occur in the survivors if tuberculous meningitis is not recognized and treated early. The case fatality rate increases with the more advanced stages of disease at the time of initiation of antituberculous therapy. Other sites of disease that may occur at least 7 to 12 months after initial infection include bones and joints, most notably the vertebrae (Pott's disease), peritoneal/intraabdominal kidneys, genital tract, eyes, and skin. Delayed recognition and treatment of these later complications may lead to chronic failure to gain weight and to deformities. These more extensive types of disease can be prevented by treatment of asymptomatic tuberculous infection or early pulmonary disease.

ETIOLOGIC AGENT

The agent that causes tuberculosis is *Mycobacterium tuberculosis*, often referred to as "M. TB" or the "tubercle bacillus." This mycobacterium is identified presumptively during light microscopic examination of body fluids that have been stained with special dyes by its "acid-fast" character and appearance as a red rod. This organism is slow growing and requires up to 6 weeks of incubation on traditional culture media before it can be isolated and identified definitively by its biochemical reactions. Automated systems (e.g., BACTEC) may allow isolation after only 1 to 2 weeks of incubation. Several different strains of *M. tuberculosis* have been distinguished by molecular typing. There are reports of the presence of two distinct molecular types in the same individual. Isolation of the infecting organism is important to allow in vitro susceptibility testing. During the 1980s, the rate of resistance to isoniazid (INH) had been approximately 7% in the United States overall but may be as high as 13 to 60% in patients who come from areas of the world (e.g., Mexico, Southeast Asia) where tuberculosis is endemic and antituberculous drugs are given frequently for an inadequate length of time. Since 1990, multi-drug resistance (MDR) has become a major concern in the United States. In 1992, a survey in New York City found resistance to one drug to be 33% and resistance to both INH and rifampin to be 19%. Nationally, 14.4% of strains were resistant to at least one drug, and 3.3% were resistant to both INH and rifampin, the most effective medicines available. However, in 1998 resistance to INH decreased to 8.2% and to both INH and rifampin to 1.1% and remained at that level in 1999 to 2000. In 1998, 49% of the MDR strains came from New York and California. The proportion of MDR TB cases occurring in foreign-born persons increased from 31% in 1993 to 72% in 2000. Case fatality rates of 70 to 90% have been associated with U.S. outbreaks of MDR disease. Within each patient, there are several different populations of organisms. Because of the varying rates of multiplication and conditions of pH, nutrient supply, etc., combination of two or more drugs is required for effective therapy. Although resistance in the United States has not increased, various resistance patterns have emerged in different areas of the world. Thus, a travel history is critical in determining the optimal combination of drugs before susceptibility testing becomes available.

EPIDEMIOLOGY

Source of the Organism.　The reservoir of *M. tuberculosis* for the child is the infected adult. Continued close contact of children with untreated adults in poorly ventilated rooms provides the greatest opportunity for transmission of infection. Although *Mycobacterium bovis* may cause disease in animals, it very rarely causes infection and illness in humans in the United States. This distinction is important because *M. bovis* is resistant to pyrazinamide. Dogs are susceptible to the human type of tubercle bacillus, but there is little evidence to support a role for dogs in the transmission of tuberculous infection to children.

High-Risk Populations.　The following factors are associated with an increased risk of development of active tuberculosis: (a) age (less than 5 years, adolescence, elderly), (b) immunosuppression associated with primary disease or chemotherapy, (c) poor nutrition, (d) weight loss, (e) poorly controlled diabetes mellitus, (f) chronic renal failure, (g) silicosis, (h) intravenous drug use, (i) ethnic groups with high rates of endemic tuberculosis (e.g., Southeast Asians, Hispanics, Haitians, Indians, and Alaskan Eskimos), (j) the homeless, and (k) health care workers. The most important risk factor for the development of active tuberculosis is the presence of HIV infection and acquired immunodeficiency syndrome (AIDS). There is a nearly 200-fold increase in the risk of active disease in patients with far advanced AIDS. Active tuberculosis occurs early in the course of AIDS and may be the illness that leads to the diagnosis of AIDS in many adults.

Children younger than 5 years of age and especially infants in the first year of life have a reduced ability to limit spread of the initial tuberculous infection to other organs. Hormonal changes associated with puberty result in poor healing of the primary focus of infection, and waning immunity of the elderly who have been infected years previously accounts for their characteristic patterns of slowly progressive disease with cavitary lesions. The reactivation of earlier tuberculous infection in young urban males with AIDS as well as recent acquisition of infection, the influx into the United States of foreign-born individuals with undiagnosed tuberculosis, and the decline in resources to support TB control programs explain the 20% increase in the number of cases of tuberculosis in the United States from 1985 to 1992. The 35% decrease in reported cases from 1992 to 1998 reflects the impact of federal funds to support directly observed therapy programs that ensure high treatment completion rates and cures. Although there has been a decrease in the number of cases reported in the United States for 6 consecutive years from 1992 to 1998, there is a continued annual increase in the proportion of cases in foreign-born individuals from 27% in 1992, to 42% in 1998, to 46% in 2000.

Mode of Spread.   *M. tuberculosis* is transmitted primarily by airborne droplet nuclei. Although repeated direct exposure to infected individuals is usually necessary, it has been shown that sharing a common air supply with a highly infective individual may be sufficient. Only 4 to 5% of individuals with active tuberculosis transmit infection to their close household contacts, and 1% are considered "dangerous disseminators" because they transmit infection to their remote as well as close contacts. The risk factors most highly associated with transmission of infection are as follows: high concentration of organisms characteristic of cavitary lesions in adults, prolonged duration and proximity of exposure, increased frequency of cough, failure to cover mouth and nose when coughing and sneezing, aerosolization of infected body fluids, and inadequate ventilation system of buildings. Of note, infants and young children are not routinely considered infective because they do not have cavitary lesions and are unable to generate a forceful cough; their sputum is usually swallowed rather than expelled and aerosolized. In any child care or preschool setting, the visiting family members and friends who may have undiagnosed active tuberculosis are more likely to infect other children than is the young child who has been diagnosed and is on appropriate therapy.

Since 1990, there have been several outbreaks of MDR tuberculosis within hospitals or correctional facilities involving highly compromised adults (usually HIV infected with highly contagious disease in poorly ventilated areas). Preschool-aged children have not been implicated in the transmission of tuberculosis. There are, in fact, few reports of transmission of tuberculosis in the child care or preschool setting. When it has occurred, spread was from adult to child rather than the usual child-to-child or child-to-adult route associated with diarrhea and viral respiratory infections in the child care center or preschool. Contact investigation of either the adult index case or the ill child identified several infected children within two separate day care homes.

Rarely, mycobacterial organisms present in purulent material that is draining from either an infected lymph node, ear, bone, or skin lesions could be transmitted to another individual either by direct contact, via hand carriage of a caretaker, or by aerosolization of organisms from the purulent drainage, especially during a wound irrigation procedure.

Incubation Period.   The incubation period from the time the mycobacteria enter the body to the time that the individual develops a positive skin test (cutaneous hypersensitivity) may vary from 2 to 10 weeks. The onset of tuberculin hypersensitivity may be accompanied by fever lasting for 1 to 3 weeks.

DIAGNOSIS

Standardized tuberculin skin testing is indicated to confirm a diagnosis of tuberculosis in the presence of one or more of the following conditions: (a) history of contact with an individual with active tuberculosis, (b) contact with immigrants from an endemic area, and (c) clinical and/or x-ray findings compatible with tuberculosis. Multiple puncture devices (Tine, Mono-Vacc, Aplitest) are no longer utilized for screening because of their inaccuracy. The intradermal (Mantoux) test in which the exact dose of antigen (i.e., 5 tuberculin units [TU]) is known and the size of the reactions can be interpreted reliably is now recommended by the Centers for Disease Control and Prevention, the American Thoracic Society, and the American Academy of Pediatrics. All tuberculin skin tests must be read by a health care professional at 48 to 72 hours after placement. Reactions occurring within the first 24 hours are not significant. A skin test is considered positive if there are 10 mm or more of induration at 48 to 72 hours. In close contacts of infective patients a skin test reaction of 5 mm or more of induration is considered positive. A 5-TU purified protein derivative (PPD) skin test that results in 10 mm or more of induration in an individual who has previously received bacillus Calmette-Guérin (BCG) vaccine is indicative of tuberculous infection. Any person with a positive skin test requires a chest x-ray and physician evaluation. Routine skin testing in low-risk groups or communities with a low prevalence of tuberculosis is not recommended.

Underlying conditions may suppress the skin test reaction; therefore, if the diagnosis of tuberculosis is strongly suspected, other methods of diagnosis must be pursued. Microscopic demonstration of M. tuberculosis in sputum, gastric aspirates, or other body fluids or tissues and isolation in culture are the definitive diagnostic techniques. Occasionally, skin test results are equivocal and must be repeated in 3 months. There is insufficient experience with the QuantiFERON Gold blood test in children to use it at this time for diagnosis.

THERAPY

All children with latent tuberculosis infection or uncomplicated primary pulmonary tuberculosis are treated with oral antituberculous medications and do not require hospitalization. For asymptomatic infection with only a positive skin test, a single drug, INH, is given daily for at least 6 months. Duration should be at least 12 months in children who are HIV-infected or otherwise immunocompromised. When there is evidence of active disease, a three-drug regimen, INH, rifampin, and pyrazinamide, is prescribed for 2 months, and then INH and rifampin are continued for at least another 4 months to complete a minimum of 6 months of therapy. These medications are given daily for the first 4 to 8 weeks. Because the mycobacteria are so slow-growing, the medications may be given twice a week for the remaining 7 to 8 months of the course. Twice-a-week regimens are particularly advantageous for those families in whom compliance cannot be assured, since it is then feasible for school, child care, or public health workers actually to administer the medications. Direct observation of patients with active disease taking their medications is recommended. Consistent implementation of directly observed therapy (DOT) programs has been one of the most important factors responsible for the decrease in new cases and drug-resistant strains in the United States in 1992 to 1998.

In the presence of extensive disease (e.g., severe pulmonary involvement, miliary tuberculosis, meningitis, bone infection) or suspected drug resistance, a minimum of four antituberculous drugs is prescribed. Such children usually require hospitalization at least for the first several days or weeks of the illness. Once the disease process has been controlled, therapy may be completed as an outpatient. The course of therapy may be extended to 12 to 18 months, depending on the clinical response and the susceptibility of the organisms to the drugs used. In cases of MDR, other antituberculous medications, such as amikacin, streptomycin, ethambutol, and ethionamide, may be added to make up a 4- to 6-drug regimen. The addition of ofloxacin is indicated for treatment of the MDR strains associated with the recent outbreaks in U.S. urban areas. Of all these antituberculosis medications, only amikacin and streptomycin cannot be given orally. Surgical drainage of localized infection may be required most frequently with bone or joint involvement. A prescribed course of therapy must be completed in order to prevent relapse or disseminated disease. Young infants with asymptomatic tuberculous infection are at great risk of developing meningitis or miliary tuberculosis if incompletely treated.

INFECTIOUS PERIOD

Children with asymptomatic or noncavitary lung disease are not infectious. Adolescents and adults with cavitary disease are infectious until effective antituberculous therapy has been initiated, the cough has decreased, and there is a diminishing number of organisms identified on acid-fast stains of their sputum. Infectivity decreases dramatically after just a few days of appropriate therapy and only rarely persists beyond 1 to 2 weeks. Because of the threat of MDR tuberculosis, high-risk patients are considered infective until there are *no* organisms seen on acid-fast stains of their sputum.

INFECTION CONTROL

Screening Prior to Entry.   Child care workers should be screened with a tuberculin skin test (preferably intracutaneous) prior to employment. In the day home setting, *all* household members must be included for screening even if some individuals will not be caring for the children directly. Any person with a positive skin test requires a chest x-ray and physician evaluation. If a staff member with active tuberculosis is identified, he or she should be reported to the public health department, treated, and excluded from the child care center or preschool until no longer considered infective by the supervising physician. A complete contact investigation must be performed.

It is preferable to screen children at age 12 to 15 months with a tuberculin skin test. If, however, in very-low-risk areas this practice is deferred, certainly any individual child from a high-risk group must be screened before enrollment. A positive skin test requires complete physician evaluation, chest x-ray, and contact investigation of the family before the child is admitted to the day care center. Routine screening every 1 to 2 years is recommended for children in high-risk settings.

Vaccine.   The BCG vaccines are derived from an attenuated strain of M. bovis and are effective in preventing serious disease resulting from tuberculous infection. These vaccines are used routinely in all newborns only in areas of the world where disease rates are excessive and surveillance and treatment of infected individuals are not possible. In the United States, the only candidates for BCG vaccine are young infants who will have repeated exposures to persistently untreated infective adults. This vaccine is given within the first few days of life.

Exclusion from Child Care or Preschool Attendance. Infants and children with tuberculosis may attend the child care setting as long as they are receiving appropriate chemotherapy according to a carefully formulated plan. The normal level of activities may be resumed once symptoms have disappeared. Infants and children with draining wounds require a physician's statement that the drainage is no longer infective. The most important control measure is the limitation of exposure of other day care children to adolescent and adult household contacts of children with tuberculous infection until the contact investigation of the family has been completed and all individuals with active tuberculosis are on appropriate chemotherapy and judged to be noninfective.

Recommendations for Other Children. The public health department should be notified and will assist in completing the contact investigation. Extent of exposure of the other children to the source adult case will determine extent of screening:

- If the source adult is a child care worker or a family member who has had regular contact with the children, the exposure is high-risk, similar to that of household contacts. All children less than 4 years of age are skin tested, have a chest x-ray performed, and begin INH preventive therapy. Any child with a negative skin test is retested at 10 to 12 weeks. If the test remains negative, the initial chest x-ray was negative, and the child is well, INH is discontinued. If either the first or second skin test is positive, INH is continued for at least 6 months. Children 6 years or older do not require INH preventive therapy in the absence of an initial positive skin test.

- If the source adult is a household contact of the infected child and has had limited or no exposure to the other children in the center, the risk of infection is minimal. All children are skin tested initially. Children with positive skin tests receive chest x-ray and INH for at least 6 months. Repeated skin testing at 10 to 12 weeks for those children who are initially negative is not recommended unless other family members with regular exposure to the child care center or other child care center attendees were discovered to have active tuberculosis during the contact investigation.

- Alternative preventive drugs will be considered if the index case is infected with an MDR strain of *M. tuberculosis.*

Recommendations for Personnel.   As for the children, the extent of contact with the source adult determines the extent of screening that is recommended. If there has been frequent exposure to the source adult, initial skin testing is performed and, if negative, repeated at 10 to 12 weeks. Initiation of INH preventive therapy for adults with a negative initial skin test is indicated only for individuals who have impaired immunity. Pregnant women are evaluated as healthy adults and are treated only when definite infectious disease has been diagnosed. INH prophylaxis for a positive skin test in the absence of disease may be deferred until after delivery unless there has been recent contact with an infectious person. If extent of exposure to the source adult is unclear, a single skin testing is recommended.

Parental Advice.   The parents must be informed of the situation and educated concerning the projected risks to their children. It is most effective to prepare a written statement in collaboration with the public health department or a physician who serves in an advisory role for the child care center or preschool, in addition to holding a group meeting. It is important to provide reassurance and education that will correct the common misconceptions that people have about tuberculosis. When the source adult is a family member who has had minimal or no contact with the other children and is not a teacher or child care worker, it should be emphasized that skin testing is a conservative precaution, and the risk of infection in the children is minimal. New enrollees should not be accepted until the tuberculin status of all adult child care workers has been determined.

Varicella-Zoster Virus
(Chickenpox, Shingles)

Anne A. Gershon

CLINICAL MANIFESTATIONS

Varicella (chickenpox) is the primary infection with varicella-zoster virus (VZV). In the prevaccine era, it usually occurred in children younger than 10 years of age; today it may develop in any age group, including older children and even adults. Symptoms include a rash that begins with maculopapular lesions that rapidly progress to vesicles, pustules, and crusts. The lesions are most concentrated on the trunk, face, and scalp. They are intensely pruritic. The illness is often accompanied by fever and lasts for about 5 days. Subclinical varicella is believed to occur in about 5% of cases. The major complication in otherwise healthy persons is bacterial superinfection of the skin. The disease is usually benign in children, unless they are immunocompromised. In severe cases the lesions may number in the thousands and become hemorrhagic. Primary varicella pneumonia is a serious complication in such patients. Generally, the extent of the skin rash is a good indication of the mildness or severity of a case of varicella; the more severe the illness, the greater the number of skin lesions. The average child with chickenpox develops 250 to 500 vesicles over about 5 days.

Zoster is a secondary infection with VZV. It occurs only in persons who have experienced a previous episode of either clinical or subclinical varicella, or, rarely, in individuals who have been vaccinated. The virus becomes latent in sensory ganglia during varicella and may remain latent for months to years. Latency probably occurs

320 Section IV. Specific Infections

much more commonly after natural infection than vaccination. In zoster, the virus infects a dermatomal area of skin, resulting in a unilateral localized vesicular eruption that may be painful. Zoster is most common in immunocompromised patients and the elderly, although children may manifest it. Children seem to be at increased risk if, while they were in utero, their mothers had varicella or they had varicella before 1 year of age. Zoster in childhood is usually a mild self-limited illness unless the child is immunocompromised.

ETIOLOGIC AGENT

VZV is a herpesvirus closely related to other agents such as herpes simplex viruses, cytomegalovirus, and Epstein-Barr virus (EBV). There is only one serotype. There is no cross-protection among these agents, although there are some shared antigens. All of the herpesviruses become latent after primary infection and may later reactivate. VZV and herpes simplex viruses become latent in sensory ganglia.

EPIDEMIOLOGY

Source of the Organism. The major source of the virus is the skin lesions of both varicella and zoster, which, when moist, are full of infectious virions. Presumably, virions become aerosolized when patients scratch the skin lesions. Although it is almost impossible to culture VZV from respiratory secretions, the respiratory tract is also probably a source of infectious virus, and children are believed to be at least somewhat contagious to others 1 to 2 days before developing the varicella rash. Varicella is extremely contagious, but zoster is less so. In both instances, varicella is transmitted to others.

High-Risk Populations. Individuals who have not previously been vaccinated or infected with natural VZV and who therefore have no antibodies or cell-mediated immunity to VZV are at risk to develop varicella following exposure to someone with either varicella or zoster. Second attacks of varicella are unusual, and if they occur, they are likely to be mild. Mild cases of varicella are thought to occur in 10 to 15% of vaccinated children following close exposure to individuals infected with the natural virus. Subclinical reinfection of persons who have had varicella is common following subsequent exposure.

Patients with defects in cellular immunity are at additional risk to develop severe varicella if they have not had the infection previously. Newborn infants whose mothers have the onset of varicella between 5 days before and 2 days after delivery are also at high risk to develop severe varicella. They should be given passive immunization and/or antiviral therapy (see Therapy).

Mode of Spread.   The virus is spread by the airborne route. Varicella is not spread by fomites but requires person-to-person contact. In family settings the attack rate among susceptibles is 80 to 90%. Transmission after less intimate exposures (such as in school) is less predictable. The disease is not transmissible until 1 to 2 days prior to development of rash, and it remains transmissible until skin lesions have crusted. Vaccinated children who nevertheless develop varicella are contagious to others. There is a general direct relationship between the number of skin lesions present and the degree of contagion.

Incubation Period.   Ten to 21 days.

DIAGNOSIS

The diagnosis of both varicella and zoster can usually be made on clinical grounds based on the history of contact and the nature and distribution of the rash. When the rash is not characteristic of varicella, a scraping of a skin lesion can be obtained for staining with commercially available fluorescein-labeled monoclonal antibody to VZV and the diagnosis made within a few hours. Skin lesions may also be cultured for the presence of virus. Acute and convalescent antibody titers for VZV antibodies may also be obtained, but the diagnosis cannot be made for at least 7 to 10 days after the onset of illness by this method. The diagnosis of zoster can be made on similar grounds. There is no need to elicit a history of contact with someone with VZV, however, since zoster is the result of reactivation of latent infection.

THERAPY

Double-blind placebo-controlled studies of oral administration of acyclovir (ACV) to children and adolescents within 24 hours after onset of the rash of varicella have indicated that this therapy shortens the course of the illness in children by about a day. The dose is 20 mg/kg (maximum, 800 mg/dose) four times a day for 5 days. The American Academy of Pediatrics has published recommendations for use of ACV in children with chickenpox. One approach is to administer it to children over age 12 years and to secondary household cases that are predictably more severe than the primary case in a family. It is not recommended that ACV be given to try to prevent varicella from developing if an exposure has been recognized. Anti-viral therapy is usually unnecessary for vaccinated children who develop breakthrough varicella.

Immunocompromised children with no history of varicella should be given varicella-zoster immune globulin (VZIG) within 3 (maximum 5) days of a close exposure to someone with either varicella or zoster. Infants born to women with the onset of varicella 5 days before delivery to 2 days after delivery should also receive VZIG.

Children who develop severe varicella should be treated with intravenous ACV, 1500 mg/m^2/day, for 7 to 10 days. Immunocompromised children who develop varicella and have not received either VZIG or varicella vaccine (see below) should also be treated with intravenous ACV as early in the illness as possible, even if the disease is mild and there are few skin lesions, mainly to prevent the development of varicella pneumonia.

Usually, zoster in children does not require therapy, since it is a self-limited illness. Exceptions include zoster of the ophthalmic division of the trigeminal nerve and zoster in an immunocompromised child. Each case requires individualization. Dosages are as for treatment of varicella.

INFECTIOUS PERIOD

Patients with varicella and zoster are infectious to others until all the skin lesions have crusted; usually this occurs within 5 to 7 days, but it may be longer in immunosuppressed patients.

INFECTION CONTROL

Vaccine. A live attenuated varicella vaccine (Oka strain) was licensed by the U.S. Food and Drug Administration for use in all children over the age of 12 months and for adults who are susceptible to chickenpox in March 1995. It is recommended by both the American Academy of Pediatrics and the Centers for Disease Control and Prevention that vaccine be routinely given to varicella-susceptibles. The vaccine is extremely safe and effective for prevention of most cases of varicella. One dose is given to children from 1 to 12 years of age. Persons who have reached the 13th birthday should be given 2 doses 4 to 8 weeks apart. Children should be immunized on the basis of a negative history; individuals older than 21 years of age should be serologically tested for antibodies to VZV if they have no history of disease before vaccination. Most adults with no history of varicella are, in fact, immune. Since the vaccine cannot be given to pregnant women, and since it is recommended that women not become pregnant until at least 3 months after a dose of varicella vaccine, it is particularly important to determine if women of childbearing age with no history of varicella have detectable antibodies. Administration of vaccine inadvertently to persons who are immune to varicella is not harmful.

Exclusion from Child Care or Preschool Attendance. Children with acute natural (wild-type) varicella should not attend day care or preschool until all the lesions have crusted. This usually leads to exclusion for about 5 to 7 days. The rare child with zoster can attend day care or preschool if the skin lesions are on the trunk and can be fully covered with a sterile dressing and clothing.

Children who were immunized may develop a rash during the 6 weeks following immunization. Only 5% of vaccinated children develop a rash, and most of these rashes consist of only a few lesions that resemble insect bites. Although these children with rash may potentially transmit vaccine-type VZV to others, transmission of vaccine-type virus is highly unlikely. It should be remembered, however, that until there is universal use of varicella vaccine with resultant little circulation of wild-type VZV, some children with apparent vaccine-associated rashes may actually be in the early stages of natural varicella that was in the incubation period when they were immunized. Thus, vaccinated children who develop vesicles suggestive of varicella should not attend day care until the vesicles are dried or a diagnosis other than varicella is made, particularly in the first 2 weeks after vaccination. Transmission of vaccine-type virus is less dangerous than transmission of wild-type

VZV. It appears that the vaccine-type virus is much less able to result in transmission, and, when transmission occurs, the resultant illness is a very modified form of varicella due to the attenuated nature of the vaccine-type virus. Clinical reversion to virulence has not been observed. In general, these recommendations also apply to adults who have recently been immunized. It is strongly recommended that day care and preschool facilities prospectively develop their own policies for potential management of vaccinated children and adults; these will need to be modified periodically as the vaccine is more widely implemented.

Routine use of varicella vaccine should prevent much disease in child day care settings. However, outbreaks due to the natural virus in vaccinated children in day care have been observed. Presumably, these infrequent occurrences are in children who did not respond to the vaccine or, rarely, are possibly due to waning immunity.

Administration of vaccine to susceptibles who have already been exposed is now acceptable ("postexposure prophylaxis"). Varicella vaccine has been useful in terminating outbreaks of the infection, including those occurring in day care settings.

Recommendations for Other Children. VZIG is recommended only for immunocompromised children at high risk to develop severe varicella. "Regular" immune globulin is not useful unless given in massive doses, and its use is therefore strongly discouraged.

Recommendations for Personnel. Adults who have never had varicella should be immunized before being exposed to VZV. Adults (and children who have already reached the 13th birthday) should be given 2 doses of vaccine 4 to 8 weeks apart. This will result in a seroconversion (measured by the latex agglutination assay for VZV antibodies) in about 90% of adults. Those who do not seroconvert after 2 doses may be given a third dose and be retested for development of antibodies. Adults who fail to seroconvert after 3 doses of vaccine are unlikely to respond to a fourth dose and must be regarded as varicella-susceptible. Most adults who seroconvert after two doses can be expected to be protected against varicella. About 70% will achieve complete protection; the remaining 30% may develop modified varicella with an average of 50 skin lesions and rapid recovery. About 10% of adult seroconverters lose detectable antibodies within several years after varicella; those who do are among the 30% who are at risk to develop breakthrough varicella. It is possible for physicians to arrange for testing of VZV lesions to determine whether they are due to wild- or vaccine-type VZV. Adult vaccinees who remain seropositive are highly unlikely to develop breakthrough varicella following exposure to the wild-type virus. Varicella-susceptible pregnant women who develop wild-type chickenpox in the first or second trimester of pregnancy have a 2% risk of delivering a child with the characteristic constellation of birth defects (skin, nervous system, and eyes) of the congenital varicella syndrome. This syndrome has not been observed to be caused by the vaccine-type virus. Presumably, the attenuated vaccine-type virus poses less of a risk.

Parental Advice. Parents should be notified of the occurrence of varicella in an attendee or staff member in case there is a varicella-susceptible pregnant woman or immunocompromised person in the family.

66

Yersinia

William J. Rodriguez*
Barbara A. Jantausch

CLINICAL MANIFESTATIONS

Yersinia pestis is responsible for human plague. *Yersinia enterocolitica* and *Yersinia pseudotuberculosis* cause gastrointestinal illness that is collectively called yersiniosis. *Y. enterocolitica* primarily causes diarrhea, nausea, and fever and also can cause mesenteric adenitis. It is the cause of large epidemics of enteritis. Children with *Y. enterocolitica* infections may have fever to 40°C with bloody diarrhea, nausea, vomiting, and colicky abdominal pain. Stools may be watery but are more often mucoid. Illness may last from a few days to 1 month, but it usually is present for less than 10 days. Infection may be asymptomatic. *Y. pseudotuberculosis* causes abdominal pain and mesenteric adenitis. *Y. enterocolitica* and *Y. pseudotuberculosis* can be responsible for a pseudoappendicitis syndrome, prompting appendectomy that in most cases yields a normal appendix and suppurative mesenteric lymph nodes.

Extraintestinal manifestations of *Yersinia* infections include reactive arthritis, erythema nodosum, Reiter's syndrome, thrombocytopenia, bacteremia, and meningitis. Asymptomatic infections occur rarely.

ETIOLOGIC AGENT

Yersinia is an enteric, nonlactose-fermenting, gram-negative bacillus belonging to the family Enterobacteriaceae. The genus *Yersinia* contains

---

*No official support or endorsement of any product or study or the content of these chapters by the U.S. Food and Drug Administration is provided or should be inferred. No commercial interest or other conflict of interest exists between Dr. Rodriguez and the manufacturers of any of the products mentioned.

three species: *Y. pestis*, *Y. pseudotuberculosis*, and *Y. enterocolitica*. *Y. pseudotuberculosis* has at least 11 serogroups distinguished on the basis of the somatic O antigen; *Y. enterocolitica* has over 50 distinguishable O serotypes, with O:3 and O:9 causing the majority of cases of diarrhea.

EPIDEMIOLOGY

Source of the Organism. Primary reservoirs for *Yersinia* are contaminated food and water and animal carriers, specifically, dogs, cats (especially those who have stayed in animal shelters), pigs, cows, goats, horses, rabbits, squirrels, rodents, domestic fowl, and fish. A recognized cause of yersiniosis in young infants is contact with an adult who has handled pork intestines (chitterlings). *Y. enterocolitica* is more common in winter than summer.

High-Risk Populations. Children with hemolytic conditions such as those leading to increased storage of iron may be at high risk, as are those on immunosuppressive therapy. Nosocomial transmission of *Y. enterocolitica* has been reported.

Mode of Spread. Food or water contaminated by feces or urine from animals is probably the main mode of spread; others include the fecal-oral route and person-to-person transmission. The organism is able to survive in refrigerated milk.

Incubation Period. The incubation period is 2 to 11 days, with an average of 5 days, but may extend up to 3 weeks.

DIAGNOSIS

Y. enterocolitica may be isolated from stool cultures by using enteric media with incubation at room temperature to facilitate growth. Cold enrichment by inoculation of broth cultures and incubation at 4° to 6°C for a few weeks may enhance recovery of organisms, but it is usually too time-consuming to be considered practical in an acute clinical situation. *Y. pseudotuberculosis* is rarely recovered from stool cultures; in cases of mesenteric adenitis it has been grown from infected lymph nodes. In disseminated infection, *Yersinia* can be readily recovered from standard media such as blood agar, which supports the growth of gram-negative organisms. A fourfold rise in antibody titer specific against the offending serotype can be diagnostic.

THERAPY

Despite the fact that antibiotic therapy has not proved to be definitively effective in *Y. enterocolitica* enterocolitis, we would recommend the use of effective oral antimicrobial agents (as determined by antibiogram) in symptomatic patients. *Y. enterocolitica* is usually sensitive to aminoglycosides, third-generation cephalosporins, chloramphenicol, fluoroquinolones, and trimethoprim-sulfamethoxazole. For those older than 9 years of age, tetracyclines can be used if the organism is susceptible. Treatment of enteric disease without invasion should be with absorbable antimicrobials for 5 to 7 days. Patients with septicemia or disseminated infection may require parenteral antibiotic therapy for a longer period of time.

INFECTIOUS PERIOD

Y. enterocolitica has been recovered from the stool 4 to 79 days (average, 27 days) after symptoms have resolved and for as long as 6 weeks after antimicrobial therapy.

INFECTION CONTROL

Vaccine.   None available.

Exclusion from Child Care or Preschool Attendance. Although the period of communicability is unknown and patients may shed the organism even after antibiotic therapy is completed, it seems reasonable to keep the child out of the center only while symptomatic.

Recommendations for Other Children.   Children should avoid contact with feces. Other children in the setting who become symptomatic with diarrhea should be removed from the setting and have their stools cultured for *Yersinia*.

Recommendations for Personnel.   Personnel who become symptomatic should remain at home and have their stools cultured for *Yersinia*. All personnel should practice good handwashing. Diapers should be disposed of properly, and separate diaper and food preparation areas provided. Toys that the infected child played with should be disinfected. New children should not be enrolled during an outbreak.

Parental Advice. Parents should observe their child for symptoms of enteritis. Symptomatic children should be removed from day care, seen by their pediatrician, and have their stools cultured. The physician should be informed of what is going on at the child care center or preschool.

INDEX

Page numbers followed by *t* indicate tables.

331